Bloom

&

Blossom

D1285057

GARDEN LIBRARY
PLANTING FIELDS ARBORETUM

BOOKS BY MARY SWANDER

Nonfiction
Out of This World: A Woman's Life Among the Amish
Parsnips in the Snow (with Jane Staw)

Poetry
Heaven-and-Earth House
Driving the Body Back
Succession

Edited Collections
Land of the Fragile Giants (with Cornelia Mutel)

Bloom
&
Blossom

THE
READER'S GUIDE
TO GARDENING

EDITED BY
MARY SWANDER

THE ECCO PRESS

#0596 4/27/03 gift of Patricia Spacorur $5.00

Selection and Introduction Copyright © 1997 by Mary Swander
All rights reserved

THE ECCO PRESS
100 West Broad Street
Hopewell, New Jersey 08525

Published simultaneously in Canada by
Penguin Books Canada Ltd., Ontario
Printed in the United States of America

Library of Congress Cataloging-in-Publication Data
Bloom & blossom : the reader's guide to gardening / edited by Mary Swander.—1st ed.
     p.   cm.
  ISBN 0-88001-473-3
  ISBN 0-88001-565-9 (paperback)
   1. Gardens—Literary collections. 2. Gardening—Literary collections.
 I. Swander, Mary
 PN6071.G27B59   1997
 810.8'036—dc20   96-26828

Pages 277 to 279 constitute an extension of this copyright page
Designed by Barbara Cohen Aronica

The text of this book is set in Weiss

9   8   7   6   5   4   3   2   1

FIRST PAPERBACK EDITION 1998

to Boo

ACKNOWLEDGMENTS

The editor would like to thank Lisa Dowling, Carla Homeister, Barbara Moss, and Susan Wiley for their help in the preparation of the manuscript for this book. Special thanks to Elizabeth Grossman for helping me conceive of the book's structure and for her support through the project. Thanks, too, to Iowa State University for its assistance and the Seed Savers Exchange for the use of its library.

Part of the proceeds of this book will be donated to the Seed Savers Exchange, a nonprofit organization.

CONTENTS

III

IV

GOOD KEEPERS

AN INTRODUCTION

A forty-mile-an-hour wind blasts snow against the house. The windows rattle. The electrical wires sag and snap. The bare limbs of the trees laden with ice break off, crashing to the ground. It's late January in Iowa where, in a matter of hours, the temperature can plunge fifty degrees and stay there for weeks at a time. Early this Saturday morning, we reached ten below zero and, with eight inches of fresh snow, the Governor declared a state of emergency. The National Guard has been called in to help plow the roads, and the State Meteorologist has issued a wind chill factor alert.

"Are you all right?" a friend telephones. "Are you warm enough?" he wants to know. "Do you have enough wood?"

I live on an isolated gravel road in the country in the middle of the Amish territory and nothing—neither car, truck, buggy, nor sleigh—has passed by for the last twenty-four hours. Last night, my neighbor tried driving the fourteen-mile commute home from his job in town. He made it to the ten-mile mark—the Amish cheese factory—but when he tried to round the corner, he careened into a gigantic drift that came at him like a tidal wave. He had to pull himself out and drive all the way back to town.

But, yes, I'm okay. Thursday, before the storm started, I loaded the woodbox with stacks of oak and hickory. Now I sit by the fire staring out the long windows in this old one-room schoolhouse, watching Bear, a huge white mutt of mixed Arctic breeds, sleep in the middle of the yard while the snow drifts around him. Only his head pops up above the swirling whiteness.

"Do you have enough food to make it through the weekend?" my friend asks.

Another large snowfall is predicted for Sunday night. It will be at least Monday morning before the plows will appear to deposit their enormous scrapings into the ditches. It will be Monday morning before the mail carrier will skid down the road in his jeep and the mailbox will be stuffed full of outdated newspapers and letters that begged to be answered yesterday. It will be Monday morning before Scalawag, the goat, ventures out from the warm nest she's made in the manger and, with a blend of curiosity and bewilderment, Katie, the donkey, minces her way down the hill to the water tank, then back up to the barn for some fresh hay.

But, yes, I'm fine. I have enough food stocked up here to last me through the winter. I have a freezer full of the lamb I raised in the pasture this summer, and several large chunks of halibut a friend brought from Alaska. I have turkeys, ducks, and geese from my own coop. And I am surrounded by vegetables. This is the month that seems the furthest removed from the gardening season, yet the one that brings me closest to realizing its bounty. The shelves on my wall are lined with mason jars full of homemade sauerkraut and pickled peppers. The bins next to the stove contain hundreds of bags of dried corn, tomatoes, and zucchini "chips." Strings of dried cayennes hang from the ceiling beams. Next to them dangle braids of onions and garlic.

Once the wind has died down a bit, I will pull on my long underwear, down vest, coat, hat, and mittens and go out to my "root cellar" where I'll return with a bucket full of potatoes, beets, carrots, and rutabagas—vegetables that will look, amazingly enough, as fresh as the day I harvested them in October. My root cellar is really a metal garbage can sunk down three and a half feet into a pit in the ground. Lined with straw, it holds layers of vegetables, keeping them at just the right moisture and temperature for a good six months.

"Don't the carrots mold? Don't the turnips rot?" people ask.

Oh, sometimes by March, the potatoes begin to grow a few sprouts but, for the most part, the root cellar creates just the right conditions for preservation of most tubers. And there's no fuss. No muss. No long hours bending over hot kettles of water on already steamy August days, no threat of botulism and inspections of properly sealed lids, no pressure cookers blowing their gaskets. Root cellaring is a cinch—safe, easy, and reliable. Over the years, I've learned to perfect my system. I've learned when to harvest the vegetables, not too early, not too late. I've learned how to layer the straw just right, no one crop touching another. And, most importantly, I've learned to grow good keepers.

Every February when I sit down to order my seeds, I hunt through the gardening catalogues searching for just the right varieties. I scan the descriptions for those mentioned as "good keepers." The varieties that grow fast and plump in the spring are fine for starters. In June, I love to gobble up a salad of new potatoes, dressed in oil and vinegar, a sprinkling of fresh chives on the top. Yet in the fall, I'm after something different, those varieties that are dense and solid—the danvers half long carrots, the purple-topped rutabagas, the table ace acorn squash—the vegetables that will still be around in April when I begin planting my garden again.

In making the selections for this anthology, I used the same method. I chose pieces that I thought would hold up for years to come. Some were old standbys. Focused on contemporary American gardening, the book begins each section with a piece of writing from the early days of horticulture on the North American continent. L. H. Bailey, Henry Ward Beecher, Henry David Thoreau, and Waheenee set the tone and themes for their respective succeeding pages.

Other pieces like those of Michael Pollan and Eleanor Perenyi have become contemporary "classics" in garden literature. However, it was fun to include poetry and fiction alongside the more expected ranks of nonfiction writers. A host of writers, like

Maxine Kumin, Stanley Kunitz, and Louise Glück, are well-known for their garden themes and help provide a welcome balance to the list.

Still other pieces were real discoveries in terms of garden writing. In my search, I came across some authors who wowed me and begged to be included. Stanley Crawford, Judith Larner Lowry, and Cathrine Sneed, in their own unique ways, called to me with commanding voices. I had long been familiar with authors like Jane Smiley, but now was able to think of them in different terms. Finally, other selections were products of my own propagation. I solicited several pieces from writers like Thomas Fox Averill and Barbara Robinette Moss who I knew had special stories to tell.

In the same way that I layer my tubers in straw, I tried to layer the pieces of this book. One next to another, each with its own special shape and color, the selections keep their own integrity yet at the same time blend together, ultimately creating a delicious literary stew, their aromas mixing and merging, enticing us to take just one more bite. When we pick up an anthology, we often reach in and pick out one piece here, one there, to savor and read, skipping around in the text to those that most interest us. *Bloom & Blossom* can be perused in that way. However, the book is designed to be read as a whole, progressing piece by piece, section by section, layer by layer, creating a life of its own.

My life began with gardening. As soon as I could walk, I remember toddling after my grandmother when she worked in her little plot, the tomatoes tangling up around their stakes. Her legs wrapped in newspaper to prevent her fair skin from sunburn, "Boo" moved among the rows in her calico housedress, reaching down to pinch a squash bug or to harvest a pepper and a cucumber, then carrying them back to the house in the folds of her apron. In the fall, she toted bushel baskets and gunnysacks full of tubers to her root cellar, a cave dug into a rise in the yard, its top mounded with dirt and growing violets, its interior lined with bricks.

When we opened the heavy wooden door of the cave, it

banged to the ground from its own weight. Then into the darkness we descended, cobwebs brushing my face, my feet feeling for the three wooden steps that took us down into the depths. There, frightened yet fascinated to be in such an enclosure, I received my first lessons in mortality, in paradox and irony. In this spooky place, worms crawling across the floor and the dank smell of decay all around, things were kept alive, vegetables that would nourish us through the long, dark winter. My grandmother, a woman in her seventies who would know fewer and fewer winters, a woman who had worked the soil her whole life, was connecting future generations to the land. In that way, as Theodore Roethke says in his poem about his childhood, "Root Cellar,"

> Nothing would give up life:
> Even the dirt kept on breathing a small breath.

My grandmother died when I was fourteen, and my early gardening life stopped. We moved away from her house to a treeless development in a city, where most gardening took place in round redwood tubs and had more to do with petunias and impatiens than with potatoes and turnips. It wasn't until my late twenties, when I bought a house of my own, that gardening came back into my reality. Then, when I worked in my yard, whether turning over a spadeful of dirt in the vegetable plot or hoeing around the crocuses that bloomed under the lilac shrub, I was ever reminded of those sunny summer days trailing after my grandmother. In my adult life, the preservation of my crops became a preservation of the past, a link to my maternal line.

Scratch the dirt under most gardeners and you'll find a similar story. Gardening, like any complicated skill, is frequently learned through trial and error and reference books, but the love of plants is often a notion that is passed down through the generations. "Much of gardening is a return," Michael Pollan says, "an effort at recovering remembered landscapes." Gardening naturally evokes family and, since Genesis, it has created a setting for intimacy. The writers in Section I of this book explore these human connections (and disconnections).

L.H. Bailey tells us that "Every family can have a garden," and that the satisfaction of the endeavor "depends upon the temper of the person." Michael Pollan and Lee May bond to their fathers through their gardens, while Kathleen Norris bonds to her grandmother. Katha Pollitt meditates on the specialness of the tomato, while Eleanor Perenyi contemplates the specialness of women in the garden. "It may come as a surprise that sexism should play any part in horticulture, but the more you read of gardening history the more convincing the case for it becomes," Perenyi observes, while the romantic pull and tug of the garden place become the seed of Stanley Kunitz's and Julia Alvarez's poems.

Did I say seed? In Section II, Henry Ward Beecher gives us an historical glimpse into seed saving. Gerald Stern launches a metaphorical exploration of seeds and later Carl H. Klaus brings it to closure. "I give myself / to the first flower," Stern writes in his poem; then, as he reaches out his left hand, "I let it tremble./ I looked at the sun, it was a kind of dandelion." By the end of his poem, Stern's speaker, like the dandelion itself, is "winged and scattered." In Carl Klaus' gardening journal, the metaphor of the dandelion becomes much more menacing as it is appropriated by the medical profession.

At the end of his selection, Klaus chastises himself for not confronting his wife's doctor. "And why didn't I tell him that his dandelion analogy was badly chosen, for the body is not like a lawn any more than a cancer cell is like a dandelion seed? Maybe, it's because the dandelion analogy did embody a germ of common sense—that some things are so small they cannot be detected even by the most sophisticated technology. But a germ of sense doesn't necessarily lead to an epidemic of truth."

In between this frame, seeds become anything but metaphorical for Barbara Moss. Boyce Rensberger is the only writer in the book whose piece is not set in the United States, but I thought his tale of the nine Soviet botanists who starved for the sake of their seeds was so gripping that it deserved inclusion. Roger B. Swain introduces us to the idea of seed saving and the safeguarding of endangered varieties. Jane Anne Staw and I profile a gardener who makes the absolute most of his garden savings, and Jane Smiley finds the seed for her novella in her neighbor's plot.

As seeds develop and ripen, young tendrils lifting their heads above the soil, so do gardeners evolve and mature. In my late thirties, I moved to the country where my garden grew bigger and my methods became more sophisticated. I stood on top of the hill staking out my plot, tilling the soil by hand, surveying the whole valley below. From this vantage point, I slowly gained a better sense of my place in the region, the ecosystem, and the natural world as a whole.

From my garden, I looked out on rolling fields of corn and beans and could imagine what had come before the plow—the vast expanses of prairie, a complex system of interdependent plants and animals that lived in ecological balance. I gazed on the cultivated crops and realized that what had taken eons to form had been eliminated in only about fifty years. Each turn of the potato fork made me acutely aware that, in my small way, I was a part of an agricultural movement that had forever changed my environment. This realization allowed me to lift my head up above the single vegetable, flower, or weed to try to comprehend the bigger picture, how all of nature once fit together in harmony.

Section III of *Bloom & Blossom* examines the place of gardening in the larger scope of the natural world. Henry David Thoreau, the Transcendentalist who found peace in the natural setting of Walden Pond, goes to war with the weeds in his cultivated bean field. Gene Logsdon and Judith Larner Lowry blur the boundaries between the garden and the wilderness. "Maybe my piece of land is neither the wildlands nor a garden," Lowry says of her tract in California, "and maybe the activities involved aren't really gardening at all but more like inserting yourself into the long dream of this solemn, fogbound, silvered land." Stanley Plumly echoes these sentiments when writing of a once-cultivated field struggling to return to a more primitive state. "Wild has its skills," Plumly states in the beginning of "Lapsed Meadow."

Allen Lacy and Maxine Kumin bend to the continuum of growing things, questioning the labels we use to distinguish and value certain plants above others, the battles we wage against some and the trouble we invite into our lives with the distribution of others. "O children, citizens, my wayward jungly dears/ you are all to be celebrated," Kumin writes in "An Insider's View of the Garden." Then, addressing vegetables, weeds and wild flowers alike, she concludes:

> For all of you, whether eaten or extirpated
> I plan to spend the rest of my life on my knees.

Stanley Crawford celebrates a link among three seemingly disjointed things: crops, words, and movies; Sara Stein shows us how we can mend the disjointedness in our own backyards. "I want to change the whole suburban landscape," Stein says modestly. "I want to walk into any roadside nursery and see wild roses. I want every landscaper to know their local berries like they know the alphabet. I want wildflower societies to treasure native grasses like they treasure the flowers that grow in it. I want growers to see trees as woodlands, shrubs as hedgerows, perennials as meadows. I want professionals not just to landscape with native plants, but to landscape with native ecosystems."

In the country, I began to treasure the big and little bluestem grasses, as well as the purple cone flowers, milkweed, and compass plants, all inhabitants of the prairie patch I restored in "my own backyard." I learned how a Native American woman who had lost her knitting needles improvised from a set of big bluestem grasses, how the Chippewa used the grass as a medicine for indigestion and stomach pains, how the Omaha made a concoction of the lower leaf blades to treat general debility from an unknown cause. I began to understand that Native Americans had a knowledge and understanding of the ecosystem that stretched way beyond anything that the Euro-Americans had ever tapped. I meditated on the past caretakers of the land and tried to project the future.

Section IV of *Bloom & Blossom* begins with a tribute to our Native American past, then contemplates the future of gardening. Garrison Keillor sings the praises of sweet corn, a gift from such people as Waheenee, or Buffalo-Bird-Woman, a Hidatsa gardener born around 1839 whose memoir of corn planting gives us a peek into the practices of more prehistoric peoples. Thomas Fox Averill's gardening life cycled back to indigenous plants, and his gifts to us are recipes for such things as Black Bean and Gooseberry Enchiladas.

Gary Nabhan digs back further in gardening history to trace the disruption of native farming and the way in which the takeover of the American Indians' land produced a reduction in crop diversity. Gene Logsdon offers us a vision of the future of farming. Contrary to the more prevalent notions of agribusiness ventures run by machinery, Logsdon foresees the cultivation of small acreages and garden-sized plots that produce labor-intensive specialty crops. Louise Glück's "Daisies" does her take on machines and gardens, while Cathrine Sneed documents her work with prisoners— the sort of gardening that seems to fulfill Logsdon's predictions.

Finally, Wendell Berry closes by expounding on "The Pleasures of Eating" and how we can all eat responsibly. Berry says that, "Eating with the fullest pleasure—pleasure, that is, that does not depend on ignorance—is perhaps the profoundest enactment of our connection with the world. In this pleasure we experience and celebrate our dependence and our gratitude, for we are living from mystery, from creatures we did not make and powers we cannot comprehend."

If I can comprehend anything about gardening, it's that of preservation. In an activity that is so ephemeral, we find long-lasting traditions and paths for living "the good life." When I kneel down before my root cellar with my potatoes in my hands, I am preserving one vegetable for the winter, one gardener's health. I am also preserving the crop's diversity. I save a few extra spuds for seeds for planting the next spring. With these and with the soil-saving gardening techniques I've learned to use, I will preserve my little piece of the larger world, what's come before me and what will be left behind.

Preserved here within the folds of this book, the literary works collected in *Bloom & Blossom* call forth with their own power. They connect us to ourselves and to all the mysteries surrounding us. Let us celebrate these authors. With pleasure and gratitude.

I have often thought that if heaven had given me choice of my position and calling, it should have been on a rich spot of earth, well watered, and near a good market for the production of the garden. No occupation is so delightful to me as the culture of the earth, and no culture comparable to that of the garden. Such a variety of subjects, some one always comming to perfection, the failure of one thing repaired by the success of another, and instead of one harvest a continued one through the year. Under a total want of demand except for our family table, I am still devoted to the garden. But though an old man, I am but a young gardener.

—Thomas Jefferson to
Charles Willson Peale
Poplar Forest, August 20, 1811

Bloom

&

Blossom

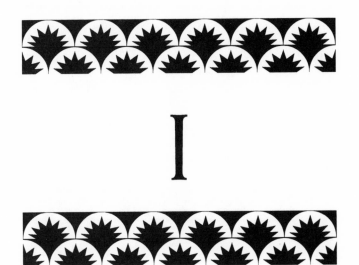

I

L. H. Bailey

GENERAL ADVICE

Every family can have a garden. If there is not a foot of land, there are porches or windows. Wherever there is sunlight, plants may be made to grow; and one plant in a tin-can may be a more helpful and inspiring garden to some minds than a whole acre of lawn and flowers may be to another. The satisfaction of a garden does not depend upon the area, nor, happily, upon the cost or rarity of the plants. It depends upon the temper of the person. One must first seek to love plants and nature, and then to cultivate that happy peace of mind which is satisfied with little. He will be happier if he has no rigid and arbitrary ideals, for gardens are coquettish, particularly with the novice. If plants grow and thrive, he should be happy; and if the plants which thrive chance not to be the ones which he planted, they are plants nevertheless, and nature is satisfied with them. We are apt to covet the things which we cannot have; but we are happier when we love the things which grow because they must. A patch of lusty pigweeds, growing and crowding in luxuriant abandon, may be a better and more worthy object of affection than a bed of coleuses in which every spark of life and spirit and individuality has been sheared out and suppressed. The man who worries morning and night about the dandelions in the lawn will find great relief in loving the dandelions. Each blossom is worth more than a gold coin, as it shimmers in the exuberant sunlight of the growing spring, and attracts the bees to its bosom. Little children love the dandelions: why may not we? Love the things nearest at hand; and love intensely. If I were to write a motto over the

gate of a garden, I should choose the remark which Socrates
made as he saw the luxuries in the market, "How much there is in
the world that I do not want!"

TWO GARDENS

My first garden was a place no grown-up ever knew about, even though it was in the backyard of a quarter-acre suburban plot. Behind our house in Farmingdale, on Long Island, stood a rough hedge of lilac and forsythia that had been planted to hide the neighbor's slat wood fence. My garden, which I shared with my sister and our friends, consisted of the strip of unplanted ground between the hedge and the fence. I say that no grown-up knew about it because in an adult's picture of this landscape, the hedge runs flush against the fence. To a four-year-old, though, the space made by the vaulting branches of a forsythia is as grand as the inside of a cathedral, and there is room enough for a world between a lilac and a wall. Whenever I needed to be out of range of adult radar, I'd crawl beneath two lilac bushes, and find myself safe and alone in my own green room.

I think of this place today as a garden not only because it offered an enclosed and privileged space out-of-doors but also because it was here that I first actually grew something. Most of the pictures I can retrieve from that time are sketchy and brittle, but this one unspools like a strip of celluloid. It must be September. I am by myself behind the hedge, maybe hiding from my sister or just poking around, when I catch sight of a stippled green football sitting in a tangle of vines and broad leaves. It's a watermelon. The feeling is of finding treasure—a right-angled change of fortune, an unexpected boon. Then I make the big connection between this melon and a seed I planted, or at least spit out and buried, months before: *I made this happen.* For a moment I'm torn between leaving the melon to ripen and the surging desire to publicize my achievement: *Mom has got to see this.* So I break the cord attaching the melon to the vine, cradle it in my arms and run for the house, screaming my head off the whole way. The watermelon weighs a ton, though, and just as I hit the back steps I lose my balance. The melon squirts from my arms and smashes in a pink explosion on the cement.

Watermelon perfume fills the air and then the memory stalls. I can't remember but I must have cried—to see so fine a triumph snatched away, to feel Humpty-Dumpty suddenly crash onto my four-year-old conscience. Memories of one kind or another play around the edges of every garden, giving them much of their resonance and savor. I've spent thousands of hours in the garden since that afternoon, and there is perhaps some sense in which all this time has been spent trying to recover that watermelon and the flush of pride that attended its discovery.

I can't recall whether I tried to salvage any part of the melon to show my father when he got home from work, but I can assume he would not have been greatly impressed. My father was not much for gardening, and the postage-stamp yard of our ranch house showed it. The lawn was patchy and always in need of a mowing, the hedges were unclipped and scraggly, and in summer hordes of Japanese beetles dined on our rosebushes without challenge. My father was a Bronx boy who had been swept to the suburbs in the postwar migration. Buying a house with a yard on Long Island was simply what you did then, part of how you said who you were when you were a lawyer or a dentist (he was a lawyer) just starting out in the fifties. Certainly it was no great love of fresh air that drove him from the city. I have a few memories of my father standing with his Salem and a highball glass on the concrete patio behind the house, but, with a single exception I will come to, not one of him out in the yard mowing the lawn or pulling weeds or otherwise acting the part of a suburban dad.

I remember him as strictly an indoor dad, moving around the house in his year-round uniform of button-down shirt, black socks and tie shoes, and boxer shorts. Maybe it was the fact that he hated to wear pants that kept him indoors, or perhaps the boxers were a way to avoid having to go outside. Either way, my mother was left with the choice of her husband doing the yard work in his underwear, or not doing it at all, which in the suburbs is not much of a choice. So while the boxers kept Dad pinned to the kitchen table, the yard steadily deteriorated to the point where it became something of a neighborhood and family scandal.

My mother's father lived a few miles away in Babylon, in a big house with beautiful, manicured gardens, and the condition of our yard could be counted on to make him crazy—something it may well have been calculated to do. My grandfather was a somewhat overbearing patriarch whom my father could not stand. Grandpa, who would live to be ninety-six, had come to Long Island from Russia shortly before the First World War. Starting out with nothing, selling vegetables from a horse wagon, he eventually built a fortune, first in the produce business and later in real estate. In choosing my father, my mother had married a notch or two beneath her station, and Grandpa made it his business to minimize his eldest daughter's sacrifice—or, looked at from another angle, to highlight my father's shortcomings. This meant giving my father large quantities of unsolicited career advice, unsolicited business opportunities (invariably bum deals, according to my father), and unsolicited landscape services.

In the same way some people send flowers, Grandpa sent whole gardens. These usually arrived unexpectedly, by truck caravan. Two or three flatbeds appeared at the curb and a crew of Italian laborers fanned out across the property to execute whatever new plan Grandpa had dreamed up. One time he sent a rose garden that ran the length of our property, from curb to back fence. But it wasn't enough to send the rosebushes; Grandpa held my father's very soil in low esteem; no plant of *his* could be expected to grow in it. So he had his men dig a fifty-foot trench three feet wide and a foot deep, remove the soil by hand, and then replace it with soil trucked in from his own garden. This way the roses (which also came from Grandpa's garden) would suffer no undue stress and my father's poor, neglected soil would be at least partly redeemed. Sometimes it seemed as if my grandfather was bent on replacing every bit of earth around our house, a square foot at a time.

Now any good gardener cares as much about soil as plants, but my grandfather's obsession with this particular patch of earth probably went deeper than that. No doubt my father, who was the first in his family to own his own house, viewed his father-in-law's desire to replace our soil with his own as a challenge to the very ground on which his independence stood. And maybe there was something to this: Grandpa had given my parents the money for the down payment ($4,000, the house had cost $11,000), and like most of his gifts, this one was not unencumbered. The unsolicited landscaping services, like Grandpa's habit of occasionally pounding on the house's walls as if to check on its upkeep, suggest that his feelings about our house were more than a little proprietary. It was as a landlord that Grandpa felt most comfortable in the world, and as long as my father declined to think of himself as a tenant, they were bound not to get along.

But probably his concern for our soil was also an extension of his genuine and deeply felt love of land. I don't mean love of *the* land, in the nature-lover's sense. *The* land is abstract and in some final sense unpossessable by any individual. Grandpa loved land as a reliable if somewhat mystical source of private wealth. No matter what happened in the world, no matter what folly the government perpetrated, land could be counted on to hold and multiply its value. At the worst a plot could yield a marketable crop and, at least on Long Island for most of this century, it could be resold for a profit. "They can print more money," he liked to say, "and they can print new stocks and bonds, but they can't print more land."

In his mind, the Old World peasant and the real estate developer existed side by side; he was both men and perceived no contradiction. Each looked at a piece of land and saw potential wealth: it made no difference that one saw a field of potatoes and the other a housing development. Grandpa could be perfectly happy spending his mornings tenderly cultivating the land and his afternoons despoiling it. Thoreau, planting his bean field, said he aimed to make the earth "speak beans." Some days my grandfather made the earth speak vegetables; other days it was shopping centers.

Grandpa started out in the teens wholesaling produce in Suffolk County, which was mostly farmland then. He would buy fruits and vegetables from the farmers and sell them to restaurants and, later, to the military bases that sprang up on Long Island during the war. He managed to make money straight through the Depression, and used his savings to buy farmland at Depression prices. When after the Second World War the suburbs started to boom, he saw his opportunity. Suffolk County was generally considered too far from the city for commuters, but Grandpa was confident that sooner or later the suburban tide would reach his shore. His faith in the area was so emphatic that (according to his obituary in *Newsday*) he was known in business circles as Mr. Suffolk.

Grandpa worked the leading edge of the suburban advance, speculating in the land that suburbanization was steadily translating from farm into tract house and shopping center. He grasped the powerful impulses that drove New Yorkers farther and farther out east because he shared them. There was the fear and contempt for city ways—the usual gloss on the suburban outlook—but there was also a nobler motive: to build a middle-class utopia, impelled by a Jeffersonian hunger for independence and a drive to create an ideal world for one's children. The suburbs, where you could keep one foot on the land and the other in the city, was without a doubt the best way to live, and Grandpa possessed an almost evangelical faith that we would all live this way eventually. Every time he bought a hundred acres of North Fork potato field, he knew it was only a matter of time before its utopian destiny would be fulfilled. Grandpa had nothing against potatoes, but who could deny that the ultimate Long Island crop was a suburban development? The fact that every home in that development could have a patch of potatoes in the backyard was proof that progress had no cost.

His own suburban utopia was a sprawling ranch house on five acres of waterfront in Babylon, on the south shore. My grandfather had enough money to live nearly anywhere, and for a time the family lived in a very grand mansion in Westbury. But he preferred to live in one of Long Island's new developments, and after his children were grown he and my grandmother moved into one where the fancy homes on their big plots nevertheless hewed to the dictates of middle-class suburban taste. The houses were set well back from the road and their massive expanses of unhedged front lawn ran together to create the impression of a single park-like landscape. Here in front of each house was at least an acre of land on which no one but the hired gardener ever stepped, an extravagance of unused acreage that must have rubbed against Grandpa's grain. But front yards in the suburbs are supposed to contribute to a kind of visual commons, and to honor this convention, Grandpa was willing to deny himself the satisfaction of fully exploiting an entire acre of prime real estate.

At least until I was a teenager, visits to Grandma and Grandpa's were always sweet occasions. The anticipation would start to build as we turned onto Peninsula Drive and began the long, slow ride through that Great Common Lawn, a perfection of green relieved only by evergreen punctuation marks and the fine curves of driveways drawn in jet-black asphalt. Eager as we were to get there, we always made Mom slow down (Dad hardly ever made the trip) in the hope of spotting the one celebrity who lived on my grandparents' road: Bob Keeshan, known to every child of that time as Captain Kangaroo. One time we did see the Captain, dressed in his civilian clothes, digging in his garden.

There is something about a lush, fresh-cut lawn that compels children to break into a sprint, and after the long ride we couldn't wait to spill out of the station wagon and fan out across the backyard. The grass always seemed to have a fresh crew cut, and it was so springy and uniform that you wanted to run your hand across it and bring your face close. My sisters could spend the whole afternoon practicing their cartwheels on it, but sooner or later Grandma would lure them indoors, into what was emphatically her realm. Except for the garage and a small den with a TV, where Grandpa passed rainy days stretched out on the sofa, the house brimmed with grandmotherness: glass cases full of tiny ceramic figurines, billowy pink chiffon curtains, dressing tables with crystal atomizers and silver hairbrushes, lacquered boxes stuffed with earrings, ornately framed portraits of my mother and aunt. I remember it as a very queenly place, a suburban Versailles, and it absorbed my sisters for hours at a time.

Grandpa's realm was outside, where he and his gardener, Andy, had made what I judged a paradise. Beginning at the driveway, the lawn described a broad, curving avenue that wound around the back of the house. On one side of it was the flagstone patio and rock garden, and on the other a wilder area planted with shrubs and small trees; this enclosed the backyard, screening it from the bay. A stepping-stone path conducted you through this area, passing beneath a small rose arbor and issuing with an unfailingly pleasing surprise onto the bright white beach. Plunked in the middle of the lawn was a gazebo, a silly confection of a building that was hardly ever used. Arrayed around it in a neat crescent was a collection of the latest roses, enormous blooms on spindly stems with names like Chrysler and Eisenhower and Peace. In June they looked like members of a small orchestra, performing for visitors in the garden.

The area between the lawn and the beach was twenty or thirty feet deep, thickly planted, and it formed a kind of wilderness we could explore out of sight of the adults on the patio. Here were mature rhododendrons and fruit trees, including a famous peach that Grandpa was said to have planted from seed. It was an impressive tree, too, weighed down in late summer with bushels of fruit. The tree was a dwarf, so we could reach the downy yellow globes ourselves. Hoping to repeat Grandpa's achievement, we carefully buried the pit of every peach we ate. (Probably it was his example that inspired my experiment with watermelon seeds.) But ripe fruit was only one of the surprises of Grandpa's wild garden. There was another we always looked for, only sometimes found. Creeping among the rhododendrons and dwarf trees, we would on lucky days come upon a small, shaded glade where, on a low mound, a concrete statue stood. It was a boy with his hand on his penis, peeing. This scandalous little scene never failed to set off peals of laughter when we were in a group; alone, the feelings were more complicated. In one way or another Eros operates in every garden; here was where he held sway in Grandpa's.

Back out in daylight, you could continue along the avenue of lawn until you came to an area of formal hedges clipped as tall as a ten-year-old, and forming an alley perhaps ten feet wide and forty feet long. At one end was a regulation-size shuffleboard court paved in sleek, painted concrete (it felt cool to bare feet all summer), and, at the other, a pair of horseshoe pins. Some visits these games held my interest for a while, but usually I made straight for the break in the hedge that gave onto what was unquestionably my favorite and my grandfather's proudest part of the garden—indeed, the only part of the property I ever heard anybody call a garden: his vegetable garden.

Vegetables had given Grandpa his earliest success, and the older he got, the more devoted to them he became. Eventually care of the ornamental gardens fell to Andy, and Grandpa spent the better part of his days among his vegetables, each spring adding to the garden and subtracting from the lawn. It's quite possible that, had Grandpa lived another twenty years, his suburban spread would have reverted entirely to farm. As it was, Grandpa had at least a half-acre planted in vegetables—virtually a truck farm, and a totally unreasonable garden for an elderly couple. I have a photograph of him from the seventies, standing proudly among his vegetables in his double-knits, and I can count more than twenty-five tomato plants and at least a dozen zucchini plants. You can't see the corn—row upon row of sweet corn—or the string beans, cucumbers, cantaloupes, peppers, and onions, but there had to be enough here to supply a farm stand.

The garden was bordered by a curving brick kneewall that ran right along the water, a location that ensured a long growing season since the bay held heat well into the fall forestalling frost. Grandpa could afford to be extravagant with space, and no two plants in his garden ever touched one another. I don't think a more meticulous vegetable garden ever existed; my grandfather hoed it every morning, and no weed dared raise its head above that black, loamy floor. Grandpa brought the same precision to the planting of string beans and tomatoes that Le Nôtre brought to the planting of chestnut trees in the Tuileries. The rows, which followed the curves of the garden wall, might as well have been laid out by a surveyor, and the space between each plant was uniform and exact. Taken as a whole, the garden looked like nothing so much as a scale model for one of the latest suburban developments: the rows were roads, and each freestanding vegetable plant was a single-family house. Here in the garden one of the unacknowledged contradictions of Grandpa's life was symbolically resolved: the farmer and the developer became one.

But what could have possessed my grandfather to plant such a *big* vegetable garden? Even cooking and canning and pickling at her furious clip, there was no way my grandmother could keep up with his garden's vast daily yield. Eventually she cracked and went on strike: she refused to process any more of his harvest, and true to her word, never again pickled a cucumber or canned a tomato. But even then he would not be deterred, and the garden continued to expand.

I suspect that this crisis of overproduction suited Grandpa just fine. He was foremost a capitalist and, to borrow a pair of terms from Marx, was ultimately less interested in the use value of his produce than in its exchange value. I don't mean to suggest that he took no immediate pleasure in his vegetables; his tomatoes, especially, pleased him enormously. He liked to slice his beefsteaks into thick pink slabs and go at them with a knife and fork. Watching him dine on one, you understood immediately how a tomato could come to be named for a cut of meat. "Sweet-as-sugar," he would announce between bites, his accent mushing the three words together into one incantatory sound. Of course he would say the same thing about his Bermuda onions, his corn, even his bell peppers. Grandpa's vocabulary of English superlatives was limited, and "sweet-as-sugar" was the highest compliment you could pay a vegetable.

Eating beefsteaks was one pleasure, but calculating their market value and giving them away was even better. Having spent many years in the produce business, Grandpa had set aside a place in his mind where he maintained the current retail price of every vegetable in the supermarket; even in his nineties he would drop by the Waldbaum's produce section from time to time to update his mental price list. Harvesting alongside him, I can remember Grandpa holding a tomato aloft and, instead of exclaiming over its size or perfect color, he'd quote its market price: *Thirty-nine cents a pound!* (Whatever the amount, it was always an outrage.) Probably when he gazed out over his garden he could see in his mind's eye those little white placards stapled to tongue depressors listing the going per-pound price of every crop. And given the speed with which he could tally a column of figures in his head, I am sure he could mentally translate the entire tomato plant. To work in his garden was to commune with nature without ever leaving the marketplace.

By growing much more produce than he and Grandma could ever hope to consume, Grandpa transformed his vegetables into commodities. And to make sure of this elevated status, he planted exclusively those varieties sold by the supermarket chains: beefsteaks, iceberg lettuce, Blue Lake string beans, Marketmore cukes. Never mind that these were usually varieties distinguished less for their flavor than their fitness for transcontinental shipment; he preferred a (theoretically) marketable crop to a tasty one. Of course selling the vegetables wasn't a realistic option; he appreciated that an eighty-five-year-old real estate magnate couldn't very well open a farm stand, as much as he might have liked to. Still, he needed distribution channels, so he worked hard at giving the stuff away. All summer, before he got dressed for work (he never retired), Grandpa harvested the garden and loaded the trunk and backseat of his Lincoln with bushel baskets of produce. As he went on his rounds—visiting tenants, haggling with bankers and brokers, buying low and selling high—he'd give away baskets of vegetables. Now my grandfather never gave away anything that didn't have at least some slender string attached to it, and no doubt he believed that his sweet-as-sugar beefsteaks put these businessmen in his debt, gave him some slight edge. And probably this was so. At the least, the traveling produce show put the suits off their guard, making Grandpa seem more like some benign Old World bumpkin than the shark he really was.

It took a long time before I understood the satisfaction of giving away vegetables, but the pleasures of harvesting them I acquired immediately. A good visit to Grandma and Grandpa's was one on a day he hadn't already harvested. On these occasions I could barely wait for Grandpa to hand me a basket and dispatch me to the garden to start the picking. Alone was best—when Grandpa came along, he would invariably browbeat me about some fault in my technique, so I made sure to get out there before he finished small-talking with Mom. Ripe vegetables were magic to me. Unharvested, the garden bristled with possibility. I would quicken at the sight of a ripe tomato, sounding its redness from deep amidst the undifferentiated green. To lift a bean plant's hood of heart-shaped leaves and discover a clutch of long, slender pods hanging underneath could make me catch my breath. Cradling the globe of a cantaloupe warmed in the sun, or pulling orange spears straight from his sandy soil—these were the keenest of pleasures, and even today in the garden they're accessible to me, dulled only slightly by familiarity.

At the time this pleasure had nothing to do with eating. I didn't like vegetables any better than most kids do (tomatoes I considered disgusting, acceptable only in the form of ketchup), yet there it was: the vegetable sublime. Probably I had absorbed my grandfather's reverence for produce, the sense that this was precious stuff and here it was, growing, for all purposes, on trees. I may have had no use for tomatoes and cucumbers, but the fact that adults did conferred value on them in my eyes. The vegetable garden in summer made an enchanted landscape, mined with hidden surprises, dabs of unexpected color and unlikely forms that my grandfather had taught me to regard as treasures. My favorite board game as a child was Candyland, in which throws of the dice advanced your man through a stupendous landscape of lollipop trees, milk-chocolate swamps, shrubs made of gumdrops. Candyland posited a version of nature that answered to a child's every wish—a landscape hospitable in the extreme, which is one definition of a garden—and my grandfather's vegetable patch in summer offered a fair copy of that paradise.

This was Grandpa's garden. If I could look at it and see Candyland, he probably saw Monopoly; in both our eyes, this was a landscape full of meaning, one that answered to wishes and somehow spoke in a human language. As a child I could always attend more closely to gardens than to forests, probably because forests contain so little of the human information that I craved then, and gardens so much. One of the things childhood is is a process of learning about the various paths that lead out of nature and into culture, and the garden contains many of these. I can't imagine a wilderness that would have had as much to say to me as Grandpa's garden did: the floral scents that intimated something about the ways of ladies as well as flowers, the peach trees that made legible the whole of the idea of fruit and seed, the vegetable that had so much to say about the getting of food and money, and the summer lawns that could not have better expressed the hospitality of nature to human habitation.

My parents' yard (you would not call it a garden) had a lot to say too, but it wasn't until I was much older that I could appreciate this. Landscapes can carry a whole other set of meanings, having to do with social or even political questions, and these are usually beyond the ken of young children. My father's unmowed front lawn was a clear message to our neighbors and his father-in-law, but at the time I was too young to comprehend it fully. I understood our yard as a source of some friction between my parents, and I knew enough to be vaguely embarrassed by it. Conformity is something children seem to grasp almost instinctively, and the fact that our front yard was different from everybody else's made me feel our family was odd. I couldn't understand why my father couldn't be more like other dads in the neighborhood.

One summer he let the lawn go altogether. The grasses grew tall enough to flower and set seed; the lawn rippled in the breeze like a context. Stuck in the middle of a row of tract houses on Long Island, the lawn said *turpitude* rather than *meadow*, even though that is strictly speaking what it had become. It also said, to the neighbors, *fuck you.*

A case could be made that the front lawn is the most characteristic institution of the American suburb, and my father's lack of respect for it probably expressed his general ambivalence about the suburban way of life. In the suburbs, the front lawn is, at least visually, a part of a collective landscape; while not exactly public land, it isn't entirely private either. In this it reflects one of the foundations of the suburban experiment, which Lewis Mumford once defined as "a collective effort to live a private life." The private part was simple enough; the suburban dream turns on the primacy of family life and private property; these being the two greatest goods in my father's moral universe, he was eager to sign up. But "owning your own home" turned out to be only half of it: a suburb is a place where you undertake to do this in concert with hundreds of other "like-minded" couples. Without reading the small print, my father had signed on for the whole middle-class utopia package, and there were heavy dues to pay.

The front lawn symbolized the collective face of suburbia,

the backyard its private aspect. In the back, you could do pretty much whatever you wanted, but out front you had to take account of the community's wishes and its self-image. Fences and hedges were out of the question: they were considered antisocial, unmistakable symbols of alienation from the group. One lawn should flow unimpeded into another, obscuring the boundaries between homes and contributing to the sense of community. It was here in the front lawn that "like-mindedness" received its clearest expression. The conventional design of a suburban street is meant to forge the multitude of equal individual parcels of land into a single vista—a democratic landscape. To maintain your portion of this landscape was part of your civic duty. You voted each November, joined the PTA, and mowed the lawn every Saturday.

Of course the democratic system can cope with the nonvoter far more easily than the democratic landscape can cope with the nonmower. A single unmowed lawn ruins the whole effect, announcing to the world that all is not well here in utopia. My father couldn't have cared less. He owned the land; he could do whatever he wanted with it. As for the neighbors, he felt he owed them nothing. Ours was virtually the only Jewish family in a largely Catholic neighborhood, and with one or two exceptions, the neighbors had always treated us coolly. Why should he pretend to share their values? If they considered our lawn a dissent from the common will, that was a fair interpretation. And if it also happened to rankle his father-in-law, well, that only counted in its favor. (One should be careful, however, not to minimize the influence of laziness on my father's philosophy of lawn care.)

The summer he stopped mowing altogether, I felt the hot breath of a tyrannical majority for the first time. Nobody would say anything, but you heard it anyway: *Mow your lawn.* Cars would slow down as they drove by our house. Probably some of the drivers were merely curious: they saw the unmowed lawn and wondered if perhaps someone had left in a hurry, or died. But others drove by in a manner that was unmistakably expressive, slowing down as they drew near and then hitting the gas angrily as they passed—this was pithy driving, the sort of move that is second nature to a Klansman.

The message came by other media, too. George Hackett, our next-door neighbor and my father's only friend in the development, was charged by the neighbors with conveying the sense of the community to my father. George didn't necessarily hold with the majority on this question, but he was the only conceivable intermediary and he was susceptible to pressure. George was a small, somewhat timid man—he was probably the least intimidating adult in my world at the time—and I'm sure the others twisted his arm fairly hard before he agreed to do their bidding. It was early on a summer evening that he came by to deliver the message. I don't remember it all, but I can imagine him taking a drink from my mother, squeaking out what he had been deputized to say, and then waiting for my father—who next to George was a bear—to respond.

My father's reply could not have been more eloquent. He went to the garage and cranked up the rusty old Toro for the first time since spring; it is a miracle the thing started. He pushed it out to the curb and then started back across the lawn to the house, but not in a straight line; he swerved right, then left, then right again. He had made an *S* in the tall grass. Then he made an *M* and finally a *P.* These were his initials, and as soon as he finished writing them, he wheeled the lawn mower back to the garage, never to start it up again.

It wasn't long after this incident that we moved out of Farmingdale. The year was 1961, I was six, and my father was by now doing well enough to afford a house on the more affluent north shore, in a town called Woodbury. We bought one of the first houses in a new development called the Gates: the development was going in on the site of an old estate, and the builder had preserved the gigantic wrought-iron entrance gates in order to lend the new neighborhood a bit of aristocratic tone.

To the builder goes the privilege of naming the streets in his development, and the common practice then was to follow a theme. Most neighborhoods had streets named for trees and flowers, but the Gates from the start pictured itself as a different kind of development—grander, more forward-looking—so it would have a different kind of street name. Alaska had recently been made the fiftieth state, and this developer, regarding himself perhaps as a pioneer or empire builder, decided to name all his streets after places there; our house was at the corner of Juneau Boulevard and Fairbanks Drive. (The word street, with its urban connotation, is not a part of the suburban vocabulary.) The incongruity of remote, frontierish, place names attached to prissy "boulevards" and "drives" and "courts" never seemed to bother anybody.

With a new development, you chose your plot of land, one of the three available house types (ranch, colonial, or split-level), and then they built it for you. We chose a wooded acre (a vast tract compared to what we had in Farmingdale) that sloped down from Juneau Boulevard into a hollow. The topography afforded some privacy, but it meant that the floor of our basement was usually under several inches of water. As for house type, there could be no question: we always lived in ranch houses. There were two reasons for this. First, a ranch was the most "modern" kind of house, and my parents regarded themselves as modern. The second reason had to do with safety: my mother believed you simply did not raise children in a house with a staircase. You might as well invite the Long Island Railroad to lay its tracks through your backyard.

After the contract had been signed, my father would drive my sister and me to Woodbury each weekend to follow the progress of our new house. We watched as the wooded acre was partially cleared and staked out by surveyors with tripods. My parents had chosen this plot because of its deep oak forest, and we tied ribbons to the trees we wanted saved, including a great big two-trunked oak that would stand outside our front door for the rest of my childhood. We felt like pioneers, watching as the woods gave way to bulldozers and a whole new landscape began to take shape. I remember being deeply impressed by what the heavy equipment could accomplish; who knew a forest could be turned into a yard, or a hill made to disappear? I'd never seen land change like this. The day they came to pour the foundation, my father gave us pennies to drop in the fresh concrete for good luck.

Though only twenty minutes away from Farmingdale, the Gates was a different world. Farmingdale was a blue-collar neighborhood, inhabited by electricians, engineers, and aerospace workers for whom a suburban home was the first and perhaps the only proof of membership in the American middle class. It may have been the tenuousness of our neighbors' grip on that identity that made them so touchy about lawns and Jews. The people who bought into the Gates, on the other hand, were the sons and daughters of the lower middle class, which in the fifties and sixties meant they were on their way to becoming quite affluent; they were lawyers and doctors and the owners of small businesses. This was a more confident class, and they sought a suburban home that would reflect their ascendancy and sophistication. Already in the early 1960s, the suburbs had acquired a reputation for conformity and squareness, and the Gates appealed to people who wanted to live in a suburb that didn't look like one. The streets were broad and, instead of being laid out in a tight grid, they curved in unpredictable ways. There was no practical reason for this, of course; the streets didn't curve around anything. They curved strictly to give an impression of ruralness and age. A sort of antisuburban suburban aesthetic ruled the development: the plots had been cut into irregular shapes, sidewalks had been eliminated, and roads ended in cul-de-sacs (these were the "courts").

Compared to Farmingdale, the landscaping in the Gates was wildly expressive. Not that the tyranny of the front lawn had been overturned. But even within that tight constraint, many families managed, in a phrase you were beginning to hear a lot, to do their own thing. Most of the landscaping styles were vaguely aristocratic, recalling the look of British country estates or, even more improbably, southern plantations. Circular driveways were very big. These broad crescents, scrupulously outlined in shrubbery, would curve right up to the front door. The planting served to emphasize the asphalt, which would be repainted each year with driveway sealer to restore its inky sheen. These driveways made a visitor feel he was driving up to a mansion rather than a split-level; you half expected someone in livery to open the car door for you. But the true purpose of the circular driveway was to provide a glittering setting for the family jewel, which was usually a Cadillac or Lincoln. Circular driveways made it socially acceptable to park your car right in the middle of the front yard where no one could possibly miss it.

The Rosenblums, a few doors up Juneau Boulevard from us, had *two* driveways, one on each side of the biggest, flattest, most pristine lawn in the development. Their aloof white colonial stood squarely in the middle of this vast green rectangle, framed by the two dead-straight black pavements. One driveway delivered family members to the garage and the other brought guests to a somewhat more formal entrance. The facade of the house was vaguely Greek Revival, but immense, with four ridiculous Doric columns and a giant wrought-iron chandelier hanging in the middle. It always reminded me of Tara. Just what kind of fantasy Mr. Rosenblum was working out here I have no idea, but I do remember he would get hopping mad whenever anyone used the wrong driveway.

It must have been obvious to my parents that the "S.M.P." approach to lawn care and gardening would not go over in the Gates. Fortunately, they could now afford to buy a fancy landscaping job and, even more important, a maintenance contract that would help keep my father on the right side of his new neighbors. It's important to understand that my parents were not indifferent to the landscape; even my father cared about his trees and shrubs. He simply didn't like lawns and preferred to deal with the rest of the garden at a remove, ideally through a window. But with money came a new approach to gardening, one that replaced laborious, direct involvement with the earth and plants with practices more to his liking: supervision, deal making, shopping, technological tinkering, negotiation. One must enlarge the definition of gardening a bit before his quasi-horticultural accomplishments can be fully appreciated. Perhaps the greatest of these involved the weeping birch that stood in the middle of our backyard in Farmingdale, forming what looked like a cascading green fountain. This somewhat rare specimen was my mother's favorite tree, and she wanted very badly to bring it with us to Woodbury. So as soon as the contract to sell the house in Farmingdale had been signed, but before the new owners had moved in, my father arranged to have Walter Schikelhaus, my grandfather's landscape man, dig it out and truck it to Woodbury. But the tree was so distinctive, and occupied such a pivotal position in the backyard, that the new owners were bound to miss it. So my father had Walter plant in its place a weeping willow. Then he instructed Walter to paint the willow's bark white and carefully prune its branches to resemble a weeping birch. After mowing his initials in Farmingdale, this was perhaps my father's greatest achievement as a gardener, a strikingly original synthesis of topiary and fraud.

The man my parents hired to design, plant, and maintain our yard must have been a renegade among Long Island landscapers. Taking his cues from my father, he came up with a radical, low-maintenance design that included only a slender, curving ribbon of lawn. This narrow lane of sod wound an unpredictable path among every alternative to grass then known to landscaping: broad islands of shrubbery underplanted with pachysandra; flagstone patios; substantial wooded areas; and even a Japanese section paved in imported white pebbles. It was all very modern, and though it defied the conventions of suburban landscape design, it did so with taste. Overall, the front yard had far more ground cover than grass. Instead of foundation planting, most of the shrubs (rhododendron and azalea, in the main) were planted close to the street, forming a rough, irregular hedge that obscured the house. The retaining wall along the driveway was a terraced affair made out of railroad ties, which at the time were still a novelty in landscape design. (They weren't commercially available then, but my father arranged to buy them off trucks from LILCO and LIRR employees.) Much of the property was left wooded. And the Toro stayed behind, in Farmingdale. We may have been the only family on Long Island that didn't own a lawn mower.

Since my father's line on watering was more or less the same as his line on mowing, he decided to order a state-of-the-art sprinkler system. From his command post in the garage he would be able to monitor and water every corner of his acre, one zone at a time. An elaborate timer, working in conjunction with a device that judged the moisture content of the soil, was supposed to ensure that the grass and pachysandra enjoyed optimum conditions. But it soon became clear that the sprinkler man had taken my father for an expensive ride. We had hundreds more sprinkler heads than we could possibly need; every six feet another bronze mushroom poked out of the ground. And the system never worked properly. Often in the middle of the night, or during a rainstorm, the sprinkler heads would suddenly start hissing and spitting in unison, as if under the direction of some alien intelligence. From some heads the spray roared like Niagara, but most of them dribbled pathetically. My father would spend hours at a time in the garage, standing in his boxer shorts at the control panel, trying vainly to rein in the system's perversity.

From my point of view, my father's remote-controlled landscape was sorely lacking. Once the crew finished planting the shrubs and laying down the carpet of sod, there was nothing left to do but look at it. For all its banality, the conventional suburban landscape, like the suburbs themselves, was tailored to the needs of children. As a place to play, nothing surpasses a lawn. Beautiful as it was, my parents' yard, with its sliver of lawn and masses of shade trees, was inhospitable to children; it was a spectator's landscape, its picturesque views best appreciated indoors, in boxers. You certainly couldn't play in pachysandra.

But what it lacked most was a garden. True, considered whole, it *was* a garden, but to my mind (as in the common American usage) a garden was a small plot of flowers or vegetables; everything else was a "yard." A yard was just a place; a garden was somehow more specific and, best of all as far as I was concerned, it was productive: it did something. I wanted something more like my grandfather's garden, a place where I could put my hands on the land and make it do things. I'd also been spending a lot of time watching workmen revolutionize the landscape all around me as they created this new development: every day, it seemed, forests turned into lawns, fresh black roads bisected the nearby farm fields, sumps were being dug, whole hills were *moving*. Everywhere you looked the landscape seemed to be in flux, and I was taken with the whole idea of reshaping earth. Meanwhile our own acre had suddenly fossilized. All you could do was go to the garage and fiddle with the sprinkler controls. I wanted to *dig*.

Most of our yard now came under the jurisdiction of the maintenance crews that showed up every Friday, but there were still a few corners that escaped their attention. The lawn never took in the backyard, along the narrow corridor between the house and the woods; no matter what blend of seed they tried, the shade eventually defeated the grass. When the landscapers finally gave up on this patch I was allowed to dig in it. Of course the shade precluded my planting a garden, but I had another idea: to give the property a badly needed body of water. I ran a hose underground from the house and constructed a watercourse: a streambed lined with stones passed through a complex network of pools and culminated in a spectacular waterfall, at least eight inches tall. I spent whole afternoons observing the water as it inscribed new paths in the ground on its infinitely variable yet inevitable journey toward the woods. I was learning to think like water, a knack that would serve me well in the garden later on. I experimented with various stones to produce different sounds and motions, and no doubt wasted an obscene amount of water. Though I judged it a miniature landscape of extraordinary beauty, my water garden may have really been little more than a mud patch; I'm not sure.

When I tired of my water garden, I ripped it out and built a cemetery in its place. We had lots of pets, and they were constantly dying. Not just cats and dogs, but canaries and chicks, turtles and ducklings, gerbils and hamsters. Whenever one of these animals expired, my sister and I would organize elaborate funerals. And if all our pets happened to be in good health, there were always roadkills in need of decent burial. After we interred the shoe-box-caskets, we would rake and reseed the ground and plant another homemade wooden cross above the grave. I understood that crosses were for Christians. But a Star of David was beyond my carpentry skills, and anyway I was inclined to think of pets as gentiles. To a child growing up Jewish, the Other, in all its forms, was presumed to be Christian.

My usual partner in all these various landscaping endeavors was Jimmy Brancato, an uncannily hapless boy who lived down the street with his problematic parents. Mr. Brancato was a vaguely gangsterish character who owned a car wash in Hempstead, and who, it was rumored, had once spent time in jail in another state. Mrs. Brancato, who wore her bleach-blond hair in a monumental do and looked a lot like a gun moll, was a champion screamer and worrier. She was so steadfast in the conviction that her children were destined for trouble (jail in Jimmy's case; out-of-wedlock pregnancy in his sisters') that they must have gradually come to believe there could be no alternative. And sure enough, one of the daughters eventually did get knocked up and Jimmy had a serious run-in with the law.

But that came much later; at the time I'm writing about, Jimmy was nine or ten, merely on the cusp of delinquency. As you can imagine, we both preferred to hang out at my house. Jimmy loved my mother, probably for the simple reason that she didn't see prison stripes when she looked at him. And I was too terrified of Jimmy's parents to go near them voluntarily. I liked Jimmy because, compared to me, he was bold and fearless; he liked me because, compared to him, I had a brain. We made a good team.

We both liked to garden, though it's possible Jimmy was just following my lead here. I usually set the agenda, explaining to Jimmy where we were going to dig or what we were going to plant that day, citing my grandfather whenever I needed to bolster my authority. Our first garden, which we called a farm, was terraced: the railroad-tie retaining wall rose from the driveway in a series of four or five steps, each of which made a perfect garden bed. We'd plant strawberries on one level, watermelons on another, and on a third some cucumbers, eggplants, and peppers. But strawberries were by far our favorite crop. They had the drama of tomatoes (the brilliant red fruit), they came back every year by themselves (something we thought was very cool), *and* they were edible. Our goal, though, was to harvest enough strawberries to sell—this being a farm—and anytime we could get six or seven ripe ones at a time, we'd put them in a Dixie cup and sell them to my mother. Eventually we hoped to open a farm stand on Juneau Boulevard. Jimmy always worked like a dog. Even after I'd be called in for dinner, he'd stay out there digging and hoeing until his mother stuck her head out of their kitchen window and started hollering for him to come home.

As much as he seemed to enjoy it, this form of gardening didn't fully satisfy Jimmy's taste for adventure; perhaps he sensed that it would be hard to realize his destiny in the vegetable patch (though in fact he eventually would find a way to do exactly that). Jimmy held a relatively broad concept of gardening, embracing as it did such unconventional practices as the harvesting of other people's crops in their absence. Bordering our development was a pumpkin field, and several times each fall Jimmy insisted I accompany him on a mission to steal as many pumpkins as we could pile in our wagons. Going along was the price I paid for Jimmy's help on the farm.

The pumpkin field in October was a weirdly beautiful place, with its vast web of green vines blanketing the gorgeous orange orbs for as far as you could see. Here was the vegetable sublime again, but now its experience was fraught with danger. I'd been taught that trespassing was a heinous crime, and the NO TRESPASS-

ING sign we had to drag our wagons past choked me with fear. In the suburbs private property was such a sacrosanct institution that even young children felt its force. Jimmy claimed—probably just to scare me but you never knew for sure—that the farmers had rifles that fired bullets made of salt, and if they saw us they would be fully within their rights to shoot since *we were on their property*. These salt pellets were said to cause excruciating pain. (As if getting shot with steel bullets wouldn't have been enough.) We managed to get out alive every time, but I have to say I wasn't entirely disappointed the year the pumpkin field gave way to a new housing development.

After we arrived safely at home with our pumpkins (we'd always go to Jimmy's; my mother would have flipped out if we'd shown up with hot pumpkins), we'd divvy up the loot and then Jimmy would proceed methodically to smash his share. This was a pleasure I could not comprehend. But clearly the kick for Jimmy came in stealing the pumpkins, not owning them. Watching him get off bashing his pumpkins, you would think he'd been possessed. And the longer I knew him, the more I began to sense that he had an almost mystical attraction to trouble. One summer while my family was away on vacation, Jimmy was running some routine experiments with matches when he accidentally burned down the forest behind our house. All kids chucked snowballs at passing cars, but when Jimmy did it he would smash a windshield and then actually get caught. He wasn't a bad kid, not at all; it's just that he had some sort of tropism that bent him toward disaster as naturally as a plant bends toward sunlight.

Years after we had gone our separate ways, Jimmy figured out a way to combine what I'd taught him about gardening with his penchant for trouble. It must have been around 1970, when he was in the ninth grade, that Jimmy decided to start his own farm, one that might actually make some money. He planted a small field of marijuana. Jimmy had considered all the angles and went to great lengths to avoid detection. Growing pot on his parents' property was obviously out of the question, so he cleared a plot down by the Manor House, the abandoned mansion on whose grounds the Gates had been built. The developer had promised to turn the Manor House into a community center, but he had skipped town long ago and the place had devolved into a kind of no-man's-land, a gothic ruin surrounded by old refrigerators and derelict shopping carts. Brambles and sumac choked any spot not occupied by a stripped Impala, and clearing a patch for a garden must have been back-breaking work. Most of us didn't dare go near the Manor House during the day, let alone after dark. But each night, after midnight, Jimmy would slip out of his house, ride his bicycle down to the Manor House, and tend to his precious crop by flashlight.

Getting caught wasn't going to be easy, but Jimmy managed to pull it off.

Shortly before Jimmy planned to begin his harvest, a neighborhood boy riding his bicycle around the Manor House happened upon his garden. Today, the leaf pattern and silhouette of a pot plant is as familiar as a maple's, but this was not yet the case in 1970. Unfortunately for Jimmy, this particular boy had recently attended an assembly at school where a policeman had shown the kids how to recognize marijuana. The boy raced home and told his mother what he'd seen and his mother called the police.

Jimmy had by now been in enough scrapes to be well known to the local police and I'm sure they immediately settled on him as a prime suspect. In the version of the story I heard, when the cops dropped by to question Jimmy and his mother, he kept cool, admitting nothing. Since they had no evidence linking Jimmy to the marijuana plants, that should have been the end of it. But the police had aroused Mrs. Brancato's suspicions and she decided to conduct a search of Jimmy's room.

Of the seven deadly sins, surely it is pride that most commonly afflicts the gardener. Jimmy was justly proud of his garden, and though he knew better than to invite anyone to visit it, he apparently couldn't resist taking a few snapshots of his eight-foot beauties in their prime. Mrs. Brancato found the incriminating photographs and, concluding it would be best for her son in the long run, turned them in to the police. No charges were brought, but Jimmy was packed off to military school, and I lost track of him.

My own gardening career remained well within the bounds of the law, if not always of propriety. Around the same time Jimmy was tending his plot down at the Manor House, I moved the farm from the cramped quarters of the retaining wall to a more spacious plot I had cajoled from my parents alongside the foundation of our house. This would be my last garden in the Gates. Even the most devoted young gardener will find that his interest fades around the time of high school, and soon mine did. But the summer before I got my driver's license I made my most ambitious garden yet. I persuaded my parents to buy me a few yards of topsoil, and in the space of a hundred square feet I crammed a dozen different crops: tomatoes (just then become edible), peppers, eggplants, strawberries, corn, squash, melons (watermelon and cantaloupe), string beans, peas. Everything but lettuce, which, since it bore no fruit, held not nearly enough drama for me. Why would anyone ever want to grow *leaves*?

Years later when I read about European techniques of intensive agriculture, I realized this is what I had been doing without knowing it. I enriched the soil with bags of peat moss and manure, tilled it deeply, and then planted my seedlings virtually cheek-by-jowl. Since the bed was long and narrow, I decided to dispense with rows and planted most of the seedlings no more than six inches apart, in a pattern you would have to call free-form. Everything thrived: by August, my postage-stamp garden, haphazard though it was, was yielding bushels of produce.

Even my parents took note of this garden, marveling at the peppers and tomatoes I brought to the dinner table. But the person I really wanted to impress was my grandfather. By this point, my relationship with Grandpa was badly frayed. I wore my hair long and had grown a beard, and this deeply troubled him. By the time I turned fifteen, I could do nothing right by him, and visits to Babylon, which had held some of the sweetest hours of my childhood, had become an ordeal. From the moment I arrived, he would berate me about the beard, my studiously sloppy clothes, the braided leather bracelet I wore, and any other shred of evidence that I had become one of those despised 'ippies, as he used to spit out the word. I figured that if there was one place where an elderly reactionary and an aspiring hippie could find a bit of common ground, it was in the vegetable garden. I had finally made a garden he'd be proud of, and when he and Grandma made one of their infrequent visits to our house that summer, I couldn't wait to take him around back and show him what I'd achieved.

But Grandpa never even saw the garden I had made. All he saw were weeds and disorder. You call this a garden? he barked. It's all too close together—your plants are going to choke each other out. And where are your rows? *There have to be rows.* This isn't a vegetable garden—what you've got here is a weed garden! The big red beefsteaks, the boxy green peppers, the watermelons now bigger than footballs: everything was invisible to him but the weeds. He looked at my garden and saw in it everything about me—indeed, everything about America in 1970—that he could not stand. He saw the collapse of order, disrespect for authority, laziness, the unchecked march of disreputable elements. He was acting like a jerk, it's true, but he was my grandfather, an old man in a bad time to be old, and when he got down on his knees and started furiously pulling weeds, I did feel ashamed.

So I guess you could say that Jimmy and I were expelled from our gardens at around the same time. But that would be too neat. For all I know, Jimmy today tends twenty acres of the finest sinse in Humboldt County. In my case, the arrival of my driver's license did more to push me out of the garden than my grandfather's intemperate attack on my technique. If gardening is an exploration of a place close to home, being a teenager is an exploration of mobility, and these two approaches to place, or home, are bound sooner or later to come into conflict. For at least a decade I probably didn't think once about plants or even notice a landscape. Eventually, though, I came back to the garden, which is probably how it usually goes. Much of gardening is a return, an effort at recovering remembered landscapes. I was lucky that when I took up gardening again my grandfather was still alive. He was over ninety by the time I had my own house, and he never did get to see it. But I would bring him pictures, carefully culled to give an impression of neatness and order, and, after examining them closely for evidence of weeds, he would pronounce his approval. By then, his own garden consisted of a half-dozen tomatoes planted by the back door of a small condominium. I would help him weed and harvest; he still grew enough beefsteaks to give a few away. He would ask me to describe my garden, and I would, choosing my words with care, painting a picture of a place that he would find hospitable. The garden I described was largely imaginary, combining elements of my actual garden with memories of Babylon and the kind of pictures that I suppose are common to every gardener's dream. It was one of those places that is neither exactly in the past nor in the future, but that anyone who gardens is ever moving toward. It was somewhere we could still travel together. On one of my last visits to see him, he told me I could have his Dutch hoe, declaring it was the best tool for weeding he had ever found. Grandpa was ninety-six, three times my age exactly, and though his step by then was uncertain, he took me outside and showed me how to use it.

Lee May

from

IN MY
FATHER'S GARDEN

MERIDIAN, MISSISSIPPI
JUNE 20, 1989

The narrow concrete walk-way stretches barely twenty feet from the street to the porch, but this nervous-making visit made the distance seem more like a mile.

I had come to my father's home. Once, it was mine, too. On this scorching, Mississippi-dusty June day, the house on 30th Street seemed one of the few things in life that had not changed; it still was small. Two bedrooms, a kitchen and living room, its shell sheathed in those white asbestos shingles. On the faded bur-gundy-painted concrete floor sat two green metal chairs, the kind that spring back and forth as you rock your body.

Getting out of my little rental car, I peered up the walk to see my father, sitting still in one of the chairs. He was wearing a tiny smile, a light-colored shirt and newish overalls that floated around his body. He seemed so old. And so thin. So changed.

No wonder, I told myself as I yelled, "Hey! How ya doin'?" and started the long walk toward the porch. No wonder. Now, June 20, 1989, it had been thirty-nine years since I was last at this house. And since I last saw my father, eighty years old by this time. I was forty-eight.

"I'm doing tolerable well. How you?" Ples Mae answered. During those decades in which I had not seen him, I always wondered about his name. His first name is pronounced *Plez*, and his last name is spelled differently from mine. Someday, I would always think, I'll find out why.

But that could wait. It was time to walk that mile, a journey through almost four decades, through tons of events, memories and lives. My father and my mother, Riller, split up in 1950, when I, their only child, was nine. They both remarried. He to Mary Sterdivant, she to Milton Walker, the man I called Dad. The word stepfather would not have done him justice. My mother and dad and I moved from Meridian to East St. Louis, Illinois, in 1955, severing all contact with my father. Funny how seeing him after all these years recalled memories of my other two parents. Ironic that this was the eve of what would have been my mother's sixty-seventh birthday.

As I reached the porch, I did not know what to expect. Would we hug? We did not. My father did not rise. We shook hands. I sat. On one level this first meeting went as if we had seen each other just days before. There was no rush of questions about the past, no obvious look to gauge what the years had done. Weirdly, it was natural. How could we possibly catch the years we had lost? Better to go from now.

But Mary was much more demonstrative. She rushed through the door with a large grin and yelled, "Sonny! Sonny! I'm so glad you're here to see your Daddy! You don't know how many years I've prayed for this to happen." My father looked a little sheepish as Mary, a thinly built woman, hard of hearing but not hard to hear, darted back inside the house, talking over her shoulder: "Y'all talk. Go on and talk. I'm fixing dinner. Sonny, you got to eat something. We got butter beans outta the garden. Frozen fresh."

Just as I was unprepared for him to be so old, I also did not expect to see so much of myself in him. I noted that we were about the same height, six feet, and our facial structures, along with balding hair pattern, showed our connections.

Physical similarities aside, we had lived two disparate lives, worlds apart in many ways. Mine had been spread over many addresses, while most of my father's had unfolded right here. Sitting on the front porch, we made small talk to try bridging that time gap. I looked out onto 30th Avenue, then across the street, trying to recapture long-lost memories of my years in this neighborhood.

Searching for lost memories of my father, I felt a flush of discomfort and doubt. Was it really possible to make any meaning of a relationship that had not existed for forty years? Was coming here a bad idea after all?

"Been a hot one today," I said, wiping my forehead. "Hadn't been much rain."

"Yeah, I been having to water every day."

After about half an hour that felt like much longer, Mary appeared at the front door, calling us in to a wonderfully intoxicating meal—gifts from the garden. Around noonday, this meal was dinner to many Southerners, while the meal I would eat later, around 7 P.M., was supper. As Mary had advertised, there were butter beans mixed with peas, tomatoes, collards, okra, and corn bread, washed down with sodas.

Pretty soon, we took a stroll, to see what he was having to water. I was amazed at how orderly was his garden, rows straight and clean as arrows.

"Those tomatoes oughta be ready to eat any day," I said.

"If the squirrels don't get 'em first," he replied.

That first walk in my father's garden was filled with so much of my past. In that space, that deep, narrow lot, I could see the cages of rabbits that had infatuated me as a child, revolted me when I realized we were supposed to eat them. My dachshund, Pup Pup, had trotted from one end of the lot to the other, under the cages, among the vegetables.

And just as it had done almost forty years earlier, the sun-drenched garden grew just about everything a family might need. Collards, corn, butter beans, peas, tomatoes, peppers, squash, watermelon, potatoes. And amazingly, peanuts, their vines twirling out of a network of old car tires. Proudly, my father pointed out each crop, giving me a rundown on its progress, how well he expected it to bear.

"Now, this okra gonna make more than we can eat," he said in a voice that combined deep tones and heavy punctuations, one that must reflect something from his western Alabama upbringing. "And we gonna freeze these butter beans and peas, 'cause we get so many. Always do. We eat 'em all year long."

From the peanuts in the front of the garden, near the house, to the gnarled grapevine at the garden's end, near the spot where mosses and ferns grow in the wet, we walked during that visit and each subsequent one, looking, talking—a lot about gardening but also about my journalism career, neighbors long gone and half forgotten, politics, his health; he had long suffered from high blood pressure, alerting me to a danger I had feared for years, as mine had been borderline.

We must have been in the garden for about thirty minutes when he introduced me to his garden shed. A small corrugated-tin structure near the house, it contained the usual assortment of hoes, picks, shovels and trowels. All were clean and oiled. There also was a monstrous gasoline-powered plow that he was later to offer me—an offer I took as a huge measure of affection but had to decline as my space would not accommodate it.

Suddenly, my father grabbed a BB gun that was leaning against the shed's wall. Striding a few feet from the shed, he turned and fired, "Ping!," striking a tin can fifteen paces away. The proud father had shown off, just as his son might have forty years earlier. "You got to be able to shoot straight to get them rats," he said, all but blowing across the top of the gun barrel. I was impressed.

I was glad I had come.

I had decided to reach out to my father when a writing assignment brought me from Washington, D.C., where I was living, to Meridian. The story centered on the twenty-fifth anniversary of the murders of three civil rights workers in nearby Philadelphia, Mississippi.

Also, I knew then that my wife, Lyn, and I would in a few weeks be moving from Washington to Atlanta, as I was being promoted from correspondent in the *Los Angeles Times* Washington bureau to chief of its Southern bureau. This meant that my father and I would be only three hundred miles apart.

But such practical reasons were nothing compared to the emotional ones. I wanted some questions answered. Who is this man? Would seeing him show me what I might become? Could I learn what afflictions might strike me? Should I worry about my borderline high blood pressure, my over-two-hundred cholesterol?

As Mother and Dad both were dead, shouldn't I have some sort of relationship with my sole surviving parent?

I had looked up his telephone number and made the call, knowing that this could backfire, that I might be awakening a bad relationship. Through all the years, he never wrote, phoned, or tried to visit. And neither did I. Why is impossible to know. Fear of rejection? Pride? Anger? Fear of nothing to say? Fear of intrusion? When I got him on the phone, neither of us brought up the whys.

And we did not bring them up during the visit. Nor did we confront one another about the gulf that so long separated us.

I hoped that our meeting would represent a kind of closure, or at least the beginning of one, resolving questions about what kind of father and son we might have been.

We met much like two strangers, but strangers with a history. In a couple of hours, we touched on highlights of the previous thirty-some years. It seemed unrealistic to reach for more than highlights at that time.

Then, visit by visit, talk by talk, we found kinship in our love for growing plants, gradually expanding that to include other parts of our lives. This first meeting, tough as it started out to be, was the start of something tender.

Katha Pollitt

TOMATO

It is the female fruit: the plush
red flesh the fat
sac of seeds and oh
those silky membranes
plump and calm
it fits your palm just so
it is that perfect softball of your childhood
the one you always lost
you can stroke the sleek skin
you can thumb
the comfortable curve beneath:
here's
all soft gum
no sheer
secret murderous teeth.

Eleanor Perenyi

WOMAN'S PLACE

There are the husband's apple and pear trees, twined by the wife's clematis; his cabbage beds fringed with her pinks and pansies; the tool-house wreathed with roses; his rougher labor adorned by her gayer fancy, all speaking loudly of their hearts and tastes. . . . We trust the cottager's wife will love and care for the flowers and we are sure if she does that her husband's love and esteem for her will be heightened and strengthened.

—From an English
gardening magazine, 1848

A charming sentiment on the face of it, but what about that veiled threat at the end? Why should the cottager's love and esteem for his wife be contingent on her care for the flowers? And if he neglected the apple and pear trees—would she then be entitled to think less of *him*? It may come as a surprise that sexism should play any part in horticulture but the more you read of gardening history the more convincing the case for it becomes, and the less you are ready to see the cottager as a chivalrous male doing the hard work while indulging his wife in her 'gayer fancy.' Divisions of labor there have been, but not nearly as simple as that, while the whole business of women's supposed devotion to flowers may need another look.

At Woburn Abbey in the seventeenth century there was a famously lifelike statue of a woman weeding, and records of English estates show that from a very early period this chore was almost exclusively performed by females. It is, says my source (who is, naturally, a man), 'a task at which they have always been preeminent,' and this is an assessment with which male gardeners have long agreed. La Quintinie, who was in charge of Louis XIV's *potagers* and otherwise an adorable person, recommended the hiring of married men rather than bachelors (as was the usual custom), on the ground that wives would be available for weeding, as well as cleaning and scraping out pots. In the Orient, women weed the rice paddies in water up to their knees. In general, it is to be observed that men plow while women sow; prune fruit and nut trees but leave the harvest to women; and most men like working with vegetables (all, that is, but the weeding). Other crops appear to be largely in the hands of women. In that part of Turkey where tobacco is grown, I saw them patting together the raised beds, setting out seedlings, and of course weeding, while the male population sat under pergolas playing tric-trac. But why pick on Turks? In other parts of the world women are thought to be preeminent at hauling brushwood on their backs. Russian grannies sweep leaves in parks and streets.

Altogether, it is pretty obvious that relative physical strength isn't the determining factor in most cases of divided labor but rather which tasks men prefer to do and which they have decided to leave to women. The man in charge of our Hungarian vineyard was the envy of the neighborhood on account of his ten terrific daughters, who could and did get through twice the work of any male, and he didn't hesitate to lay it on them. In peasant societies nobody worries very much about overtaxing women's strength. I doubt if they do in any society. Thus, La Quintinie must have known that women could be trained as well as men to perform a hundred more exacting interesting horticultural tasks than scraping out pots.

This is all the more striking when you consider that it was women who invented horticulture in the first place, women who ventured into field and forest in search of wild plants, and women who domesticated them while men were still out chasing wild beasts. Women were the first gardeners; but when men retired from the hunting field and decided in favor of agriculture instead, women steadily lost control. No longer were they the ones to decide what was planted, how, or where; and accordingly the space allotted to them diminished too, until flowers and herbs were the only plants left under their direct management, while their former power passed into myth. The inventor of agriculture became the goddess of agriculture, her daughter the bringer of spring, when plants come to life; and each of these had a flower or flowers assigned to her—almost certainly by men and as a form of propitiation. For make no mistake: Men were always half in terror of women's complicity with nature, and the power it had given them. The other face of the goddess belongs to the witch brewing her spells from plants, able to cure and also curse with her knowledge of their properties. In some societies this fear of women amounted to panic. It was believed that their mere presence could blight vegetation. Democritus wrote that a menstruating woman could kill young produce 'merely by looking at it.' On the one hand, the benign giver of life and fertility; on the other, the baneful caster of withering spells—it's a tall order and no wonder that men were inclined to confine such a dangerously two-faced influence to a safe place.

For that is how I have come to interpret the two-thousand-odd years of women's incarceration in the flower garden. The superstitious fear that women were in league with nature in some way that men were not was thus simultaneously catered to and kept in check. Flowers are of all plants the least menacing and the most useless. Their sole purpose is to be beautiful and to give pleasure—which is what one half of man wants from women (the other, it is needless to say, asks for qualities more practical and down-to-earth)—and as such they are the perfect combination of tribute and demand. A gift of flowers to a woman implies that she is as deliciously desirable as the blossoms themselves; but there may be another and hidden message, contained in old-fashioned phrases like 'shy as a violet,' 'clinging vine,' not originally conceived as pejorative, that tells more of the truth—which is that flowers are also emblems of feminine submission. In the western world, this is rarely explicit. In the Orient, where fewer bones are made about the position of women, two examples may be cited. The art of Japanese flower arrangement, *ikebanu*, whose masters are male, was originally imparted to women as a means of silent communication with stern samurai husbands to whom words, and especially plaintive words, would have been an intolerable presumption; whereas an iris and a pussy willow and perhaps a convolvulus, arranged in the right order, conveyed a world of meaning. In China, we find another example, one that borders on the atrocious: the bound foot, to be encountered as late as the 1920's. My Chinese amah's feet were bound, and filled me with fascinated horror. What unspeakable distortion lay inside that delicate little slipper that caused her to sway (seductively to men, that was the point) as she walked? She would never show me but I have seen photographs since, and learned that the hideously crushed mass of flesh and bone was compared by Chinese poets to a lotus bud.

With this in mind, one may feel that those paintings of Chinese gardens in which exquisitely clad ladies float about tending to potted peonies depict scenes less idyllic than they appear. What we are seeing is a sort of floral cage—one that in the Hindu and Moslem world was an actual prison. Purdah and the harem were mitigated for their captives by the presence of many beautiful flowers. The illiterate women in the Ottoman seraglio even devised a 'language of flowers' (described with some scorn by Lady Mary Wortley Montagu in her letters from Turkey and later all the rage among European females with nothing better to do) to take the place of written language forbidden them. But there was no escape from the famous tulip gardens of the seraglio. . . . Call them what you will— and as everybody knows the word 'paradise' derives from the Persian word for garden, an idea later expanded in Moslem usage to mean a heaven where male wants were attended to by ravishing and submissive houris—one of the principal functions of the Oriental garden from Turkey to China was the incarceration of women.

To equate European gardens with any such purpose might seem to carry feminist interpretation too far, and obviously the differences are great. Garden plans nevertheless suggest a similar if less drastic impulse on the part of men. The Roman atrium was a flower-filled enclosure chiefly for women's use, and it is in marked contrast to the pleasure ground laid out by a rich Roman gentleman and intellectual like Pliny, who makes it perfectly clear that his were entirely for male diversion. Those pavilions for reading and sunbathing, dining with friends, those philosopher's walks, were for himself and his male companions. Possibly there was somewhere an inner courtyard where the women of the household could spend their leisure time, and more than likely it was filled with flowers, if only those that would be picked for the house; but except for his violet bed, he doesn't speak of flowers—or of women.

Medieval gardens repeat the pattern of the *hortus conclusus*, with the difference that they are more elaborate and better adapted to feminine comfort. Trellised walks, turf seats, tiny flower beds, all mark a female presence that is borne out in the illuminations and tapestries where we almost invariably see a lady stooping to pluck a strawberry, a rose, or at her ease with embroidery and lute. So plainly were they designed for women that they even convey an illusion of female supremacy at last—and it wasn't entirely an illusion. The mass folly of the Crusades occupied European men for the better part of two hundred years, and with her lord away at the wars the chatelaine did often manage his estate at home, and not badly either. She lived behind fortified walls nevertheless, and it isn't hard to conjecture that her garden was in the nature of a chastity belt, locking her in until the return of her lord and master. 'A garden inclosed is my sister, my spouse; a spring shut up, a foundation sealed,' says the Song of Solomon—to all of course but him. That feminine purity is only to be preserved within four walls is another ancient idea, and in the late Middle Ages it found indirect expression in those curious paintings of so-called Mary gardens, which show the Virgin seated in a castellated enclosure surrounded by richly symbolic fruit, vines and flowers. But the fortified walls came down with the return of something like peace and leisure, and the Renaissance garden with its magical perspectives, its cascades and fountains, was another story altogether—a celebration of humanism—except that in Italy at least it always had an odd little appendix attached, as it were, to the grand design: the *giardino segreto*.

Garden histories don't try to account for the *giardini segreti* except to note that flowers, largely absent in the rest of the garden, grew in them. To me it is at least plausible that these fossilized remnants of the medieval garden were for women, intended to be so, and that in fact they kept alive the tradition of the flower-filled feminine ghetto.

'Know that it doesn't displease but rather pleases me that you should have roses to grow and violets to care for,' wrote a fifteenth-century French merchant to his wife, sounding the note to be heard again and again for the next three hundred years. From 1500 to 1800 was the great age of garden design: visions of what a garden should be shifted like scenery upon a stage, theories multiplied and books on the subject poured from the presses. But in England only two were in all that time specifically directed to women, and both assume her province to be flowers and herbs. Lawson's *Countrie Housewife* (1618) gives her a list of sixteen flowers for nosegays, five kinds of bulbs including 'Tulippos,' and twenty-six herbs. Charles Evelyn's *Lady's Recreation* (1707) discusses most of the same flowers while permitting a fountain and 'an excellent contriv'd statue.' He also allows her a wilderness where 'being no longer pleas'd with a solitary Amusement you come out into a large Road, where you have the Diversion of seeing Travellers pass by, to compleat your Variety.' Why she should be solitary and driven to watch travelers in the road he doesn't say. His whole tone, however, is one of a patronage that is echoed elsewhere. Sir William Temple (*Garden of Epicurus*, 1685): 'I will not enter upon any account of flowers, having only pleased myself with seeing or smelling them, and not troubled myself with the care, which is more the ladies' part than the men's. . . . ' John Lawrence (*New System . . . a complete Body of Husbandry and Gardening*, 1726) adds to patronage something like a scolding: 'I flatter myself the Ladies would soon think that their vacant Hours in the Culture of the Flower-Garden would be more innocently spent and with greater Satisfaction than the common Talk over a Tea-Table where Envy and Detraction so commonly preside. Whereas when Opportunity and Weather invite them amongst their Flowers, there they may dress, and admire and cultivate Beauties like themselves without envying or being envied.' Here the argument for keeping women shut up with flowers is almost entirely trivialized. The Virgin's bower is now a school for decorum.

What amazes me is the way female scholars have failed to notice the implications of statements like these. Eleanor Sinclair Rohde (*The Story of the Garden*, 1932), to whom I am indebted for many of my quotations, gives no hint that she catches their drift. She takes no umbrage at her adored Parkinson (or perhaps doesn't choose to understand him) when she quotes a passage like this from the *Paradisus*: 'Gentlewomen, these pleasures are the delights of leasure [sic], which hath bred your love and liking to them, and although you are not herein predominant, yet cannot they be barred from your beloved, who I doubt not, will share with you in the delight as much as is fit.' Not the cleanest prose in the world, and Mrs. Rohde construes it as a tribute to the central place of women in seventeenth-century gardening. I read it as the opposite: a warning to wives with ideas about garden layout to leave that area to their husbands, who know best but will, if not aggravated, allow a share in the result.

Whichever of us is right, history is on my side. Not until the twentieth century did any woman play a recognizable part in garden design. We know why, of course. The great gardens of the world have been reflections of men's intellectual and spiritual experience: visions of Arcadia, hymns to rationalism or the divine right of kings, Zen parables—and the well-known reasons for our failure to compose symphonies, paint masterpieces, conceive the Einstein theory, apply equally to our failure to produce a feminine incarnation of, say, Le Nôtre. One or two great gardens were made for women, who were queens or the equivalent; but as they were always in the prevailing fashion it isn't possible to tell to what extent they conformed to the client's particular wishes. In one case we know they didn't. Marie de Medici's ideas for Luxembourg were resolutely opposed by her designer, the incomparable Boyceau, and he had his way (much to posterity's gain, it should be said). We know, too, that Marie Antoinette's *hameau,* arranged in what she imagined to be the English style, was done in a taste all her own, but that sad spot, so out of place at Versailles, doesn't say much in favor of feminine theories about design.

Malmaison might be a happier example. It, too, was laid out for a woman, and given the Empress Josephine's character, one can be sure she got what she wanted. Malmaison, however, isn't outstanding for its design but for the millions of roses that grew there, probably the greatest collection the world has ever seen; and this was generally true of all gardens made by or for women of which we have any record. Flowers were, and until the twentieth century remained, the theme. In the eighteenth, the Duchess of Beaufort grew exotics, as did Mme. de Pompadour in all the many ravishing gardens given her by Louis XV—she adored the white, highly scented tropicals, gardenias and jasmine especially, brought to her from all parts of the French empire. Lady Broughton specialized in alpines, and was one of the first to grow them outdoors in a rock garden; Lady Holland introduced dahlias to England and grew them in her greenhouses.

Here, a new note was introduced, for it was about this time that women were allowed to embark on the study of botany—not too seriously and rather late in the day; and it is notable that various writers should have seen their studies in much the same light as pottering in the flower garden itself. J. C. Loudon, for one, recommended botany as 'a charming and instructive female exercise,' or a grade or two above the netting of purses, and in the hands of the upper-class young ladies who went in for it, that was about what these studies amounted to. In fact, they mostly consisted in the coloring of flower engravings, and counting stamens according to the newly introduced Linnaean system of classification, which made everything wonderfully simple. Honorable exceptions there were, mostly royal. The dowager Princess of Wales founded the great botanic at Kew in 1761; and Queen Charlotte was accounted a passionate student, though how she found time for her researches in the course of bearing her sixteen children is a wonder. The *Strelitzia* or bird-of-paradise flower, however, is named for her (she was born Mecklenberg-Strelitz), as were four varieties of apple—hence, it is said, Apple Charlotte, the dessert.

Women in humbler positions, who might have contributed rather more to the science, did not fare so well. One of them was Jane Colden, the daughter of a lieutenant-governor of New York, who lived near Newburgh-on-Hudson and who ventured into the wilderness at a time when that was neither easy nor safe. By 1758 she had compiled a manuscript describing four hundred local plants and their uses, illustrated by herself. It was never published. During the Revolution it fell into the hands of a Hessian officer who was interested in botany. He took it back to Germany where it was preserved at the University of Göttingen. Evidently where it was important enough to have been purchased at a later date by Sir Joseph Banks, the most influential botanist of his time; but he didn't try to have it published and it reposes in the British Museum to this day. Nor is any flower called *Coldenia*, the accolade regularly bestowed by botanists on those of their tribe who have made important contributions to science. (That those standards have been less than strict is, however, obvious even where men's names are concerned: the *Montanoa*, a species of shrub, appears to have been named for a Mexican bandit-politician. As applied to women, names seem chiefly to have been bows to rank: *Victoria amazonica*, that water-lily whose pad is the size of a dinner table, was of course named for the dear queen; while the *Cinchona*, from whose bark quinine is derived, was called after the Condesa de Cinchon, Vicerene of Peru, who in 1638 was cured of malaria by a decoction of what had previously been called Peruvian bark.)

Given the circumstances, circumscribed travel, the reluctance to admit that female minds could cope seriously with science—it isn't surprising that no woman made a name for herself in botany. That her accomplishments in the breeding and cultivating of plants should also be a well-kept secret is another matter. 'In March and in April from morning till night/In sowing and seeding good housewives delight,' sang Thomas Tusser (1524–1580) in his rhyming calendar for gardeners. Even in Tudor times England was famous for the beauty of its flowers, especially doubled varieties—columbines, primroses, violets, marigolds and campanula—but also striped and unusual colors, which included sorts such as a reddish lily-of-the-valley. Foreigners attributed these variations to the damp English climate which allowed for year-around planting, but also noted that the selection and cultivation were done by housewives rather than professionals—at that period well behind their French and Dutch colleagues. In the seventeenth century, the great age of English plantsmanship, when collectors like the Tradescants began to range the world, these accomplishments receded into the background—where they remained for another two hundred years. What the Victorians called 'old-fashioned' flowers were really housewives' flowers, grown continuously and in defiance or ignorance of fashion—including the landscape movement that destroyed so many of England's finest and most characteristic gardens and prohibited so much as a cowslip from showing its pretty head above ground. In the feminine domain called the cottage garden, which a modern state might designate as a preserve with plants whose removal would be punishable by law, grew such otherwise lost rarities as blue primroses, Parkinson's 'stately Crown Imperial,' and the fairy rose (not to be confused with the modern polyantha of that name), many violas and pinks long since vanished from cultivation in the gardens of the rich and those desiring to be à la page.

The cottage garden was rediscovered toward the end of the nineteenth century—mostly by women like Mrs. Juliana Horatia Ewing, who founded a Parkinson Society 'to search out and cultivate old flowers which have become scarce,' and of course Gertrude Jekyll, who reintroduced the fairy rose. But although these gardens clearly pointed to the role of women as important conservators as well as breeders and cultivators of plant species, no one pursued the obvious conclusion that what had happened in the nineteenth century might also be presumed to have occurred in others as well. No writer I know of has, for example, enlarged the thesis that in the Dark Ages it was monks in monasteries who preserved such species as survived in those parts of Europe not fortunate enough to be conquered by the garden-loving Arabs (Spain, Sicily, etc.). Why not also nuns in nunneries? It is known that they grew flowers in profusion for the adornment of churches and herbs for simples, just as the monks did. Indeed it was one of their functions to school ladies in the uses of cooking and medicinal herbs (which then included flowers like marigolds, poppies, even roses and honeysuckle), especially the latter because it was the lady of the manor who compounded and administered medicines, though she wasn't of course honored with the title of physician, and the few venturesome women who did try to set themselves up as doctors were promptly squelched.

With all the vast amount of writing about gardens that has appeared in the last hundred years, much of it by women, you might expect somebody to have devoted a book to women's place in gardening history. If anyone has, I haven't heard of it, and it must be admitted that the difficulties of research would be formidable. Where would the documentation come from? In England, the earliest herbal published by a woman was Elizabeth Blackwell's in 1737. The earliest essay on gardening itself is probably Lady Charlotte Murray's *British Garden* (1799); in America, Mrs. Martha Logan's *Gardener's Kalender* (known only through republication in a magazine around 1798). What the library stacks of other countries would yield I can't say; the pickings would presumably be even slimmer. Private correspondence would be a richer source, if one knew where to look. (There are, for instance, tantalizing hints in Mme. de Sévigné's letters that in the age dominated by Le Nôtre's geometry she had ideas about *la nature* that anticipated Rousseau's—as when she told her daughter that she had spent the morning on her country estate 'in the dew up to my knees laying lines; I am making winding *allées* all around my park . . . ') Novels by women could also be studied in this light. Jane Austen has a great deal about the theory and practice of gardening, especially in *Mansfield Park*, where a part of the plot hinges on Mr. Rushworth's determination to have Mr. Repton remodel his grounds, though in fact every novel has its gardens and each is made to say something about the character and social situation of the owner. (Elizabeth Bennet isn't entirely joking when she says she must date her falling in love with Mr. Darcy to her visit to his 'beautiful grounds at Pemberely.')

Diaries and notebooks would be another source, not forgetting *The Pillow Book of Sei Shōnagon*. In the remoter past, the body of feminine knowledge was locked away under the anonymous heading of old wives' tales, a phrase I have always found offensive. Assume that 'old' doesn't mean the woman gardener was a crone but refers to 'old times.' The expression still implies a combination of ignorance and superstition peculiarly female—and never mind that a thirteenth-century church father like the Abbott of Beauvais testified that a decoction of heliotrope could produce invisibility or that St. Gregory the Great believed the devil hid in lettuce heads. Women will have shed their superstitions at about the same time men did, and what many an old wives' tale really refers to is orally transmitted information, as often as not the result of illiteracy, not inborn backwardness. Women weren't stupider than men; they lacked the means of expressing themselves, and instead of writing herbals or treatises on what is called (note this) husbandry, they told one another what experience had taught them about plants, medicines and many other things. This is also called folk wisdom, and it can be as discriminatory as the rest of human history: How many people know, for instance, that the subtly constructed tents of the Plains Indians were designed and set up entirely by women?

To remedy these deficiencies wouldn't be easy, but I wish somebody would try. The story could end well, too—up to a point. In the spring of 1980 a symposium was held at Dumbarton Oaks whose subject was 'Beatrix Jones Farrand (1872–1959) and Fifty Years of American Landscape Architecture.' The setting was appropriate: Mrs. Farrand designed the beautiful garden at Dumbarton Oaks and many other famous ones as well. She was the only woman among the eleven original members of the American Society of Landscape Architects, founded in 1899, and the first to demonstrate that women could design gardens as well as plant flowers. (Jekyll, remember, worked in collaboration with the architect Edwin Lutyens.) She was a thorough professional and inaugurated a period of great brilliance for women as landscape architects. Ellen Biddle Shipman, another of them, told a reporter in 1938 that 'until women took up landscaping, gardening in this country was at its lowest ebb. The renaissance was due largely to the fact that women, instead of working over their boards, used plants as if they were painting pictures and as an artist would. Today women are at the top of the profession.'

That, alas, is no longer true. Not only are the gardens designed by those women for the most part in a sad state of neglect, the profession itself leaves something to be desired. It has, so it seems, gone back to the drawing boards. Many universities now separate courses in design and horticulture into different academic departments. We are where we were in earlier centuries when the designer and the plantsman lived in different worlds—an extraordinary step backward. Does it also represent a resurgence of male chauvinism, a return of the old idea that flowers and plants are a province less worthy than that of stone and water? Not overtly so perhaps. But the lack of interest in horticulture shown by liberated women architects suggests that they recognize, however subconsciously, the link between flowering plants and old-style femininity as opposed to feminism, and if forced to choose between the two courses, as I gather the students more or less must, would opt for the 'higher' (i.e., male-dominated) one of landscaping. If so, though we have come a long way from the statue of the female weeder and cottager's wife, it isn't far enough.

Kathleen Norris

THE GARDEN

My garden, even more than most, is an exercise in faith. And in failure. I inherited it when I moved to my grandmother's house, but scarely knew what I had. Her perennial flowers were up and in bud in the wet spring when we moved into the house. I had memories of the garden as a child, of weeding and thinning the leaf lettuce that we would eat sprinkled with vinegar and sugar, of helping my grandmother pick tomatoes and string beans. Visiting her flowers, admiring the day lilies, lily-of-the-valley, painted daisies, columbines, and other flowers whose names I forget, was one of the joys of summer when I was a child.

In the first years I was in the house, I felt that I should care for the flowers, but didn't know how. Advice from neighbors helped, but not enough. Advice from books was sometimes of use, but often it only reinforced my sense of myself as a hopeless gardener. I'd weed around the flowers and usually pull some flowers by mistake. Often, in the spring, I was working away from home, and the weeds got away from me. I was mightily impressed that the columbines and painted daisies never failed to come back up, no matter how I neglected them. They came to seem like unloseable friends.

My grandmother had a small stand of mint that she used for making mint jelly. I recall that she used to call mint "near a weed," and she was careful to keep it within bounds. In my twenty-one years of struggling with the garden, I've let the mint take over. It keeps the real weeds down. I use it in sun tea all summer, and often send it, fresh or dried, to my urban friends for whom it is a luxury.

I do try to keep it from overrunning the columbines, my grandmother's favorite flower, and mine, a flower that can withstand both bitter cold winters and the wild storms of summer. The delicate whimsey of the columbine is deceiving. After violent hail and wind, I've seen the flowers, long spikes intact, blooming in the mud, the long stems bowed down but not broken.

In the half of the garden where my grandmother grew her vegetables, I've given up on tomatoes—end rot, no matter what I tried—and in some years have simply let the weeds take over. When I manage to be at home in the early spring, I have a friend till the ground, and plant basil, lettuce, and snow peas. In a recent fit of optimism, I've tried to establish parsley (having killed off my grandmother's patch years ago), chives, sorrel, rosemary, and thyme. The thyme died before the summer was out, as did much of the tarragon patch a friend helped me establish years ago. Some of it seemed to have survived, and I hope it will be up next spring, along with the rosemary, parsley, sorrel and chives. I wouldn't put money on any of it.

My parents were never much for gardening, and oddly enough, it was when I lived in New York City as a young adult that I first felt compelled to work with the earth. I had friends with a country place in Rhode Island, and I looked forward each spring to getting my hands into the warm soil, and doing whatever job they had for me to do. I'd visit several times a summer and on into fall, shoveling manure and compost, gathering seaweed at a nearby beach for the compost pile, hoeing, weeding, picking potato bugs and releasing lady bugs, picking the ripened corn and tomatoes and eggplant just before it was time to cook them.

In the medieval era gardens were designed to suffice for the loss of Eden. The garden I've grown into, in my middle-age, seems more of a kind of Purgatory, but I love it. It's a ratty little garden, not much at all. But I can call it mine.

Stanley Kunitz

TOUCH ME

Summer is late, my heart.
Words plucked out of the air
some forty years ago
when I was wild with love
and torn almost in two
scatter like leaves this night
of whistling wind and rain.
It is my heart that's late,
it is my song that's flown.
Outdoors all afternoon
under a gunmetal sky
staking my garden down,
I kneeled to the crickets trilling
underfoot as if about
to burst from their crusty shells;
and like a child again

marvelled to hear so clear
and brave a music pour
from such a small machine.
What makes the engine go?
Desire, desire, desire.
The longing for the dance

stirs in the buried life.
One season only,

         and it's done.

So let the battered old willow
thrash against the windowpanes
and the house timbers creak.
Darling, do you remember
the man you married? Touch
me,
remind me who I am.

Julia Alvarez

WHAT GOES WRONG

All the plants you give me die.
I try my darndest setting their finicky pots
now on one sill, now on another spot,
hoping the Jew will wander
and the smug mums yak with color
in this indoor garden.

In the *What Went Wrong* chart
of my plant book, wilting is a symptom
of prolonged soil dryness and then guilty
waterlogging, too little and then too much—
the capricious gardener.
I stand forewarned,

thinking of my bouts of loving
then sudden withdrawing as if some gauge
is off and only too much gives
the signal of what's enough.
My love, how shall I keep you
safe from my love?

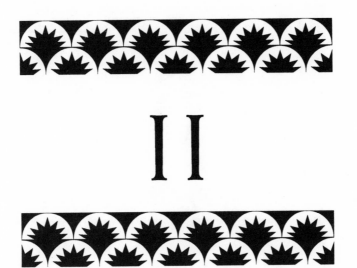

II

SEED SAVING

The seeds of cucumber, melon, etc., are better, at any rate, when four or five years old than when fresh; and we have well authenticated instances of seeds retaining their vitality much longer than this. There is *no* fixed period during which seeds will keep. There is no reason to suppose that they would lose their vitality in any assignable number of years *if the proper conditions were observed.* De Candolle says that M. Gerardin raised kidney beans, obtained from Tournefort's herbarium, which were at least a hundred years old; but beans left to the chances of the atmosphere are not good the second year, and hardly worth planting in the third. Professor Lindley raised raspberry plants from seed not less than sixteen or seventeen hundred years old. Multitudes of other instances might be given. In reply to the first question, it may, then, be said, that the length of time through which seeds will keep depends upon the method of preserving them.

We do not suppose it to be essential to inclose apple, pear, and quince seeds in earth for the purpose of preserving their vitality during a single winter. But if exposed to the air, the rind becomes so hard and rigid as to make germination very difficult from mere mechanical reasons. The moisture of the soil keeps the covering in a tender state, and it is easily ruptured by the expansion of the seed.

The shell of peach, plum, and other stone-fruit seeds would form, if left to dry and harden, a yet more hopeless prison. If kept for two years, the most stone-fruit pips, it is to be presumed, would not germinate. Some, however, would have vigor enough to grow even then. We have forgotten who it was, but believe it to have been a reliable person, recently mentioned the fact, that a peach or apricot stone was for several years kept as a child's plaything; but upon being planted, grew, and is now a healthy tree. Such cases are, however, rare.

The intercourse between Great Britain and her distant colonies, and the various expeditions fitted out from her shores for purposes of botanical research and for the acquisition of new plants from distant regions, have made the subject of seed-saving at sea a matter of much experiment.

In general, the conditions of preservation are three; a low temperature, dryness, and exclusion of air. But it often happens, that all these cannot be had, and then a choice must be made between them. Heat and moisture will either germinate the seeds or corrupt them. In long voyages, and in warm regions, *moisture contained in the seed*, if in a close bottle, is sufficient to destroy the seed. Glass bottles have therefore been rejected. Seeds for long voyages, or for long preservation, are thoroughly ripened and thoroughly dried; but dried without raising the *temperature* of the air, as this would impair their vitality. They are then wrapped in coarse paper, and put, loosely, in a coarse canvas bag, and hung up in a cool and airy place. In this way seeds will be as nearly secure from heat and moisture—their two worst enemies—as may be. It is probable that some seeds have but a short period of vitality under any circumstances of preservation. Seeds containing much oil, are peculiarly liable to spoil. Lindley suggests that the oil becomes rancid.

The preservation of seeds from one season to another, for home use, is not difficult, and may be described in three sentences: ripen them well, dry them thoroughly, and keep them aired and cool.

D I D I S A Y ?

This time of year I kneel on my jacket. The ice
is almost solid. The groaning has ended. There is
an inch of fresh snow. A bush has turned to glass.

I take my left glove off, finger by finger.
There is a pocket in which I wait. I break
a twig. I pull at the bark. I give myself

to the first flower, something streaked with pink
and three dark leaves as a kind of foil, something
just two or three inches tall. As soon as it melts

the snow will turn to water; I will scrape
the ground a little; I will clean it. I am
cloven; I was split in two; I opened

because of the water, because of the seed. I thought
the knowledge had started—for half a day. I thought
the light was in one place, the dark in another.

I reached my left hand out; I let it tremble.
I looked at the sun, it was a kind of dandelion,
though smaller, it was a snowdrop, one of the leaves

was shaped like a goat, we stood and butted, I was
one side, he was the other, I ate the horns,
I ate the flattened eyes; light will cover

darkness—in a day or two—the flower
will be a snowdrop—did I say that?—the petals,
they are like rays. I walked for an hour struggling

with this and that; the split is harder and harder
every year. I wrenched my shoulder—did I say that
too? Did I say I was winged and scattered?

Roger B. Swain

CULTIVATING
DIVERSITY

On the main floor of the barn, between the workbench and the rack where we hang our shovels, hoes, and rakes, sits a great wooden trunk. It's a double trunk. Under the outer cover with its dovetailed corners is a hinged panel that conceals the trunk's tin-lined interior. Cool, dry, and mouse-proof—this is where we keep our old vegetable seeds, the seeds of gardens past. In theory, this is a storehouse of varieties, a vault of genes. In reality, the contents of the trunk are a shambles. If there is a lesson to be found in our muddle of seeds, it is that vegetable diversity is easier to celebrate than it is to keep.

The individual packets—some with colored pictures, others with plain text—are torn, muddied, and rain-speckled. They bear the marks of having been hastily reclosed by dirty fingers and carried about in a hip or shirt pocket before being dumped unceremoniously into the trunk. Here is a record, thoroughly shuffled, of every vegetable we have raised or planned to raise: 'Armenian' cucumber, 'Royalty Purple Pod' beans, 'Harper Hybrid' muskmelon, 'Thai Hot' pepper, 'Detroit Dark Red' beets. The dozen different onion packets, still held together by a brittle rubber band, hark back to the year we hosted the Olympic onion ring trials. An unopened half-pound of 'Silver Queen' corn is a reminder of a spring when the ground didn't dry out in time for us to plant this ninety-day variety.

Neither Elisabeth nor I consult this box often enough, or we would have found the corn and used it before we ordered more.

We should long since have inventoried the contents of the trunk and thrown out the junk. Why are we still hanging on to my father's 'Yellow Plum' tomato packet from 1953? And even if the 'Green Globe' artichoke seed is still viable, haven't we finally given up trying to raise artichokes in New Hampshire? At the very least, can't we pitch what has spilled—those little black beads, the brown commas, the God only knows what kind of squash?

The conditions inside our trunk are adequate for storing seeds, but they aren't great. The seeds would stay viable longer if we dried them down to five percent moisture level with a silica gel desiccant, packed them inside airtight glass jars, and then put those jars in our freezer. We would then be careful whenever we opened a jar to let it reach room temperature so that moisture wouldn't condense inside. And we would open them as infrequently as possible, because fluctuations in temperature reduce the viability of seeds. Seeds are tiny living, breathing organisms. They need the right conditions or they'll die, and much of what's in our trunk is by now fit only for feeding birds or turning into baked beans.

I'm still proud of the blue ribbon that we won one year for having eighty-five different kinds of vegetables at the Hillsborough County Agricultural Fair. And we continue to plant almost that many each spring. Not only does this give us plenty of opportunity for crop rotation, it lets us do our bit toward conserving endangered varieties. Orchids growing in the canopies of the tropical forests aren't the only threatened plants. There are thousands of varieties of garden vegetables that could disappear unless someone keeps them growing. The Harvard professor Edward O. Wilson, who has been one of my mentors, has been widely quoted for stating that the loss of genetic diversity is "the folly our descendants are least likely to forgive us." And some of that diversity is included in the vegetables that I used to carry into his laboratory as a graduate student.

The problem is that the vegetable varieties that aren't suited for mass cultivation or refrigerated storage, that don't fit neatly into containers, that can't be shipped long distances, that aren't dark green or bright red, aren't of much interest to commercial growers. Yet these oddball varieties are our horticultural heritage, a legacy of plant selection going back ten thousand years. The smooth-seeded 'Alaska' peas date back to 1880, before the appearance of the mutant wrinkled pea whose higher sugar content now dominates the class. 'Taos Pueblo' blue corn has been handed down from generation to generation by native Americans in New Mexico.

The term "heirloom variety" reflects the fact that many of these vegetable varieties have been family-held and -perpetuated ones. And many of them were treasured because they were so well adapted to the needs and conditions of a particular family or people. When you find a vegetable that does well in your specific climate or soil, that suits your palate and needs, you stick with it.

So why do we keep buying new vegetable seeds every year? Why not choose a variety and let some of it go to seed each year to start next year's plants? Partly it's because we are curious, eager to plant things that we've never tried. Also it's because I'm not sure that we have what it takes to do a good job of saving our own seeds. The problem is that most of the vegetables we raise are annuals. A few, like peppers and eggplants, are actually perennials, but we raise them from seed each year as though they were annuals. And seeds are a perishable commodity. Squash and cucumber seeds can remain viable for a decade, but parsnip and onion seeds have a shelf life of only a year. Keeping seeds viable for longer than that means sowing them, raising the plants, letting them go to seed, and harvesting the seeds.

However, only the seeds gathered from standard, or open-pollinated, varieties will come true, producing plants that carry all the genes of the previous generation. And even with these standard varieties, genetic purity depends on preventing accidental hybridization between two different standard varieties. Accidental or deliberate, the progeny of such a cross is hybrid seed—a sort of gene soup.

Hybrid vegetable plants have been a boon to agriculture with their vigor, their uniformity, and the fact that seed companies can sell hybrid seed year after year to farmers and gardeners who are unable to reproduce it themselves. But hybrids are trouble for the back-yard seed saver who doesn't want to get into the process of plant breeding, raising generation after generation of some new variety of vegetable until once again it comes true from seed. For the amateur seed saver, hybrids are to be avoided.

Some vegetables, such as beans, are largely self-pollinating, which means that hybrids almost never occur, even when two different kinds are grown in close proximity. That is why the late John Withee of Lynnfield, Massachusetts, was able to maintain a collection of over a thousand varieties of beans, planting out several hundred of them in the same garden, each year.

If the vegetable is corn or squash, however, which rely on wind or insects to carry pollen from male to female flowers, cross-pollination is a certainty. Unless the gardener is growing only a single variety and no other varieties are being grown within a quarter of a mile, it's necessary to take steps to control fertilization. Cages and blossom bags and hand pollination are all ways to keep seed pure. The recently published book *Seed to Seed*, written by Susanne Ashworth and edited by Kent Whealy, is an essential guide and reference for anyone setting out to save his or her own seed. Here is information about pollination, isolation distance, and caging, as well as harvesting, drying, and storage, for a hundred and sixty different vegetables. There are by now thousands of back-yard gardeners across the country saving their own seed, and they are making a very real contribution to the conservation of biodiversity.

Kent Whealy is the founder of the Seed Savers Exchange (headquartered in Decorah, Iowa), whose members—seven thousand strong—are dedicated to preserving vanishing varieties of edible plants. In 1990 he was given one of the prestigious MacArthur fellowships for his work, as was a colleague of his, Gary Paul Nabhan, whose organization, Native Seeds/SEARCH, in Tucson, Arizona, is similarly dedicated to preserving the traditional native crops of the southwestern United States and northern Mexico. Both men are passionate about the importance of these plants to the future of gardening—not just as a source of rare genes for future breeding but as plants that in their current form already contribute to a more sustainable agriculture.

As for my own reluctance to plunge in and muddy up the gene pool, Whealy allows that back-yard seed saving isn't for everyone. Given that ninety percent of vegetable gardeners buy their seeds from racks in garden centers and hardware stores, where the offering is limited, gardeners who simply order their seeds from catalogs are already doing something to preserve the diversity of offerings, as Whealy points out. To make this easier, he publishes the *Garden Seed Inventory*; now in its third edition, it lists all the standard (nonhybrid) varieties of vegetable seed currently available from two hundred and twenty-three mail-order catalogs and notes source codes for the company or companies offering each.

So what Elisabeth and I are doing is letting seed companies keep the lines pure, letting them test the seed to make sure that it meets the federally mandated levels for minimum germination. We in turn are creating a market for some lesser-known varieties, such as 'Mandan Bride,' a multicolored, short-season flour corn that was once grown by the Mandan tribe in what is now North Dakota and that doubles for us as Halloween decoration and a source of whole hominy. As I see it, every such seed order, whether for white tomatoes or black radishes, helps to persuade the seller that the variety is worth carrying and thus preserving. We are doing something worthwhile even if we never get the seed into the ground. With this perspective, none of those seeds in the trunk have died in vain.

I will admit that we are perpetuating fifteen different varieties of potatoes—varieties that we have collected from people over the years, varieties with names like 'Ruby Crescent' and 'Russian Banana.' But these are vegetatively propagated. We simply have to replant the smaller potatoes left over from the previous year's harvest to assure a new crop that's true to type. We also have a dozen or so varieties of garlic, shallots, horseradish, Jerusalem artichoke, and rhubarb, but these aren't raised from seed either.

Although it's the exception among vegetables, vegetative propagation is the rule for fruit. The time we save by letting others preserve the diversity of our vegetable plot we more than spend in our vineyard, orchard, and bramble patches. At last count we had just under a hundred different named selections of strawberries, raspberries, black raspberries, blackberries. Also blueberries, cranberries, and elderberries, grapes and hardy kiwi vines. Not to mention peaches, pears, plums, and apples. In terms of the diversity that exists, we've only scratched the surface. But we are proud of them all, from the 'Brandywine' purple raspberry, which makes the world's best jam, to the 'Chenango Strawberry' apple, which ripens its fruit gradually over a month-long stretch, making it useless for the commercial grower but ideal for the homeowner.

Now that these perennials are established, they will all be here a long time. Some of them will likely outlast us. And there's a good chance we'll forget which is which long before our demise. This would be unfortunate, because from each of these plants, an unerring copy could readily be made by anyone. That is the beauty of vegetative propagation. The 'Baldwin' apple has been the same ever since the original seedling was discovered in Wilmington, Massachusetts, in 1793 by Samuel Thompson, as he surveyed the route of the Middlesex Canal. The same is true of all the other cultivated varieties of fruit, no matter whether they derive from a chance seedling or from the most deliberate and controlled breeding. Whether the propagation is by grafting, as in the case of apples, or cuttings, as in the case of grapes, or the more recent tissue culture, used for raspberries, vegetative propagation (as opposed to seed propagation) leaves no chance for genetic confusion.

Where confusion shows up is in the matter of labeling. Once the name of a variety is misplaced, it is extremely difficult to get it reapplied correctly. Even careful scrutiny by an expert in the group may not prove definitive. Since there can be fifty years between a grapevine's planting and someone's request for a cutting, good labels are of critical importance. Records of what is growing where will let future generations know what things are.

The best advice, actually, is not to rely entirely on labels. Paper records survive far longer, and for safety you need two of them. One should be a map of what is planted where on the property. The other should be a catalog—a collection of index cards will do—with each entry describing the particular plant and including directions about its location. I keep ours in different places. If the map is lost, the catalog will still exist, and vice versa. Both are far more likely to survive than anything outdoors.

Peter Del Tredici, at Harvard University's Arnold Arboretum, likes to say that the limb you put the label on is the limb that dies. Every time. He doesn't know why. Labels can be attached to the trunk, of course, but then the tree may be girdled or the label swallowed up in bark. The smaller the plant, the more difficult it is to attach the label directly. But unless the label is attached to something, it tends to walk away, showing up where it doesn't belong or vanishing for good. Even well-intentioned photographers may lift a label and return it to the wrong place when they have taken the picture.

But first there is the matter of finding a label that lasts. Black laundry marker on white plastic fades, and the plastic degrades in sunlight. Wood labels rot. Black pencil on roughened aluminum is far more permanent. Our blueberries are all tagged with pieces of aluminum flashing stamped with a pin punch, spelling out the various names. The Arnold Arboretum uses an old Addressograph machine that embosses letters on a strip of zinc. Someday we might decide to buy a few of the engraved plastic labels that botanical gardens use for display labels, where the underlying white plastic is exposed by cutting through a colored layer. Or better still, the aluminum labels that are photo-printed.

Perhaps the most durable label of all has been devised by a fruit collector named Bill Vose in Paw Paw, Illinois. Describing his method in an issue of *Pomona*, the journal of the North American Fruit Explorers, Vose explains that he uses a thin wire to slice three-eighths- to half-inch-thick slabs from a block of stoneware clay. Then, after letting the pieces dry to a leathery consistency, he stamps them with the fruit's name, variety, interstem (if present), and rootstock, the scion source, and the date planted. Vose has the labels fired in a local hobbyist's kiln. Staining the letters with a dark clay slip and firing the labels a second time makes the printing even more visible. The weak point of Vose's system is the twelve-gauge plastic-coated electric wire that he uses to attach his labels to the trees. But barring a gunshot or other shattering impact, the labels themselves should be around for future archaeologists to discover.

Labels, of course, are useless without the plants themselves. For a guide to finding specific varieties of fruit and nuts, again we have the Seed Savers Exchange to thank. The *Fruit, Berry, and Nut Inventory* (second edition) lists all of the varieties currently available by mail order in the United States and tells you which of the three hundred and nine nurseries has each in stock. Alternatively, gardeners can turn to the even larger *Cornucopia: A Source Book of Edible Plants*, by Stephen Facciola, which identifies sources for three thousand species of edible plants (and their varieties), listing 1,350 firms and institutions.

In the end, even the right name is optional. Yes, the problems of synonymy can be nightmarish for taxonomists charged with assigning the correct name to a particular plant. Is a mulberry being sold as 'Wellington' actually the old variety 'New American,' which was also sold many years ago as 'Downing'? We may never know. But saving the name isn't really what preservation is about. We can live with the loss of a variety's name as long as we save the variety itself.

Jane Anne Staw
and
Mary Swander

SUCCESSION

"Lawrence man gets by on only $120 a year," Bill Hatke read the headline, then the lead paragraph from the *Kansas City Times* feature on him. "I have no electricity, phone, running water, TV, stereo or other money-gobbling habits. And I'm the happiest guy in the world for it."

Photographs of Bill accompanied the article: one of Bill's smoke-stained Ph.D. diploma nailed to the wall above the wood-burning stove he uses for cooking meals and heating his four-room house; another of the bearded Bill reading by the light of an oil lamp, with his thicket of curls bent close to the page; and a third of Bill, lean and muscular, in one of his seven gardens. Here, he is barefoot and bare-chested, his head thrown back as he pours water from an old jug into his mouth.

"You know, of all the things I told that reporter, I thought what she published was rather odd. See, she interviewed me for two days, and we talked about almost every God-awful thing you can possibly imagine. I mean, the whole focus of her article was, 'He has no utilities. He doesn't even have a car.' Now, I ask you, why would she focus on that when we talked about so many other subjects? We talked about Zen Buddhism. We talked about the dropouts of the sixties. And, my God, we talked about gardening. We talked about sweet corn and squash bugs. And I told her all about my methods for storage. But none of that appears."

For Bill, any listener is an opportunity to perform. Like an actor in the commedia dell'arte, he struts, he swaggers, he sways, he giggles, flashing his white teeth, his voice high-pitched and sing-song one minute, deep and resonant the next. His costume: a washed-out football jersey and castaway chinos, crudely cut off at the knees and splotched with an accretion of food and gardening stains, the crotch loosely patched with childlike stitches in black thread. The setting: Bill's front yard, a jumble of vegetables—okra fanning out over the steps to his house, green beans winding around the fence and gate, zucchini sprawling up and over the curb and, here and there, patches of beets and carrots poling through open spaces between the vines.

"I mean, the woman from the *Kansas City Times* never even ex-plained why I started to garden. I'm a University of Kansas drop-out. I have my Ph.D. in sociology. Well, I guess the article says that. But I decided I didn't want to work in my field—criminology. There were plenty of jobs, but it was basically working with the leftovers of society. And this society has a way of creating so many leftovers and so much waste in terms of human beings. I didn't want to be part of that, and I decided to find another way to live.

"I always knew how to garden, and for me it was a catharsis. When I was finishing my courses at the university, I was pretty in-volved with the intellectual stuff. Gardening was a way to get away from that—to get back to something that was purely physi-cal, something that would respond. I guess I needed some kind of therapy, so I started growing things and I liked it so much, I thought, Why don't you just do this for a living?"

Bill's hands swooped through the air, gliding, soaring, then dropping until they settled on his dense beard, the fingertips mas-saging his jaw and chin. At his feet, a cabbage butterfly flitted among the cucumber vines. On his ankle, where he had scratched a chigger bite, a trickle of blood thickened and turned dark.

"I learned to garden when I was six years old in northern Idaho. My mother pretty well supported a family of eight kids on what she grew. Dad produced the beef cattle and the deer and the hogs. But my mother did all the vegetables and fruits. And then when I was thirteen, I worked for some years in a convent garden with Benedictine nuns. It was Saint Gertrude's Convent and Academy in Cottonwood, Idaho. They had a huge garden and it was a private school. They charged, well, at that time it was only $125 a semester. What I did was, I earned that and my book money by working in the garden.

"Of course, the convent garden was different from my mother's. The school was out on a prairie, so the sisters could grow many crops my mother couldn't—for example, corn and pumpkins, cantaloupe, cucumbers and beans. Where I grew up, we were higher in the mountain valley. My mother raised all the cold-weather crops: peas, lettuce, spinach, turnips, cabbage, rhubarb, beets. Oh, yes, and Irish potatoes.

"And then we had strawberries. The strawberry patch was on the south slope of a high hill. The draws would freeze—you know, those areas between the higher hills—so we planted strawberries and things like that up high. The draws around us were formed by runoff that eventually found its way to the Salmon River. The Snake River Gorge was about ten miles from the house."

Bill grew up in the wilderness, the old family homestead surrounded by a dense forest of pine, and white and red fir trees. On one side of the Hatkes', there were no neighbors. On the other side, the closest family lived two miles through the timber. The nearest town, Keuterville, Idaho, with a population of twenty-two, was ten miles away. Carved out of the forest, the town consisted of one street, known by the locals as the Keuterville-Cottonwood road. Today Keuterville's population has swelled to thirty-five, and the old post office and the Keuterville Tavern/ Store are still functioning. The town even boasts its own highway district headquarters.

And Keuterville still has lots of spunk. Three years ago it celebrated its centennial. Displays of quilts and saws, including several tree climbers, and an old steam engine that one of the residents hauled out of his garage, lined the road during the day. At night, after everyone had gorged themselves on hot dogs and

Coke, with the smell of pine heavy in the air, young and old danced in the streets to the music of a band imported from Cottonwood, where sometime after Bill's graduation Saint Gertrude's had metamorphosed into Prairie High School. Bill's brother Hank, who lives in a new house he built on the old family property, urged Bill to attend the celebration.

"But I wouldn't go, even if I had the money. Keuterville represents a way of life I'm not very fond of. My mother had a nervous breakdown, and because of the rural way of life so many people romanticize these days, the community just ignored her. And believe me, everybody knew my mother. My grandfather was one of the founders of Keuterville. And my father was born in the same house that my mother had her children in. Of course, the fact that my grandfather founded the town didn't mean my family prospered. We were very poor. When I got to college, I figured out that my parents raised eight kids on twelve hundred dollars a year.

"In fact, we were so poor that just about everything we ate came out of the garden or off the land. Oh, we would never buy anything but sugar or coffee. Mom made her lard and she made her soap until I was about thirteen. Then civilization arrived. Everything came later to us because of how backwoods we were. I must have been nine or ten before we got electricity. I remember sitting around the living room table with a coal lamp. And we had no tractors. We did have an old beat-up truck. That was the only mechanical thing. Everything else was moved with horses.

"We had a horse-drawn mower and wagons to bring the hay into the barn. And we manured out the barn every year by hand, too. You know, we hauled the manure down to the garden in the spring, or maybe in the fall. See, the barn just had a dirt floor, and in the wintertime, we let the horses and cattle in out of the storms. When we got to the manuring depended on how the work load was going. Manuring out the barn was something you did after you cut up all the hay, or once you had all the cattle moved and branded."

For a while after leaving home, Bill lived a cosmopolitan life, attending Loyola University of Chicago, then pursuing a degree in criminology at the University of Kansas. At one time he even owned a condominium, which he later sold to buy his four-room house in a residential neighborhood in East Lawrence, Kansas. Then he dropped out and, whether by design or happenstance, evolved a life which replicates his childhood in Idaho. He quit his two jobs, one analyzing social science surveys on computer, the other stacking paper at a printing firm, and began gardening, progressively paring down his lifestyle in order to become self-sufficient. First he eliminated the phone, then the gas. Next the pipes burst, and he never repaired the plumbing. Electricity was the last amenity Bill gave up—he knew he would miss his radio.

Now, a cistern which collects rainwater for drinking has replaced the bathtub and toilet in Bill's bathroom. In the kitchen, shelves of dusty glass canning jars take up the space where the range used to sit. And until the city made him tear them down, Bill had a greenhouse jutting out of one side of his kitchen and a chicken coop incorporated into his living room.

Self-sufficiency is not Bill's only goal. Ever since he began gardening, he has been determined not to become greedy, rarely allowing himself to be seduced by the trappings of civilization. "If I have too much money, I start wanting things." To limit his income, Bill has let certain vegetable plots lie fallow, and last summer he curtailed his gardening work to four hours per day. By reining himself in and selling his produce selectively to the Lawrence Food Co-op as well as several local restaurants, he earns just the money he needs—enough to pay his ninety-eight dollars in yearly property taxes, plus incidental expenses like instant coffee and one movie a year. What he can't pay for he barters: he babysits in exchange for use of a washing machine; he helps a stonemason in order to borrow the mason's truck for hauling; and he supplies zucchini to the friend who recharges his radio batteries.

Despite his modest needs, Bill gardens prolifically. He also gardens simply, his methods identical to those his mother taught him when he was six. "I don't plow my garden and I don't till. I work the ground by hand. People say, 'What do you mean, you work the garden by hand? Do you really go out there and get on your hands and knees?' No, I use a hoe and a rake and a shovel, for crying out loud! I just don't use any motorized mechanisms. But not all because I romanticize rural life. Only because my goal is to save money. That's why I don't fertilize, and that's why I don't irrigate, either. That's something else that costs. If it dies, it dies. For the same reason, I don't use insecticides. I support myself off my garden. That's the only income I have.

"And I'm lucky because people have always given me space. My first garden was a small plot sandwiched in between concrete slabs in downtown Lawrence. And that pattern of friends offering me plots continues. I could be talking to somebody at their house, and there might be a patch of unused land, and they would let me plant it. At one time, I was gardening about twelve or fourteen plots all over town. I counted up the other day, and since I've been here, I've gardened fifty-six different places. I ride all over on my bike, and carry my tools and harvest in a little cart attached to the rear wheels.

"I haul my wood around in my little cart, too. You see, I can get all the wood I need for my stove just riding around town. In fact, when the city came the last time, they had me get rid of some of my lumber. My pile was excessive, they said. There's some kind of code that states you can store a two-year supply, but you can't store more. Oh, yes, it's code time again. How I love those little codes!"

Once again aware of his audience, Bill impersonated the housing inspector, wagging his finger, his voice rising into falsetto as he giggled and pranced around the okra on his bare, slender toes. Then his face grew severe, his voice ministerial. "Of course, being in the middle of town, trouble with the city is unavoidable. You know, especially when you have neighbors to the south who complain. Mine have two or three domestic arguments a day, and I have to listen to them screaming about *me*. 'There used to be a nice lawn over there. Now look what he's done to it. I can't stand it anymore. I have allergies. I just can't stand it.' But I want you to know something. The way I grow things *does* make sense."

Bill's backyard is where he makes sense of gardening, and the yard is a microcosm of his life. It expresses all the passion, skills, ingenuity and expertise he has acquired since he worked with his mother on the family homestead, deep in the woods at the base of the arm where Idaho reaches up toward British Columbia, and the Nez Percé used to roam. In the 50 × 100-foot lot behind his house, Bill has created a one-man agricultural economy—planting, cultivating, harvesting and storing the nourishment he needs to survive, as well as recycling his own wastes. There are beehives by the back door and piles of corn drying on the ground, the husks splitting open. There are beans, okra, peppers, butternut squash, tomatoes, asparagus and strawberries growing in cages, on poles, in patches, in mounds. There are ladders leaning up against pear and apple trees, and shovels, spades and hoes resting on the ground. There are a cache pit (a hole dug into the ground for storing vegetables), a woodpile and a composting toilet, all bounded by a back fence patched from old boards, pieces of cardboard, carpeting and corrugated metal.

"You can see this garden doesn't follow any recognizable plan. I plant as space comes open. First, I planted everything in carrots and beets on one side. And on the other side, I had leeks and onions and garlic. And of course, there are strawberry beds running through. What's happened then is these crops give out, and then I plant the later stuff. I put in peppers and eggplant with the carrots and beans. Then I put watermelon where the leeks and onions were. I also scattered okra helter-skelter. Then, if I see another spot open, I put something else in. What I put in depends on the time of the year, but I never plant in rows. Some people will go to the seed catalogue in February and start designing their little gardens. I never lay out a plan. I garden more like this: Well, now it's the beginning of March and I need to get all my peas planted.

"But this kind of gardening really works. Look over there at those butternut squash. There are fifteen of them all from one hill. Most people don't get any squash because of the bugs. I've tried to deal with them manually in years past. What I do now is plant my squash early. Then I have something planted right next to it. Like this year it was peppers. Peppers do real well growing in the shade of the squash. When the squash dies, the peppers take over the area."

Bill follows the same method with lettuce and spinach. Once these cool-weather crops begin to die back, he plants cantaloupe and watermelon among the drying plants, allowing the melons to rush out and cover the ground in late spring. Then, at the end of the summer, triggered by the cooler temperature of the earth, the lettuce and spinach seeds from the first planting sprout. "It's got to get pretty cold, actually. When the soil reaches 50 degrees, the cantaloupe and watermelon die and the other plants are free to grow. And I cultivate peas that way, too.

"I guess I've invented this method, although all I did was notice it happening. Once I planted peas, then watermelon over them. In the fall, I noticed that the peas grew right up through the melon vines. Now, the books tell you to plant peas in the middle of August, but my peas start growing about mid-July. Oh, and this is very important, you just let the pea patch die down, and then they plant themselves. So for peas, lettuce and spinach, you basically weed the area by planting melons."

Most of Bill's gardening revolves around this succession method of planting. He sows black-eyed peas or beans and straw-berries together, the legumes shading the berries and protecting them from heat and drought. He also plants sweet corn and cherry tomatoes in the same area, reaping an early harvest of corn by mid-July, as the tomatoes continue to climb up the stalks. The sweet corn keeps the sun from hitting the tomatoes directly and protects them from scorch. And Bill pairs sweet potatoes and turnips, leaving one turnip from his spring garden to go to seed, then in June planting sweet potatoes, where the turnips once flourished. Later, when the frost kills the sweet potato crop, the turnips begin maturing all over again.

"You know, I really like thinking about these succession plantings because I've been working with them for so long now. All I have to do is think about the different gardens I've had and what worked well together, and I could talk about it forever. Of course, when I'm talking succession, I'm talking early crop, late crop. I say to myself, What am I going to plant here in the spring that will be taken over in the summer and will come back again in the fall?"

There are some vegetables, Bill warns, that do not work well together. Onions and leeks have a tendency to stunt beans. And peanuts do poorly with anything, like okra, that grows above them, or like watermelon or cantaloupe, that vines around them. Peanuts need room to spread as they grow. And Bill has discovered that planting corn and beans together is counterproductive. The corn ends up blocking too much of the sun and the beans do not produce very well. "Unless, of course, you do what the old-timers did. Do corn, four to a hill, maybe four feet between hills. Then, around the corn put Kentucky Wonder pole beans, the beans being planted, oh, approximately four weeks after the corn. Then the corn will mature and the beans will wrap themselves around the stalks, using them as poles. The trick to this combination is all in the coordinating. If you plant the beans too early, they drag the corn down. And if you plant them too late, they can't sprout before the corn begins to shade them."

Bill's planting techniques are genial, the inventions of imagination and a finely honed faculty for observation. But more than anything else, these methods are sparked by a paradoxical combination of choice and necessity—by Bill's quest to live outside of convention, yet at the same time to sustain himself with the income of garden plots borrowed from friends and acquaintances all around Lawrence.

The same impetus led Bill to begin saving his seeds. "Why spend money for something you can get for free?" To harvest seeds, Bill simply lets many of his vegetables grow for a full year, leaving everything in the ground during the winter, mulched with hay at least a foot deep to keep the plants from freezing. As with most of Bill's gardening, the key to this method is timing. He spreads the mulch only at the very end of the season, after a good freeze, and removes it as soon as the ground begins to warm in the spring so the plants can begin growing again and eventually produce their seed pods. Beets and carrots were the first plants Bill insulated in this manner, the carrots surprising him by sending up exquisite lacelike clusters of miniature white flowers.

"Of course, with carrots, the real trick is just to get there at the right moment. They shoot up and start maturing, and there's about a week period when the seeds will stay in the pod. And if you don't get them immediately, they'll just blow away. Actually, what I do is, just as the carrot's about to mature, I pull it out and bring it inside the house and set it on newspaper. Then I shake it and the seeds come out. Sometimes I've screwed up. I've been busy, and two days after the carrots are ready, we get this big downpour, and *pshhhhtt*, there they are in the ground already. Of course, you can just let this turn into a carrot patch the next year."

Like carrots, onions, leeks and garlic also send up seed pods which Bill sets on paper in his house. He collects tomato seeds the same way. "If you don't want it to take too long, you should squish the tomatoes so the juice runs out and the seeds can dry faster. With peppers, let them get real red, then strip the membrane off. At the bottom, you'll have a little ball of seeds. Let that dry, and when you rub, the seeds will pop off."

Bill also recycles his sweet potatoes. But unlike most gardeners he doesn't cut up last year's crop for starts. Instead, he takes his smallest potatoes and plants entire tubers, digging down nine inches and covering them with three inches of dirt. He leaves at least one foot between plants and five feet between rows. With this method, Bill reaps twelve to fourteen huge potatoes from each plant.

"I learned about this from an old black man who used to live right across the street. He also told me to go out about a foot and a half from the hill and whack everything off the last week in August or the first week in September. That way all the energy goes back into the plant, and not the leaves. I do this in my garden and people ask, 'What in the world are you doing?' Well, I can tell you,

you get gigantic potatoes that way. I get some that can make a meal for at least five people. I can also tell you it's convenient when you go to harvest. You don't have to go digging around a large area searching for the potatoes. They're all right there."

The lay and scale of Bill's backyard are too small and cluttered for sweet potatoes, which he cultivates a mile south of his house in a lot behind the backyard of the novelist William S. Burroughs, where the half-acre plot creates a radically different backdrop for Bill's expertise and sensibilities. Serene and verdant even at high noon, this garden is laid out in rows and clearly defined patches, okra on the two long sides, beans, sweet potatoes, peas, strawberries in the center. A stand of raspberries and blackberries, their brambles thick and tangled, runs along the western border.

The earth here is rich and black, the result of Bill's no-till, constant-weed method. For the five years he has gardened this plot, Bill has kept it weed free. And because he works only with hand tools, he has not disturbed the weed seeds, which often lie deep and can remain alive for as long as forty years. Bill also protects the soil in this plot by leaving most of the plants to die in place. Throughout the winter, okra, tomato and sweet potato stalks and foliage blanket the earth, breaking the rain as it beats down and keeping the soil from compacting. For additional protection, Bill might add a small layer of mulch—some leftover straw from the sale barn, but mostly lawn clippings. He also discovered that if he plants garlic throughout the rows in the spring, the sprouting bulbs help soften the ground for the next season. "And of course, I leave some of my root vegetables in over the winter. That helps the soil, too."

Bill has named the Burroughs plot his "Berry-Garlic Garden," and in it he practices what he calls his berry philosophy. He never irrigates and he never prunes. Instead, he allows foliage, either from the plant itself or from neighboring plants, to help conserve moisture. "See how green those strawberries are growing under the black-eyed peas? And we're in the middle of a drought! And then let me show you my raspberries and blackberries. With those I never cut the canes. I just let them mass and get real thick. That way they keep enough moisture in the ground to continue growing, even when there's no rain. Of course, with the blackberries, I'll whack them back so I can get a path through. But I won't prune them. You can't treat strawberries the same way, though. You need to let those move. The strawberry plant will send down a root that has a tendency to wooden and die. So, at least every two years I wipe out one whole section of strawberries and let another section grow."

Bill bent over and yanked out a tuft of lamb's-quarters, which he stuck under his left arm. Then he bent again, this time over a clump of crab grass. And again, over wild oats, each time poking the weeds under his left arm and plucking with his right hand, the fingers soon caked with dirt. "I'm sorry. I shouldn't be doing this with you here. But I can't help myself." Then he bent again, straightening seconds later, another clump of crab grass dangling from his hand. "This is my cleanest garden. Actually, all of my gardens are unique. I try to concentrate on growing different things in each one. You should see my corn-melon garden. That's really a sight!"

To reach this third garden, which is on the far north side of town, we followed Bill as he rode his bike, his implements clattering in the cart behind him, first down oak- and elm-shaded residential streets, then through Lawrence's red-brick, Tudor-style downtown, past the Eldridge Hotel, originally built in 1854 as a Free State hotel, and the old Bowersock Opera House, past the Round Corner Drug and the Paradise Cafe. As Bill pedaled, the limestone buildings of the University of Kansas rose on his left, at the summit of Mount Oread, overlooking the Kansas River valley to the north and the Wakarusa valley to the south. North of the courthouse and shopping area, and beyond Massachusetts Street, Bill reached the industrial section of town, then crossed the Kansas River and the railroad tracks, where once again he navigated residential streets, these more spread out and less solidly middle-class than those closer to the downtown and the university. On one house, the front porch was caving in. Strips of siding hung loose on another. A junked car hulked in the driveway of a third.

"This area is what they call the sandy bottom. It's the kind of soil watermelon does so well in. According to the theory, the glacier came to the river's edge and then stopped. Everything on this side of the river is glacier deposits. They say you can go down seventeen feet and have nothing but good fertile soil. Over on the other side of town where I live, you quickly run into clay."

A large field abutting a tiny frame house, this third garden is situated on the open Kansas prairie. Here every contour of the earth, every knoll, rise, flat and hollow seemed magnified. The sky, filled with deflated cumulus clouds, paralleled the land, dropping to meet it at the horizon line—houses and barns, trees, even blades of grass standing out sharply against the air. As if to intensify this vista, a swath of corn rose seven feet in a diagonal across the middle of the garden, while zucchini and patty pan, butternut, acorn and summer squash, cantaloupe and watermelon vines crept over the remaining surface area, their tendrils curling toward the corners of the lot. The tassels of the corn were splayed and swollen in the August heat. Under their broad, scalloped leaves, the reticulated skins of the cantaloupes turned golden, the fruit emitting a faint sticky-sweet perfume.

"All of my gardens have evolved on their own. In my Burroughs garden, along with berries and garlic I grow okra, black-eyed peas and beans, because none of those really requires rich soil. And here because of the sandy bottom, I have all my melons. And see how all that corn's growing in a band? Well, my friend the stonemason and I actually got his big dump truck stuck in the garden last year. We went to the horse farm and got a load of manure, and I told him, 'Keith, don't drive the truck down the middle there. It's really soft ground.' But he didn't listen, and we ended up shoving boards under the wheels to get them out. But once he got his truck loose, he dumped the manure just like I wanted him to. He opened up the bed, and as he drove through the garden, the manure spread itself. It was like a vision—a dump truck spreading a whole load of manure across *my* garden.

"And this year, I decided because the ground is so rich here, I'd do the heavy eaters, potatoes first, corn second, and maybe beets in the fall. And it seems to be working. Look how well the corn's doing. And there's something else I'm trying with the corn this year. I'm not popping all the suckers like I used to.

"When I worked at the convent, the nuns taught me to re-move all the suckers from the stalks in order to direct energy back into the main ears. But last year, some guy stopped by this garden one day and said, 'You know, you're wasting your time. According to the county agent, you don't have to remove the suckers any-more.' Well, I didn't believe the guy, but I told him, 'O.K. I'll do a little experiment with you. Here are ten rows of corn. I'll pop the suckers off five rows and leave the suckers on the rest. But I don't believe your cock-and-bull story.' Well, it turned out the ears with the suckers were just as big as those without, and they even had an advantage. We get these incredible winds in Kansas. You pull the suckers off, and, down go the stalks. You keep the suckers on and the corn stays up. Also, the suckers keep the weeds down. They're like a natural mulch."

Bill ducked behind a row of corn, then stuck his head out from between two stalks, and hammed a series of profiles—nose up, nose down, smiling, frowning, reflecting, winking—while he waited for us to take photographs. "You know, the cameraman from the *Times* spent eight hours taking pictures of me, but they only published three. Now don't you think that was a waste of time?" Then, with a rustle, Bill slipped down another row, popping out a few seconds later at the edge of the corn.

"You know, this garden is almost too prolific. And I don't want to have too many vegetables to sell. I want to live simply. Though not the way my parents did. People are always interpre-ting my life like that. But I tell them, if they think the country is such a great place to live, they should try it. Do you realize that in 1790, 90 percent of the population lived in rural areas, while in 1970, 90 percent lived in urban areas? And you have to assume that this was not just a matter of economic opportunity. It must also have been a question of individual taste. The rural environment is just not a very pleasant place to be. Here in Lawrence people are more tolerant, there's more individual freedom, there's more diversity, and in a strange way, there's less hypocrisy.

"Oh, the rural area can have the veneer of a tight-knit community. But when my mother had her nervous breakdown, she was basically all alone. And we knew everyone within a distance of seventy miles. And we knew everything about them. We knew who shot whose cow, who was cross-branding, and who was blotch-branding. Those were the big scandals. And then, of course, there was moonlighting. I mean, there was nothing everybody didn't know. But they all completely ignored my mother.

"In all, she had four nervous breakdowns. Who wouldn't, with eight kids to raise. The final breakdown occurred my junior year in high school. By that time, my dad had died. I was already away at school, and the kids at home fled the situation. My mother went from 145 to 85 pounds. She couldn't even get out of bed. And the neighbors knew all about it. When I got home, I discovered her like that, and I had to take her to a state mental hospital and commit her."

Overhead, a sparrow hawk circled the corn. In the full afternoon sun, Bill's face was reddish brown, the long hairs of his eyebrows bleached, his hair peppered, the curls bushy at the temples but receding back from his forehead. His beard straggled down his cheeks and neck past his Adam's apple.

"I guess you can understand how I have a jaundiced view of the rural area. There was this creed that you care about your neighbor, but then there was also a conflicting rule or complementary ethic that said, 'Mind your own business. Don't deal with other people's dirty laundry.' Well, that ethic forced me to grow up rather quickly. You might say I never even had a childhood. But here's something to note. Yes, I think that this is very important. Gardening, even back then, never did seem to disappoint me."

Bill squatted down and began gathering melons, tapping the tiny curl at the stem end to see if it was dry and the fruit ripe. Toes disappearing into the sandy loam, he waddled from vine to vine, head down, back curved, leaning toward, then away from the earth, his skin taut across his forearms. When he rose, he had a load of green-and-white-striped watermelons and rough, ribbed cantaloupes nestled in the crook of each arm.

The harvest from Bill's seven gardens is abundant. Every summer and fall he reaps far more apples, peas, berries, beans, corn, melons, potatoes, turnips, tomatoes and squash than he needs to keep himself alive. But the gardens do more than sustain Bill physically. They give him the space and variety essential for him to play out the multiple scripts in his life. Buffoon, philosopher, Zen Buddhist, skeptic, intellectual, farmer, artist, engineer, recluse, Bill has at least as many sides as he does gardens, and he moves among them nimbly, creating a dazzling one-person performance in which life and art fully coincide.

AUGUST

During the first part of the interview, when we are sitting on the porch looking down the valley, I try for exactitude more than anything—$343.67. She is impressed, which pleases me, makes me impressed with myself, and then ashamed, so I say, "And seventy-four cents of that I found, so I really made only $342.93. I suppose there might be a few more pennies somewhere, in a pocket or something." She writes it down with a kind of self-conscious flourish of her pen—a Bic "round stic," ten for ninety-nine cents, plus tax, if you buy them at the beginning of the school year—and I can see that momentary pause while she inventories all the things about her that she couldn't have if her income for last year were, like mine, $343.67. The view at the far end of the valley, the scattered houses of Moreton against the west face of Snowy Top, clears suddenly of August haze, and a minute later I feel a strong southwesterly breeze. Rain by mid-afternoon.

The other subjects in her book, some Seed-Save people, a tree-fruits fanatic, a raised-bed specialist, a guy who's breeding field corn back to its prehistoric varieties, all of them are going to be included for innovative gardening. Me I don't think she would have used if I'd had an outside job, or if Liz, my wife, had a job. We are no more up-to-date than Rodale, and she, that is, Tina, the interviewer, will know my methods from looking at the beds. But the money. That gets her. I say, "Before Tommy was born, our income usually hovered around a hundred and fifty dollars a year. But you simply can't raise a kid on a hundred and fifty dollars a year." A kid likes to have nice school supplies, for example. In September I expect to go to K-Mart and spend six dollars or so on school supplies. Tommy likes the trip. He chooses very carefully.

The gardens lie around the house in a giant horseshoe, five ranges, forty-five separate beds of plants, some neat, some shaggy, all productive. There is nothing to brag about, to her; she knows her stuff, and anyway, this time of year everyone looks like a terrific gardener. The plants are thick and hung with fruit, but not unusual. She fingers the leaves, pulls some soil out from under the mulch, looks for pests. There are a few, but not many. I rely on companion planting, crop rotation, garden sanitation. It works, but she doesn't ask about it. The praise she has to offer is in the sensuality and pleasure of her gestures, the way she lingers over each bed.

This is better. I didn't like the way the focus was so clearly on the money before. Money is the precise thing Liz and I don't focus on, which is why we earn so little. As soon as you bring up the money, I notice, conversation gets sociological, then political, then moral. I would rather talk about food, or swimming, or turkey hunting, or building furniture. The thing to do would be to get Liz to say, "Oh, Bob can make anything," in that factual way she has, explanatory rather than boastful, but Liz is offended by the whole interview process, by the light it shines on our lives and the way it makes a story of us. My promise to her was that Tina wouldn't ask her any questions and that she and Tommy wouldn't have to appear in any photographs.

The fact is, I should like this unaccustomed view of the Miller family, Robert, Elizabeth, and Thomas, on their small but remarkably productive acreage just outside Moreton, Pennsylvania. The fact is that years ago, when I had first bought the land and was building the big compost heaps behind the chicken shed, I used to imagine some interviewer just like Tina passing through, showing just her degree of dignity, respectability, and knowledgeable interest. I used to plan how I would guide her around the beds, then undug, show her through the house, then unbuilt, seat her in the chairs, feed her off the table, entertain her on the porch, and through imagining her, I saw all the details she might like. I imagined I would tell her, as I did during the interview, that imagination itself was the key—once I knew what it was specifically that I wanted, then either I would build it or it would turn up. And here she is, though I stopped looking for her long ago, right on schedule, reacting as she was destined to react. The pleasure of that is a private one, not one Liz would share, but not one I am inclined to give up, either.

It's true that I even foresaw that she would focus on the money. That's what I focused on myself then, how I had bought this great piece of land at an estate sale for only thirty-three hundred dollars, that was about sixty dollars an acre, as if all the acres were interchangeable. The bargain was precious, a good omen, a substitute for knowing what I was doing. Now the land has a personality, is without dollar value, and each acre is simply more or less useful or beautiful or ripe for improvement. The money embarrasses me. I should have been less exact. I should have said, "We made some. Enough. I don't know how much." But there is false humility in that, too, since I do know how much, since I do pay property taxes and buy school supplies and Tommy's yearly ticket on the school bus. Tina stands up and stares down the valley, then takes a deep breath. As we turn toward my workshop, she says, "This spot is paradise, isn't it?"

On my grandfather's farm in Ohio, the shop was neater than the kitchen, the tools shone more brightly than the silverware. For me, still, my workshop is apart from everything else. We try to cultivate orderly habits, but I don't mind the ebb and flow of schoolbooks, projects, articles of clothing, or toys through the house. Piles accumulate, are disposed of. Here nothing accumulates. When I am not working, the place looks like a museum exhibit—galleries of narrow shelves holding planes, chisels, knives, joiner's saws, files, hammers, mallets, rulers, gouging tools, sandpaper. Light pours through the open skylight and the window above the workbench. Each space is neatly labeled, identifying the resident tool, calling out for any absent one. The floor is swept (Liz made the broom one year, didn't like it in the house, and sent it out here). In a way this workshop IS money, since it contains an irreplaceable treasury of tools, but other than the sandpaper, every item came to me as a gift, an inheritance, or a castoff. The planes, for example, with their thick beechwood stocks and blue steel blades, have been outmoded by table saws and routers, and auctioneers at farm sales used to thank me for taking them away by the basketful. I refinished the stocks and reseated the hardware. Now I am told people ransack antique stores for old planes to give their living rooms that "country" look. I could not afford to replace these. Tina glances around politely, and says, "Lovely," before stepping back outside and staring at the gardens again. When I join her, she remarks, "The best carrot germination I ever got was fifty percent, and that was the time I nicked each seed with a file." I cough. Carrot seed is about the size of beach sand.

Liz waves to me from the porch. Lunch is ready. Although she disapproves of the interview, she wants to please the visitor. She has asked me every day about the menu for lunch, about whether she should bake the sourdough bread from whole wheat or white flour (our biggest expense after property taxes), whether I think any melons will be ready, what the chances are that Tina will be repelled by the wild foods—purslane, blackberries, angelica—that we eat routinely and enjoy. I, on the other hand, have been wanting to impress. "I built that chest from a black walnut Liz and I chopped down ourselves. I found the axle and the wheels for that wagon in the junkyard. I built the box myself. We caught these trout this morning. We gave up row planting before any books came out about it." My own bragging voice followed me around to every job for days. It cannot be done, this task I give myself, the task of communicating the pleasures of our life in this valley, even to an ear that longs to hear of them.

I would begin with the weight and cottony fragrance of the quilts we've made, an "All Hands Around" on the bed, a big log cabin in rainbow colors against black on the wall. In sixteen years we've made twelve quilts, used up one, burned a hole in another. In the winter we use two or three for warmth, and the first thing I see in the morning, in the white light of our whitewashed bedroom, is the clashing colors of the quilts spilling away from me over the bed. Then, under my feet, I feel the smooth-painted floorboards. The windows are uncurtained and unshaded, usually flat gray with morning fog. All of this is familiar and comforting.

Or I could begin with something even more inexpressible, which would be the stiffness of muscles worked the day before and sensed afresh a moment after waking. I think my consciousness must rouse before my senses, because there is always, always, a pain-free moment, and then the ache flows in. I like the ache. It tells me what I did yesterday, suggests what I might do today, even how I might do it. Farm work doesn't have to be backbreaking. It can be as aerobically sound and healthfully taxing as any other sort of exercise. Liz calls this "spading-as-sport" my private obsession, but another early morning pleasure is her sleepy, admiring rake of fingertips over my pectorals and abdominals.

Or there's Tommy's room, when I pass his doorway first thing in the morning, when Tommy is thoroughly asleep. He seems afloat in his bed, under his quilt, a green, orange, and yellow "Rail Fence." On the shelves I built are the toys we made him. He sleeps in a shirt Liz wove (I built the loom) on a straw tick the three of us stuffed. Across the room he has known since birth is the rocking cradle I copied, in local butternut, from a picture in a book I got out of the library. The headboard and footboard trim is carved with a twist, to look like a piece of rope; then the twist is repeated in the four braces that hold up the cradle. The lambskin lying across the mattress Liz made came from one of our lambs. The lamb's wool of the baby blankets was spun from some of the others. Liz's mother taught me to crochet, and I used to crochet while Liz knitted. When I look into my son's room, my pleasure is the knowledge that I have brought all of my being to bear here—not just hands and brain, but seed, too, and not just seed, but hands and brain, too. If he were really afloat, his bed would bump against the window, and he could look upon the orchard I planted, then bump against the shelves I built, where he could snatch down tops and cars and blocks and tools and dolls we've made him; this is a lovely sea, I think, tiny, enclosed, friendly, all his, and his alone.

Lunch doesn't look too weird—a plate of sliced tomatoes and green peppers, a couple of trout, cold boiled potatoes, beet greens, blackberries. Tommy follows his mother back and forth between the range and the table in a way I find annoying, and so I say, "Son, sit down!" He tenses, smiles, sits down. He is a good boy. Tina sits beside him and he offers her the pitcher of cold springwater, as he should. She looks around the room.

I can't help it. I lean back in my chair and say, "You know, it's remarkable what I've gleaned for free over the years. We have fishing rods and ponies and bicycles, a canoe, plenty of tools, sheep, two goats, lots of chickens. We tried a couple of turkeys a few years ago, and a cow, but she gave too much milk. This house has double-hung windows, figured brass doorknobs, a front door with a big pearly oval of etched glass. An old man in State College gave me that kitchen range. It's from the twenties. He found it in his barn. A guy I know in Moreton hauled it for me, in exchange for three lambs. It cooks our food and keeps the entire house warm. The first five years I lived here I spent getting to know people and offering things, then asking for things they were about to discard. Now, when people for miles around want to get rid of something, they send me a card. Incoming mail is free. Every so often I jerk loose and buy a couple of dollars' worth of stamped postcards for replies." I smile. "Compared to scrounging in Vietnam, which I did, this is no big deal."

We begin helping ourselves to the food. Tina asks, "What do you do for transportation?" Her manner is mild. I was the one looking forward to this, so I'm not sure why it puts me on edge. I say, "We think about it."

Liz doesn't like my brusqueness. She smiles and says, "He means that we plan ahead. Most days nobody goes anywhere except Tommy to school on the school bus, anyway."

"If I have a job or am trading something, part of the bargain is that they come here and pick me or it up. Besides, it's only three miles to town. We can walk or ski. Tommy can ride the pony." The tomatoes are delicious, sweet and firm and juicy. I never plant hybrids, only old fashioned varieties like Rutgers and Marglobe and Roma. I save the seed from the best plants and best fruits, selecting for hardiness and flavor. It works. "The thing is, going away should be something you contemplate, not something you do automatically."

"Could you live this way farther back in the mountains?"

"You mean, where it's colder, harder to get places, and rockier?"

"Yeah."

"You really mean, if not this extreme, then why not more extreme, as extreme as possible? Why not Alaska or the Australian outback?"

"I didn't mean that, but why not?"

"Why not really live off the land. Grubs and ants and spearing fish with a sharpened stick."

"Bob, come on," Liz says; then she turns to Tina. "We went through that about five years ago. Bob kept looking at brochures about land in Montana and British Columbia."

"We didn't ever send in the business reply cards, though. I was joking then, I'm joking now. My purposes aren't extreme, or political. My aim wasn't to choose the hardest path and prove I could do it. It was the same as everyone else's claim. It was to prosper. You don't prosper on hilly, rocky soil. It's more expensive to live outside of town. We're self-contained, not isolated and hostile."

Tommy relishes everything on his plate, not preferring the sweet to the savory, the cooked to the fresh, the domestic to the wild. He is a model eater, would devour grubs and ants and roots if they were on the table. Can Tina see what a miraculous child he is, how enthusiastic and open and receptive to guidance? Before he was born, I used to imagine a child-raising program that was purely example-setting. I would go about my work and he would accompany me, gradually assuming responsibility for the tasks that he was strong enough and smart enough for. There would be a lot of informative conversation, I thought—me explicating techniques and him asking intelligent questions. The reality is better than that. He tags along as eagerly as anyone could hope for, but he does all the talking. A lot of it is questions, but much of it is observations, remarks, little stories, bits of songs that are going through his head. There is a large category of stray sounds that simply escape his lips, from grunts to hisses to yells that I hope he has the sense to contain when he is at school but that I like for their animal quality, for their way of saying, "This organism is alive."

Which is not to say that example-setting is sufficient. I find that he does need a lot of molding and guidance, but that is another task we plan for, Liz and I.

After lunch there is a routine of work—bringing the animals into the barn out of the sun, checking water buckets, looking for eggs—that I think Tina should accompany me on, but when we sit back in our seats, Liz speaks up and says, "Tina and I will clear this up. Why don't you and Tommy come back in an hour for a swim?"

Considering that, when I asked her what she thought about this interview a couple of weeks ago, she said that she would rather chase pigs in a snowstorm, I am a little surprised. But it is a relief. Tommy runs out ahead of me, knowing that after chores he can ride the pony for half an hour before his rest time. He doesn't notice the view, but I do; every time the screen door slaps shut behind me, I pause and stare down the valley meadow toward Moreton, Snowy Top, and the dusky receding folds of the mountains beyond. My land is laid out rather deceptively—the smallest part is open field, valley floor, but all of these acres are visible from the house, and all of them are flat. The slope from the foot of the valley to the house is only three degrees, which is unusual around these parts. There has always been a farm on this site, and the barn remains, though the original house burned down in 1904—it was a big house and a big fire that the volunteer fire department could see from town but couldn't get to, because over a mile of the road was drifted in. One of the children ran burning from the house, but they rolled him in the snow and saved his life. The article took up half the front page of the Moreton *Record*. The family moved in with relatives in town, and their descendants farmed from there—keeping this land in pasture for seventy years, and running sheep and heifers and horses on it. When I bought it, the soil was so well fertilized that all I had to do the first year was turn under the turf and dig the beds. The other outbuildings were pretty up-to-date, too: the lean-to workshop beside the barn, a well-ventilated root cellar ten feet from the foundation of the old house (when I scraped dirt and caked mud off the old door, I found its surface scorched black from the fire, but the shelves inside that once held bins of vegetables were only dusty).

Most of the land I own runs up the hillsides in a bowl shape, to either side and behind the house, and that woodlot hadn't been touched or exploited in seventy, or even a hundred years. It took me three years just to drag the deadfall out, and I heated my house for seven and a half years on that. If I'd had the stone masonry built around the range that I have now, it would have lasted twice that long. What we do is build our first fire in mid-September, then make sure a small fire is in the stove every minute thereafter. All that masonry will have heated up by about mid-October, and after that we only have to keep it warm. It works. I use a lot less wood than the woodlot produces, and it's all hardwood. We even burn black walnut and cherry, wood the cabinetmaking companies would pay me for if they knew I had it. That's my luxury, my conspicuous consumption—I burn black walnut for heat.

From the house, everything is perfect. The natural landscape offers enclosed, familiar, pleasing curves, softened with August haze and prolific vegetation—sugar maple, black cherry, hickory, butternut, walnut, beech, yellow birch, and white oak are some of what I can see from here—and I respond, unfailingly, with love ("regard" and "inspiration," looking and inhaling). From everywhere else on the property, I must view my own mistake, the house. I built it—yes, I built it—mostly from brick torn out of the streets of State College, Pennsylvania, and pine pallets that I ripped the nails out of one by one. Recognizing my accomplishment doesn't mean I've ever been satisfied with it. I resent its lack of grandeur more than its lack of size. What I meant to keep simple I made humble, and I made a mistake siting it, because I thought it would be easier to use the old foundation than lay another one. If we were to add on now, we would have to add outward, creating an ungainly, flat building. If I'd built farther back—into the hillside as I first intended—it would have been easy to add on upward, just to tear off the roof and build another small house on top of the old one. And we would have been closer to the springhouse. Sometimes I can see the structure I might have built so clearly that the frustration of what I've done is explosive. Here we live, here we will always live. No gardens, barns, sheds will ever mitigate the permanence of this mistake.

Chores completed, I return. The women are sitting at the table, still, talking about home schooling. Tina looks skeptical, which makes Liz speak more assertively, expressing none of the doubts she has expressed to me. Home schooling is my idea, and her arguments are ones I've made to her. "Actually," she is saying, "studies show that they get along better with the other kids once they get to college, because they have a real sense of themselves and a sense of their own abilities."

"But don't they miss the other kids?"

"I don't know if Tom would. We sent him to kindergarten, because we felt guilty about keeping him so isolated. He gets along okay, but until you've really considered home schooling, I don't think you realize what a compromise school is, how regimented it is, and how the others expect you to act so you'll fit in. And around here there's nothing to do, so most of the high-school kids gather at one of the big ponds and drink, then drive around endangering themselves and everyone else. It's not like a big suburban school, where they might be, only might be, exposed to something new."

"Well, social life has meant a lot to Libby since she's been in kindergarten—"

Libby must be a daughter. They have covered a lot of ground in my absence, and I am sort of shocked by the name, "Libby," rather idle-rich-sounding, as if this project of Tina's is a whimsy after all, not committed or serious as it would be if she had no children, or her daughter's name was, say, Susie.

"But she's a girl. Bob was a loner in school. I wasn't. I think I missed more than he did. I just had the same experiences everyone else had. I don't feel like my life had any integrity until I came here."

"It's lovely—"

"And you know at first I hated it. I didn't have any inner resources at all. I thought I would die of loneliness, even on days when Bob would talk to me." She smiles slyly at me. "This was not how I intended to spend my life."

"I just think it takes a lot of fortitude to have your child at home, to be responsible for everything that goes into his head. What does Tommy think?"

Now I speak up. "He likes the idea, but we promised him one more year in the grammar school before we make up our minds."

Liz glances at me. I make the truthful emendation. "Well, he doesn't always like it. But his schooling is my decision to make. He understands that. Anyway, we're a closely knit family, and there's so much going on around here all the time that he doesn't want to miss anything. And as for taking responsibility for what goes into his head, that ATTRACTS me."

Tina sits back. She says, "Your lives are so completely of a piece. I admire—"

"You know, I always think I'm going to love being admired, but then I get nervous when it happens, I think because you shouldn't be admired for doing something you needed to do. I mean, until I moved here, I was so filled with frustrated yearning that it was this or suicide. When I was Tommy's age, I thought it was yearning to be on my own. When I was a teenager, I thought it was lust. When I was in the army, and in Vietnam, I thought it was the desire to go home. But it was none of those things. I never figured out what it was, but it ceased. Tommy doesn't have it. He's enthusiastic about the farm and the animals and fishing and helping us cook and grow things, everything we do here that we couldn't do if we lived in town." Just now the rain begins, steady and warm, lifting the scent of the grass, of the valley's whole morning, through the screen door—wildflowers, tomato plants, walnut leaves, pony and sheep manure, the rainwater itself. It is a smell so thick and various that I can nearly see it, and I inhale sharply. Liz laughs and leans toward Tina. "Put this in your book. Bob pretends to have opinions, but the real truth about him is that his senses are about three times sharper than normal. He's really just a farm animal scratching his back in the dust."

"Not true!" I say. "What I really am is a body attached to a pair of hands that can't stop making things. Inclination precedes conviction. I want to make, therefore I decided making is valuable. The more I want to make, the more valuable making is."

"Very nice, sweetie," says Liz, standing up and kissing the top of my head. "But running your hand down the board precedes making."

Tommy appears on the porch, dripping, but doesn't come in. He calls, "Hey, Daddy, I got the pony and the foal in before the rain started! They didn't get wet at all!"

"Did you wipe off the bridle?"

"Yes, Daddy."

"Even the corners of the bit?"

"Yes, Daddy."

Liz hands him a towel and he dries off in the doorway. He has what we call "the look." His face is too bright, his eyes too eager; a kind of rigidity seems to grip him when he is still, but when he moves, the movements are quick and broad. Liz recognizes it, too, and says, patiently, "Sweetie, time to settle down for your rest. You want some milk before you go up? Sit by Daddy, and I'll pour you some."

He might sit. He might run into the other room. He might knock over this chair. I must have had the look, too, when I was his age, because I remember the feeling perfectly, a feeling of imminent eruption, fearsome, alluring, uncontrollable. It was like standing in a dim, warm, small room and having an astonishing bright light switched on every so often, and when the light was on I couldn't remember what it was like for the light to be off. From the ages of about nine to about twelve, I worked steadily to lighten the room molecule by molecule, until the bright light no longer shocked me, and the room glowed comfortably. What I actually did I can't remember, but I remember the sensations of light, the feeling of having labored, and my father remarking that I had gotten to be a good boy after all, no longer "all over the place like a crazy person." My first real feeling of accomplishment, the first time I knew that I could master myself.

Perhaps because of Tina, Tommy sits quietly, drinks his milk, and doesn't knock over his chair until he stands up. Liz picks it up with ostentatious care and I say, "Time for your rest, son. When you come down, I want you to show me the chapter you've read."

"How many pages?"

"A whole chapter."

"Even if it's ten pages?"

"A whole chapter."

He contains himself and marches off. All of these things happen every day, and yet they seem so peculiar with Tina at the table, making notes in her head. I am tempted to apologize, but I don't know for what, so I hold my tongue.

When we are undressing that night for bed, I admit it, that the interview was a bad idea. "I mean, I hate feeling this detached from everything. Look at my foot going under the covers. Look at my hands pulling the blankets up, aren't these lovely quilts, look at my wife, 'Liz' she's called, blowing out the lamp."

Liz laughs, reaches under the covers to tickle me lightly. "She thought you were a genius."

"What?"

"You heard me."

"When did she say that?"

"After lunch, then again before she left. She said, 'Everything he touches he transforms into something beautiful and useful.'"

"What did you say?"

"I said that I agreed."

"You did?"

She runs her hand over my face in the darkness, a gesture that is tender and proprietary at the same time. She says, "I told her I hoped she put that in the book, because that's what's true about you."

After we make love, when I am nearly asleep, I feel her ease out of bed, then I feel her turn, kneel beside the bed, and begin to pray. I hear that murmuring all night, even after I know in my sleep that her solid weight is unconscious beside me.

The next day is Saturday. At breakfast, Liz says, "You remember about the church meeting this afternoon?"

"I remember."

"I'll be home about six, unless someone gives me a ride to the end of the road. I might be home by five-twenty or so."

"Fine."

"Really?"

"Liz, you don't have to ask. It's fine."

"Good. I'm looking forward to it."

About a year ago, Liz started shopping around for a church to attend. There are ten churches in Moreton and she went to every one, judging them more on ambience than on doctrine. The two Quaker congregations, having within living memory been one, were hyper-aware of each other, she said, the Episcopalians enjoyed themselves too much, the Presbyterians were engaged in easing out their minister, and on down the line, until she decided upon the "Bright Light Fellowship," a Pentecostal sect whose prophet resides in Gambier, Ohio. I was frankly astonished that my wife, a graduate of the University of Pennsylvania and a voracious reader, could feel at ease in this collection of the rural poor, the badly educated, and the nakedly enthusiastic, but that is exactly what she feels there, she says. Privately, I think she feels humbled, which is a feeling she is in favor of as a way of life. She began participating in January, and attended every Sunday. If it snowed, she went on skis; if it rained, she wore rubber boots and a poncho. She asks me if I mind. I do, but I would rather not, and I certainly don't want to influence her. Nevertheless, it has become one of those marital topics of conversation, a rift that we consciously avoid making an argument of. My own religious views are deistic, you might say. I notice that days when she goes to church, for whatever reason, are special days, obstructing the smooth flow of time that I like. She assumes that this is my main objection. I also notice that, however else she arranges and varies her time with, and communication with, Tommy and me, she never fails to kneel at bedtime and make a lengthy prayer. That, both the unfailing regularity of it, and the awkwardness of its insertion into our nightly routine, is the real bone of contention. I have been married to Liz for a long time—twelve years—and I intend to be married to her forever, so I am cautious about drawing any conclusion as to whether this issue is a passing one, one that can be resolved through compromise, or simply a large, heavy object that sits in the living room, obstructing traffic, grudgingly accommodated, year after year.

Of course I have forgotten about the church meeting, so my response, because there has to be one, is to hold a little aloof—to go out in the workshop and dive into a project of my own rather than to do something more friendly, like sort iris corms on the front porch. What I do is remind myself that I am a genius, and, when I step into the workshop, that lends even these kitchen chairs I am making the glow of loveliness. They are made from ash saplings, with woven rush seats, and my tools are, basically, my draw knife and a bucket of water. There are chairs like them in every antique store—rounded stiles, ladder-backs, four stretchers below the seat—but mine are the only comfortable ones I've ever sat in. The seat is roomier, for one thing, and I soak the stiles and angle them backward so that you don't feel like you're about to be strapped in and electrocuted. I soak all the mortise joints, too, before I put everything together, and they dry and shrink around the tenon so tightly that the whole chair might have been carved from a single piece of wood. These are almost finished. All I have left is a carving of leaves and vines into the top rung of the ladder-back.

Well, it is a pleasant day. I sit on one of the chairs I've made and decorate another one. The chestnut tree above me is alive with light and shade, the weather is warm and breezy, my wife and son go about their business with evident satisfaction. The valley that is our home is soothingly beautiful, safe, and self-contained. We eat a lunch that we have provided for ourselves, and afterward I am so involved with my carving that I forget Liz is gone until I see her come walking down the road, and then, no matter who she's been with, all I want to do is to meet her, kiss her, and walk her to the house.

"Guess what?" she says.

"I'm a genius?"

"Yeah. You know how I can tell?"

"How?"

"You forgot that school starts Tuesday."

"This Tuesday? I thought that wasn't till after Labor Day this year."

"Monday is Labor Day. It's been September for four days now."

"Tina was supposed to come on the fifteenth of August."

"Well, she was two weeks late and we didn't even notice. She ought to put that in her book."

"You went to church last Sunday. Didn't you realize what day it was?"

"It didn't come up. It's not like when you're a Catholic and you're always counting backwards or forwards to some major holiday."

"Well, I guess that shows that the prophet is a man of his time. He figures everybody knows what day it is."

"If you really want to know, what he figures is that every day might as well be the last."

We haven't talked about specifics of dogma very much, but I let it drop. Anyway, Tommy comes out of the barn where he has been haying and watering the ponies for the night, and greets his mother as if she has been gone since Christmas. She swings him up into her arms, and continues walking, his arms around her neck and his legs around her waist. The voice of my father tells me that he is too old for this, but my own voice disagrees, says that boys are isolated too soon, that as long as he seeks our bodies he should find them. And there is also this reassuring shiver of jealousy, a light touch raising the hairs on the nape of my neck, that reminds me how the pleasure of marriage and the pleasure of fatherhood take their piquancy from watching, left out, as they nuzzle and giggle and tease. He never tries to impress her; she never tries to mollify him. We haven't used birth control since our marriage and she only got pregnant once. Most of the time I forget that it could happen again. Secretly, I have only ever managed to imagine one boy child. Maybe imagination is the key there, too. "Lovely sunset," says Liz, and Tommy says, "We fried green tomatoes with basil for dinner."

"Mmm," says his mommy. "I just love that."

We stroll up the road toward the house, toward the dinner laid on the table, and this is what we expect: to eat and be satisfied, to find comfort in each other's company, to relinquish the day and receive the night, to make an orderly retreat from each boundary that contains us—the valley, the house, the room, the covers, wakefulness—in perfect serenity. Well, of course I am thankful, and of course a prayer lifts off me, but there is nothing human about it, no generalizations, nor even words, only the rightness of every thing that is present expressing itself through my appreciation.

Boyce Rensberger

FOR THE
SAKE OF SEEDS

Call them the martyrs for biodiversity.

During the terrible winter of 1941–42, while Hitler's armies were blockading Leningrad and thousands were starving to death, a small band of Soviet scientists accepted the same fate, even as they guarded tons of rice, wheat, corn, beans, and potatoes in a huge seed bank.

Nine botanists perished in the midst of plenty, thus preserving the seeds for science—and for future generations, including Americans, many of whose crops today are the result of cross-breeding with varieties the scientists saved from destruction.

The researchers were on the staff of the Vavilov Institute of Plant Industry, and their ordeal helped maintain their institute as one of the world's largest repositories of the genetic diversity of food crops.

Their story, little known in the West, was recently told in the journal *Diversity* by two institute officials, S. M. Alexanyan and V. I. Krivchenko.

When World War II came to Leningrad, now called St. Petersburg, the Vavilov Institute had accumulated seeds from 187,000 varieties of plants, of which about 40,000 were food crops. By maintaining the stock—which requires periodically replanting and harvesting fresh seed—various qualities such as resistance to particular pests or adaptability to various climates are available to be bred into existing crops.

In the fall of 1941, Nazi forces tried to take Leningrad but were held off by the Red Army. The stalemate became a siege with frequent shelling and skirmishing that would last 880 days.

"It became increasingly difficult to work in the institute," Alexanyan and Krivchenko wrote. "The building was unheated as there was neither firewood nor coal. Because of unrelenting firing on the city's center, the building's windows were broken and had to be boarded up. The institute was cold, damp and dark."

As the winter wore on and temperatures plummeted to 40 below, the potato collection was at special risk of freezing. It, like much of the collection, was also vulnerable to plunder by hungry townspeople.

Institute workers "burned everything to get heat," the authors wrote—"boxes, paper, cardboard and debris from destroyed buildings. To guard and care for the collection they established 24-hour vigils for the scientific workers at a special outpost near the potato storage area."

Working secretly, the scientists prepared a sample of the collection to be smuggled out of Leningrad. The collection was transported over a frozen lake to a storage facility in the Ural mountains. Other parts of the collection were divided into smaller lots and also smuggled out of Leningrad.

"In the dark, frozen building of the institute," Alexanyan and Krivchenko wrote, "the remaining workers intensively prepared the seeds for long-term preservation in the city. While they divided the collection into several duplicate parts, bombs and shells continued bursting around the institute. . . . Fortunately, [the institute's] safety was assured because it was located near the German consulate and the Astoria Hotel where Hitler had planned to hold a victory banquet."

The portion of the collection that stayed at the institute was put into the most secure rooms.

"No one was permitted to remain alone with the collections in these rooms," the authors wrote. "Room keys were kept in the safe of one of the institute's executives. Once a week R. Y. Kordon, the institute's keeper, opened the doors, checked the conditions of the boxes, and resealed them."

As the weeks passed, even the rats became hungrier and bolder.

"The people, barely alive from hunger and cold, boarded up the door and window sills with iron, and spread poison and shattered glass to fill up the rat holes."

Famine in the city reached major proportions, killing tens of thousands.

In January 1942, Alexander G. Stchukin, a peanut specialist, died at his writing table. Georgi K. Kriyer, who was in charge of medicinal plants, and Dmitri S. Ivanov, head of the rice collection, also succumbed.

"After Ivanov's death," the authors wrote, "workers found several thousand packs of rice in his collection that he had preserved while dying of starvation."

Others who starved to death at the institute were Liliya M. Rodina, M. Steheglov, G. Kovalesky, N. Leontjevsky, A. Malygina, and A. Korzun.

"As they slowly starved," Alexanyan and Krivchenko wrote, "they refused to eat from any of the collection containers of rice, peas, corn and wheat."

By the spring of 1942, protection of the collection called for even more ingenuity and daring: Cold and damp had weakened the seeds' viability and many had to be planted so that fresh seed could be collected.

But the Nazi siege continued and access to rural land was impossible. So a small plot was found near the outskirts of the city, not far from the front line. Lacking horses or tractors, more than seven acres were tilled by hand with spades. As shelling continued, the seeds were planted, guarded through harvest, and a new supply of seed brought into the collection.

The siege of Leningrad would continue until January, 1944. Through it all, the Vavilov collection was largely preserved. In the postwar years the institute grew and prospered as one of the world's premier facilities for the collection and preservation of plant genetic diversity.

Since the collapse of the Soviet Union, however, the Vavilov has again fallen on hard times. Sources of funding have become uncertain and, according to Jose Esquinas-Alcazar of the U.N. Food and Agriculture Organization, "the Vavilov doesn't even have money to pay its electricity bills. It would be a terrible shame if the world lost that institution."

NEAR THE CENTER
OF THE EARTH

My mother spooned the poisoned corn and beans into her mouth, ravenously, eyes closed, hands shaking. We, her seven children, sat around the table watching her for signs of death, our eyes leaving her only long enough to glance at the clock, to see how far the hands had moved. *Would she turn blue like my oldest sister Alice said?* Alice sat hunched next to me in the same white kitchen chair, our identical home-made cotton dresses blending into one. She shoved my shoulder with hers as if I were disturbing her concentration and stared unblinking at Mother. Each time Mother hesitated, spoon in mid-air, Alice's face clouded and she pushed against my shoulder.

"She's dying," Alice whispered, covering her mouth so Mother could not hear her. "I told you she was gonna die."

I ignored her and watched Mother. I wanted to taste the sweet yellow corn, to feel the kernels slide against my teeth. I didn't care if they were poisoned. I was so hungry my head throbbed. The clock ticked as loudly as the clattering train that passed beside our house every day, each tick echoing against the wall and bouncing into my head, making my heart beat in my temples and my eyes want to close. I forced my eyes to stay open, to watch my mother as she ate. I stared at her face, the light freckles smearing into a large round blur, then snapping back into focus. No one spoke or moved. My oldest brother Stewart sat next to me, hands in his lap, clenched into tight white balls; David, his chair pushed as close to Stewart's as possible, leaned forward with his arms and hands spread across the table as if to catch Mother if she fell. Willie and Doris Ann also sat together, their small legs sticking straight out, dirty bare feet dangling off the seat of the chair, Doris Ann's arms wrapped around the feather pillow from her bed. Mother held John cuddled in her lap, leaning over his head to spoon the beans into her mouth; he fussed and reached for the spoon, hungry and angry because she kept pushing his hand away.

My mother had waited all morning for a letter from my father, a letter with money for food. When, once again, no letter or money arrived, she went out to the tool shed and brought in the corn and bean seeds for next year's garden. The seeds had been coated with pesticides to keep bugs from eating them during the winter. Poison. I watched my mother split the dusty sealed brown bags with a kitchen knife and empty the contents into bowls, the seeds making sweet music as they tapped the glass. *Ting, ting, ting.* She ran her hands through the dry seeds, lifting them to her nose. *Did they smell like poison?* She rubbed a fat bean between her fingers and touched her fingers to her tongue. She spit into the sink, rinsed her mouth with cold water and spit into the sink again. She stood staring out the window above the sink, her hands limp in the bowl of seeds. She stood this way for ten minutes or more, staring out the window.

Then, as if broken from a spell, she opened the cabinet and got out two colanders. She poured the dry seeds into them: corn in one, beans in the other and ran water over and over them. She turned and rubbed each tiny seed with her fingers, wiping the cool water on her forehead, on the back of her neck, her dress already damp under the sleeves from the afternoon heat.

"Those seeds are poison, you know. Poison. If we eat them, we'll die," Alice whispered. She was eleven and knew these things. I tapped my bare feet against the kitchen chair and thought about this, decided I would eat them anyway. I was so hungry and certain that no poison could kill me. I could just tell myself not to die and I wouldn't. I was that strong.

John slid from his chair and pulled at Mother's dress, kicking, fussing, wanting to be held, wanting to be fed.

"Alice, why don't you take the kids outside for a little while," Mother said as she churned the seeds through the water. She turned towards us and caught my sister's disappointed face. "Just for a little while," she said.

We stumbled reluctantly out the back door. Alice pulled John from Mother's legs and carried him outside; he liked to be outdoors and stopped fussing. We moved into the yard, each claiming our territory. Alice took John for a walk under the trees, out of the direct sunlight, to push the leaves around and look for buckeyes. Stewart and David ran into the garden and picked corn stalks to use as weapons, to joust like the knights in our story books.

I sat on the steps with Willie and Doris Ann. I could see the tiny gas station at the bottom of the hill and farther out, barely visible, our closest neighbor. Directly in front of me was the garden, or what was supposed to be a garden. The fierce sun had baked it to a toasty brown before any vegetables had appeared, the temperature climbing over a hundred degrees every day. Twelve rows of shriveled corn, dwarfed and fruitless, so many tomato plants, twenty or more, crunchy and brown, the tiny yellow flowers dried and stiff, not bothering to form into little green balls, the tomato vines weaving in with the cucumber vines like a hot-pan holder made on a loom. Grasshoppers, increased in number due to the heat, had stripped the cucumber plants bare, the vines like curved barb-wire running through the dusty red clay, in and out of the tomato vines, in and out of the bean rows.

Nothing to put up and stack on the pantry shelves for winter, no steam from boiling kettles fogging the kitchen windows, the aroma seeping into every corner of the house: tomato sauce, soup stocks, creamed corn, sweet bread and butter pickles, succotash, green beans, white navy beans, speckled pinto beans. Not one jar to open when the coldest days arrived, when it hurt to breathe the air. There had been no summer tomato sandwiches smeared thick with mayonnaise on white bread baked in the oven, no corn on the cob dripping with butter, no crispy cucumbers to eat, straight from the garden, still warm from the sun.

That summer, in Eastaboga, Alabama, what had flourished were the day lilies: thousands of them, in the yard hovering close to the house, around the trees, alongside the road and in the ditches. My father called them ditch lilies. *Cause they live in the ditches, like beggars, returning every year—more and more of 'em. We can't grow one God damn tomato but we can grow thousands of these. Hell, we couldn't weed enough to make all these damn things disappear, even if we wanted to.* "But Solomon in all his glory was not arrayed like one of these."

My father pulled a handful of lilies up by the roots, tossed them into the sun to dry like bones, knowing my mother loved the bright red and orange lilies, knowing she did not want them to disappear.

The day lilies had not disappeared but, somehow, my father had. Alice said she had gotten out of bed one morning and he was gone and did not show up again.

"That's disappearing," she said matter-of-factly, hands on her hips. It was, after all, more mysterious to have a father who disappeared than one who had just gone somewhere. And this time, we were sure, he had not just been put in jail for the week-end. The black and white sheriff's car had not driven into the yard. The sheriff had not, this time, stepped out of the car, tipped his hat to my mother and apologized for disturbing her, telling her he would bring my father back home in a day or two. No, this time my father had been gone for weeks. We wanted to ask our mother where he was but had learned not to ask questions, not to speak of it except among ourselves.

Actually, my father had not disappeared but had gone to Baltimore, Maryland, where his brothers lived, to find work. He left no money. He took the car. Said he'd write and send money soon. Mother couldn't drive anyway so the car was not a great loss. The one time my father had tried to teach her to drive, she drove into a ditch. He never let her try again, said women weren't made to drive. They were made to take care of the home. And that's just what she did: wash clothes, iron clothes, wash dishes and cook meals for seven children.

Seven children: girl, boy, boy, girl, boy, girl, boy, like descending stairs: eleven, nine, eight, seven, six, four and two years old, several without a full year in between; four with their father's hazel eyes and dark hair and three with their mother's blue eyes, but blonds rather than redheads.

I had just turned seven years old and didn't think my father's disappearance was such a bad thing; no more dishes shattering into the wall, no more whiskey breath and smell of urine, no more fear of being discovered, of having to peek into a room before entering to see if he was slumped in a chair waiting for you to walk within his reach.

"Now I've got ya," he'd shout like he had just caught a coon raiding the corn patch, pulling his leather belt from the loops as you struggled to get free. You didn't have to do anything, anything at all to get pinched, poked, shoved or hit, just be where he could reach you when he was drunk. "You belong to me and I'll do with you what I want."

Unless, which often happened, he decided you didn't belong to him at all.

"Where did these tow-heads come from?" my father would chide, ruffling David's or Doris Ann's blond hair, pulling just hard enough to make them wince.

"I got dark hair, your Mama's got red hair. Maybe they got you mixed up at the hospital and you don't really live here. Hell, Mamie's kids look more like me than you do!"

Mamie, our closest neighbor, lived about a quarter of a mile farther down Mudd Street. We played tag and leap-frog with her children. *How could he believe Mamie's kids looked more like him than some of us? Mamie and her husband Buck and her kids—they're Negroes—how could he think they look more like him than us?*

We went straight to Mother with our questions, "Were they really mixed up at the hospital?"

"Why do I / they have blond hair?"

"How do you know they weren't really mixed up at the hospital?"

"Do Mamie's kids look more like Dad than I do?"

"Are you sure all of us are yours?"

My mother, trying to get dinner on the table, would give my father that "don't do that" look, answering as she put bowls of vegetables on the table, pulled plates from the cupboard: "Yes, I'm positive you all belong to us, nobody was mixed up at the hospital, you all belong right here."

I would not have questioned my parentage for I had dark hair and hazel eyes like my father except: *How did I get to be left-handed if neither my mother nor my father were left-handed? Maybe I was swapped for another baby girl with dark hair and hazel eyes. Maybe I was the one that didn't really live here.*

It annoyed my father that I was left-handed. He called me "South-paw," "Sinister," and sometimes "Middle-of-the-Road" because I was the middle child: three older, three younger. Just before I started to school my father decided to remedy my left-handedness.

"South-paw," my father shouted, coming in the door with a six-pack of beer and a brown bag. "South-paw, come here! I got somethin' for you." He dropped a bag on the couch. "Bring me a church-key for my beer, there, Stu," he said, pulling a beer from the carton and sending the rest with Stewart to the refrigerator.

He was sitting on the couch drinking when I ran into the room, small refined pleasurable sips, a pleasure that he seemed to get from nothing else. He put the beer on the coffee table and pulled the contents from the bag: a small blackboard, a box of chalk and a length of cord. He propped the blackboard against the large family Bible on the coffee table.

"Well, get over here," he barked. "I can't reach you from there."

I walked toward my father, my heart beating fast, breathing shallow. I didn't understand the meaning of the chalkboard or the rope. The fear crept higher. I wanted to run out the door but I knew he would catch me and more than likely hit me. I looked around for my mother but she was not there. I could hear Alice and Stewart in the next room talking. *Dad brought home a rope for Barbara.* I bit my tongue and tasted the salty blood in my mouth. *What had I done?*

"Now, Miss Sinister, we're gonna rid you of your problem," my father said, pulling me towards him and shaking me gently by the shoulders. He let go of me, took another sip of his beer and opened the box of white chalk. He took out one piece and placed it firmly in my right hand. Then he picked up the length of cord and shook it out, holding on to one end.

"What are you gonna do?" I asked, my voice barely audible. "Are you gonna tie me up?"

My father didn't answer. He took my left hand and wrapped the cord around and around my wrist.

"Where's Mom?" I asked, beginning to shake. *I must have done something . . . something terrible. . . .*

He pulled my left hand behind my back, twirled me around to wrap the cord around my waist, and wrapped it, once again, around my wrist. I dropped the chalk from my right hand as I was whirled around. It hit the hardwood floor and broke into pieces.

"It's time for you to learn the correct way to write," my father said as he tied the cord snugly, tugging at it to check for security, as if I were a prisoner that might try to escape. "You'll be off to school this fall, we can't have you still writing with your left hand. You want to be like everybody else, don't you?" He picked up a piece of the broken chalk from the floor and put it back in my right hand.

I nodded "yes" but I really didn't see why it mattered if I wrote with my left instead of my right, as long as I could read it. I felt dizzy.

"I'm gonna write your name for you," my father said, picking up another piece of the broken chalk, "and you copy it using your right hand. By the time school starts you'll know how to spell your name and you'll be using the correct hand to write with."

He wrote my name on the chalkboard using all capital letters. Mother and Alice had already taught me how to write my name with big and little letters, how to count to ten and the colors of the rainbow.

I tried to copy what my father had written, pushing up on the chalk rather than pulling down, sometimes making the letters backwards. My father would erase the entire word and make me start over. I could hear a buzzing in my head. I felt like I'd never be able to think straight again, seasick. By the time we finished the first lesson, tiny white specks floated in my eyes, white worms swimming around inside my eyes like tadpoles in the creek.

"We'll do this every evening until you've got it," my father said, erasing the letters I had worked so hard on with one quick brush of his palm.

One evening, just days before school started, I worked on the chalkboard for an hour with my father giving instructions. I was still making letters backwards, sometimes the whole word backwards. Every time I started to write with my right hand, it felt like my brain would pop—like opening a Mason jar, everything I knew spilling out into the air never to be seen again. After my father untied the cord holding my left hand behind my back, I went outside and sat on the steps. I wanted to cry but knew better than to cry around my father. He'd say, "If you're gonna cry, let me give you something to cry about." Even my mother disliked for us to cry; crying was permitted for real injuries only: a cut foot or skinned knees. There was something about tears that made them both uneasy, almost fearful, so I held my tears, but they were thick and teeming in my chest. I propped my arms on my knees, sunk my face into my hands, and thought about the only time I had seen my mother cry.

It was before I started to school. My mother was having another baby. I had been waiting for this new baby, not particularly anxiously but with curiosity. John was not a baby at all, not to me anyway; he could walk and talk a little too. And Willie and Doris Ann were certainly not babies, even though Mamie called them that when she talked to my mother. Babies smelled pretty and let you hold them in your arms like a doll; they didn't cry or tear at your hair.

Someone, I think it was Mamie, came over while Mother was gone to the clinic and dressed me in my only good clothes. All of us were dressed in our good clothes and placed on the couch in the living room, in order of birth, like ornaments: Alice, Stewart, David, me, Willie, Doris Ann and John. We sat for what felt like a long time waiting for Mother to arrive with the new baby. Mamie went home. Finally a car drove into the yard. We all ran to the door. Mother got out of a taxi, alone. She had a small suitcase but no baby.

"Where's the baby?" Alice and Stewart asked simultaneously, pushing open the screen door.

"The baby died," my mother answered, moving through the sea of children, gently pushing them aside with the suitcase and creeping toward her bedroom.

"Where's Dad?" Alice asked, turning from the screen door, directing the question to my mother's back. She didn't answer. The screen door slammed shut.

Later that evening, after my father had come home and gone back to the bar, I heard squeaks, like a caught mouse, coming from my mother's bedroom. I sneaked to the door and peered into the darkness expecting to see the cat with a mouthful of fur. Instead, I saw my mother sitting on the edge of the bed, crying bitterly, a pillow over her face to muffle the sobs.

Alice told me later, under the quilts in the dark, her warm breath in my ear, what she had overheard my mother telling Mamie: that my father had buried the new baby girl while Mother was still in the hospital. He was drunk and could not remember where he had buried her. She heard that this baby was a blue baby. *I had visions of a sky blue baby to hold, to play with, to show off to Mamie. We would surely have had the only sky blue baby had she lived.* Alice also heard that my father was watching the heart monitor at the hospital when this baby died; that this baby had hair the same color as mine, that her name was Mary Louise.

I watched an army of ants march across the step below me, lifted my feet and scooted up a step so they wouldn't be blocked. My mother came out and sat down beside me. She smoothed her skirt and ran her fingers through her hair.

"The writing lesson over?" she asked. I nodded. She watched the ants march across the steps. She picked up a leaf and placed it in the path of the ants. They marched across it without pausing.

"It's foolishness you know, you writing with your right hand when God gave *only you* in this family the ability to write with your left."

I nodded my head "yes" unable to speak. My mother did not look at me; she watched the ants and dropped another leaf in their path. This time they moved around the leaf rather than over it.

"Why don't we make this writing with the right hand a game?" she said, almost whispering. "When you're around your father—you write with your right hand—when he's not home and when you're at school—you write with your left hand. It'll be our secret, O.K.?"

I shook my head "yes" again and put my face down on my knees, a flood of relief in my chest, barely able to hold back the tears. My mother patted my back and stood up. She looked about the yard as if searching for something, ran her hands into the side pockets of her dress and began to whistle a tune. She walked slowly back inside the house, the soft serenade lingering in my ears.

After that day the right-handed writing no longer made me seasick. It was a game and I was good at games. I got better and better at it, no longer making letters backwards. My father would smile at me, so pleased with his teaching. I was so delighted to be smiled upon by my father that I worked even harder, perfecting each letter, each number. With each writing lesson, I hoped for my father to smile at me, to shake me gently as he untied the cord on my left hand as if he were tickling me, to swat at my bottom just as I moved out of his reach.

After six months my father threw away the cord that tied my left hand behind my back. My first grade year was half over. As far as he knew, I was like everyone else. We continued practicing on the chalkboard at least twice a week, moving from block letters to cursive. I began to notice that my right-handed writing was completely different than my left-handed writing, angular and sharp rather than curved and flowing, perfect lettering but not having the grace and rhythm that the left-handed writing possessed. It was as if someone else had written it.

My father's disappearance made my mother very unhappy. She did not sing the way she usually did, her sweet soprano filling the house as she washed the dishes. She did not want to read to us from our favorite book or play "hide and seek," indoors, just before bed. She filled her days, silently, with the tasks of housekeeping: stacks of dishes, mounds of clothes, sorted into jeans, colors, whites and diapers. Washed with a scrub board in the double kitchen sinks, hard Lava soap rubbed across the cloth leaving marks like a plowed field. When she wasn't working, she sat on the porch waiting for the mailman or stared out the window as if looking for my father to drive up with boxes of groceries.

Within days of my father's departure, there was nothing left to eat. Nothing. Mother harvested edible wild greens from the ditches using a stick to whack the brush and frighten away the snakes before walking into the tall weeds.

Stewart suggested we catch the snakes and sell them to the snake handlers at the holy roller church down Mudd Street. We had not actually been to this church but we had heard about it from kids at school. Snake handlers: wrapping rattle-snakes around their arms and necks praying not to be bitten. *If the snake bites you and you die then your belief in God wasn't strong enough to keep you alive.* But Mother said they liked to find their own snakes.

"Besides," she said, "I think there's something wrong with those people, using snakes to worship God. I've read enough of the Bible to know it doesn't say anything about torturing a poor snake or yourself to get to heaven. If that's what it takes to get to heaven, I'll just stay right here."

We tried to help Mother find the greens by walking along the edge of the ditch, picking what we thought looked like what she was gathering.

"No, not this, you can't eat this," she'd say taking the weeds from our hands. "Dandelion greens look like this, the curly ones, close to the ground with the tiny yellow flowers."

Our neighbor, Mamie, brought catfish on a line of rope to my mother. We had known Mamie since we moved there. My father had often gone fishing with her husband Buck.

Mamie and Buck had more children than my mother, ranging from almost grown to babies. The older ones helped care for the younger ones so Mamie could work and fish. In the afternoons, Mamie ironed clothes for white people for five cents a piece. In the mornings, she fished. She claimed she had to "feed all them young 'ens" but she really just liked to sit on the red clay bank with a can of worms and not hear a single child's voice. She fished in the pond that stood between our house and hers. Nobody knew who owned the land the pond was on. It had gone unnoticed for years, fished only by those few who had stumbled upon it. It was swarming with the biggest catfish you ever saw, catfish that churned the water when I threw in cracker crumbs.

I loved to go fishing at the pond with Mamie and this she allowed, as long as I did not speak, not one word. She'd come to the back door just as the sun lit the sky and tap lightly on the screen. If I was ready to go, fine, if not, she went on without me. She would ask me how I was doing in school or something like that but I knew that once we broke into the path toward the pond, I'd best not speak, not even a sneeze. Mamie could get on to you something fierce.

Mamie would sit right down with her big rump on the hard ground, her cotton print dress spread across her knees making a puddle in her lap for extra bobbers, a foil package of chewing tobacco and a fan with an advertisement from the local funeral parlor on the front. She wore a hat with two dozen handmade fishing lures knit into the tight straw, fished with a long cane pole and round red and white bobber, sometimes red worms. She could catch more fish than anyone I knew, even my father or Buck. Anyone.

"Don't let your shadow get in the water. Fish ain't stupid you know."

Mother didn't tell Mamie that my father was gone, that we had nothing to eat, no money to buy anything. Mamie brought catfish because she liked my mother and knew she appreciated the fish. She showed my mother how to skin a catfish with a razor-blade, how to keep from being horned when cleaning them.

"A catfish has a needle-sharp spine on its back. If he sticks you with it, the wound almost always gets infected," Mamie said to Mother as she held a squirming catfish with a pair of pliers. "Then you'll have to burn the infection out by packing gunpowder into the wound and striking a match to it." Mamie showed us scars on her hands from being horned by a catfish, black round flat scars.

Mamie had no way of knowing that the few flopping catfish, lips strung through a rope, were all we had to eat some days. Three or four catfish, fried in a cast iron skillet and divided between eight people, was not enough food for an entire day. If Mamie didn't stop by, there was nothing to eat at all.

As if a bell had rung, we filed back into the kitchen and claimed the same places we had occupied before, Alice pushing for more than her half of our shared kitchen chair. My mother had begun cooking the corn and beans. The aroma made me dizzy and as empty as my stomach was, I thought I would vomit. I put my face against the kitchen table and watched my mother's back, the curve of her thin shoulders, the red curls of wet hair licking the back of her neck. I wanted my hair to be curly and red like hers instead of dark and straight like my father's. I wanted to be able to stand at the stove and wave my wooden spoon and make hot delicious food from hard little rocks. I fell asleep.

I awoke to the sound of rustling paper. Mother was tearing a piece of paper from a brown grocery bag. John, his diaper wet and down to his knees, was pulling on my mother's dress, fussing and kicking. I put my head in my hands and yawned. Stewart came back into the kitchen with one of his short yellow school pencils and gave it to Mother. She wrote on the brown paper: letters and numbers. First grade letters and numbers that even I could read.

"This is your Aunt Janet's address and phone number in Birmingham," she said to Alice, placing the paper in her held-out hand. "I'm going to eat the corn and beans now. If I get sick, you call your Aunt Janet from the gas station and tell her to come and get you. Throw the rest of the corn and beans into the out-house before you leave the house so none of the kids eat any of them. The directions for calling collect are written right here," she pointed at the bottom of the brown paper. "Can you do this?" she asked.

"Yes ma'am," Alice answered, wadding the paper into her fist.

"If I'm not sick in two hours, we'll all eat the corn and beans. O.K.?" She looked at the faces around the table. We nodded in agreement.

"Tomorrow, I'm sure we'll receive some money in the mail from your father," she said as she picked John up and left the room. We stared at each other. Stewart shrugged his shoulders.

Alice grimaced. Mother returned with the baby in a dry diaper and the wind-up clock from her bedroom. She stood John in a kitchen chair and wound the clock, placing it in the middle of the table, the bright yellow face so everyone could see.

"When this hand reaches the three, if I'm not sick, you can eat." She walked to the stove and scooped corn from one pan, beans from the other. She put the plate on the table and sat John in her lap. She ate. Slowly. Taste and wait. Taste and wait. One bean at a time, one kernel of corn at a time. Finally she spooned the corn into her mouth and chewed, cheeks puffed and eyes closed. Just watching her made my mouth fill with saliva, my lips kiss together.

We watched my mother for signs of death. No one spoke. I could hear David breathing, in and out, in and out, as if he were keeping time by breaths, his arms spread across the table like the hands of the clock. Mother played with John's toes and seemed to have forgotten we were there, her blue eyes unfocused and weary, she seemed to drift farther and farther away. *Are her lips turning purple? Is she still breathing?* No one moved from their chairs; the tick of the clock enclosed the room. *Maybe we should touch her.* Still, no one moved. I could hear Alice's stomach rumbling loudly and I knew she could hear mine, a fierce hunger in our bones. Without taking her eyes off of Mother, she gently walked her fingers over my leg and put her hand on top of mine, the heat enough to burst wood into flames. Suddenly Stewart slapped the table with his palms and shouted, "Ten more minutes!" Mother jumped in her chair, startled, ransomed back to the present, her eyes finally focusing on what was truly visible.

John fell asleep before the ten minutes were up. Mother carried him to the living room, laid him on the couch, and covered him with an afghan from the rocking chair. We never took our eyes from her, we were wide awake now, voraciously hungry and smiling.

In the time it took Mother to put John down, Stewart had passed out spoons. Alice had a stack of chipped mismatched saucers in her arms. Willie, Doris Ann and I were squirming a dance in our chairs, spoons in hand, while David pretended to conduct our dance like a choir director. There was a sense of excitement, of celebration in the air. Mother wasn't dead and we had something to eat!

Mother scooped equal portions of corn and beans onto each saucer. Falling into the spell of David's choir directing she hummed a song we'd learned in church. She made a saucer for John, covered it with another saucer turned upside down and put it at the back of the stove. She put our saucers on the table, asking us not to begin eating until everyone was served and the food blessed. She put down the last saucer and sat between Willie and Doris Ann. After the blessing, she opened a book and began reading aloud.

"'Alice's Adventures in Wonderland'," she read, "for Alice, because she has been so brave. *Alice was beginning to get very tired of sitting by her sister. . . .*"

We ate. We laughed. We kicked one another under the table, told on each other, lined the bright yellow kernels of corn in rows, spelled our names with them. We counted each corn kernel as we put them on our tongues, and because we liked corn better, we devoured them all first before we started on the beans. Then we ate the sweet white navy beans, spearing a bean onto each tine of the fork like shoes, licking the bean juice from our saucers, chins dripping. *Down, down, down. Would the fall never come to an end? "I wonder how many miles I've fallen by this time?" Alice in Wonderland said aloud. "I must be getting somewhere near the center of the earth."*

After dinner we went outside to make wishes and watch the stars peep out of the deep Alabama sky, one at a time like tiny sparks from the fire. I found my star next to David's star. A tiny red twinkling dot. I wished for a sailboat. We had been given color pages in first grade and I had kept the one of the sailboat. I colored it red with a yellow sail, drew a black bird on the biggest sail. I told

Mother it was my best drawing all year. She taped it on the refrigerator door; it flapped like a kite every time the door was opened and closed. I saw the sailboat picture just as I woke up before dinner and thought a sailboat would be nice to go fishing with Mamie.

The next morning we got out of bed, pulled on our clothes and went to sit with Mother on the front porch to wait for the mailman. We played a game called "I spy," where someone picks something that they can see, tells what color it is, then everyone has to guess what the person picked. *"I spy something red."*

"That stop sign?"

"No."

"That red flower?"

"No."

"Is it Toot-toot's shirt?"

"Stewart's shirt is yellow, Doris Ann. It has to be red."

"Oh."

"A red bird."

"What red bird? You have to be able to see it."

"There was a red bird by the tree."

"The red sign on the gas station?"

"No."

"Mom's hair."

"Yes!"

The sun drifted from our faces to our knees. The baby whined and we were tired of the game. Stewart asked Mother to read to us but she shook her head.

"Not right now, a little later," Mother said tapping the toes of her shoes on the step. She brushed two ants from John's leg and picked him up. The toe tapping becoming a bounce, a pony ride. We went back to our game.

Mother spotted the mailman before any of us and stood up, handing the baby to Alice. She watched him, a hand over her eyes, walk slowly up the hill, sorting his letters. She smiled when he handed her the letter from my father. Waiting for the mailman to walk back down the hill, she looked carefully at the letter in her hand, at the return address, at the postage, the hand-writing.

She opened the letter, not tearing the flap, and slid the letter from the envelope. Folded neatly between a sheet of white paper were two one dollar bills. Mother dropped her hands to her sides, sucking in a quick sharp breath, the two dollars in one hand, the envelope in the other, the white paper fluttering down like a badly folded paper plane to rest on the bottom step.

Mother stood in silence a moment then abruptly walked down the steps. We followed. Alice gave John to me and ran after Mother, Stewart and David right behind her. I was pulling John by the arm trying to keep up. Willie and Doris Ann fell behind and Doris Ann began to whimper. Mother stopped in front of a thick bed of day lilies on the north side of the house, fire-red, tall and straight, in full bloom. She stood for a long time, not moving. We all stood perfectly still, not attempting to move any closer to her. She stared at the lilies.

"They're so beautiful," she said, touching a frilly petal with the corner of the envelope. "I just wish we could eat them." She burst into tears, crushing the envelope and the two one dollar bills into her face.

An hour later Mother took the crumpled brown paper with Aunt Janet's phone number on it and the two one dollar bills to the gas station at the bottom of the hill and called her sister in Birmingham to come and get her starving children.

Carl H. Klaus

from

MY VEGETABLE LOVE: JOURNAL OF A GROWING SEASON

MONDAY/MAY 15, 1995

A perfect day for gardening, with temperatures in the seventies and mild southern breezes. But I had other things on my mind. Like paying the overdue real estate taxes, taking Phoebe to the vet for an inspection of her cancerous growth, and going to the Cancer Clinic with Kate while she had a pea-sized growth removed from her chest. The taxes turned out to be the easiest part of the day.

The vet was openly surprised that Phoebe's still alive. "I never thought she'd last this long, so I wouldn't want to predict what might happen. She could go on for a while, or everything could change tomorrow, if the growth begins to interfere with things, like her ability to urinate. It's much bigger now. But she hasn't lost much weight, and she still looks good for a cat her age. Most cats don't live beyond thirteen or fourteen, and she's almost twenty." An interesting statistic, but not much solace in the long run, especially when I thought she might live to be twenty-five. So each day now seems more precious than the one before. This afternoon, she spent a few minutes lounging on the warmth of the terrace, as she used to do for days on end in the long hot summers of her youth. Tomorrow she might really take to the stones, since it's predicted to reach into the eighties for the first time this spring. But then again, who knows what she might do tomorrow?

Kate's cancer surgeon reported to her that the growth he removed was "not obviously cancerous" to him or the people in the biopsy lab, but the results won't be clear until Wednesday when they've made a permanent slide of the tissue and examine it under a microscope. If it does turn out to be cancerous, there are various options, from doing nothing to attacking it with everything. But they won't even discuss the options until a week from now if that turns out to be the case. So many uncertainties and so many delays that, all the way home in the car, I kept wishing he'd said it was "obviously not cancerous." Or words to that effect. Oh what a difference a few words can make, or just the arrangement of a couple of words.

So, except for the real estate taxes, uncertainty seems to be the rule of the day. Late this afternoon, though, when I was planting a row of shallots at the east end of the vegetable garden, I found a volunteer seedling that definitely appeared to be a sunflower, growing in exactly the same spot where a volunteer sunflower emerged last summer. I showed it to Kate, and she agreed that it was definitely a sunflower. So, there's one sure thing—at least for the moment.

TUESDAY/MAY 16, 1995

Last night at midnight when I went for a walk with Pip, the full moon was visible in the southern sky, backlighting the edges of all the nearby cumulus clouds. A sight so striking I stood in the yard and gazed at it through the walnut trees, just beginning to unfurl their leaves. But the moonlit clouds were hardly so surprising as the small flicker of light I noticed at the edge of a neighbor's lawn just a few minutes later. Could that possibly be a firefly so early in the season? I walked back a few steps to check, and as if to satisfy my curiosity, it flickered again. The first firefly of the year. Another sure thing to go with the sunflower I discovered yesterday in the garden. But I also wonder if it's a harbinger of bugs to come, given the unusually warm weather this winter.

This morning when I awoke, the sun was lighting the edges of the clouds with an aura of coral pink, as if to announce another good day for gardening. Warmer than yesterday, with temperatures in the low eighties for the first time this year. But I had to turn in final grades this morning. Besides, the soil in the back vegetable bed was still too wet and chilly for planting the tomatoes, and the tomatoes themselves still need a few more days of hardening off before they'll be ready for the garden. So, I've moved them from the terrace, now mostly shaded by the maple, to the edge of the gazebo, where they're sitting in trays with the peppers and eggplants, getting more accustomed to the sun and the breezes that constantly play across our backyard. And Kate's moved her seedlings to the top of the stone retaining wall at the edge of the terrace.

Every spring we go through this process of acclimating our seedlings to the strenuous summer climate on our west sloping lot—moving them from the house to the back porch to the terrace to the gazebo and the retaining wall and finally into the garden. A process that sometimes tries my patience to the limit, but I've learned from a few premature planting escapades that there's no point in trying to force the summer vegetables. Jim got away with it last year, but this year he lost his pepper plants to a light frost a few days after he put them in. So, a couple of days ago, when I went up to harvest the last of the early radish crop to make room for his tomatoes, he was sounding more cautious than ever before. "I'm gonna wait a few more days before putting them in. Maybe even a week. I'm not even gonna buy any yet, so I'm not tempted by having 'em around."

I wasn't tempted today, for the sudden warm-up had me hustling around to remove the row covers from the broccoli, the cauliflower, and the shell peas, lest they cook under the extra heat. And once the peas were uncovered, I had to put in all the brush for them to climb on, before the rain that moved in again late this afternoon. But the garden at last is beginning to look like a real garden of green vegetables, rather than a ghostly series of white row covers.

WEDNESDAY/MAY 17, 1995

The minute I got up this morning, I was already on edge, wondering when Kate's doctor would call with the results of the biopsy. But I put it in the back of my mind, figuring he would call soon enough. And I threw myself into the morning chores, hustling Pip and Phoebe out for some fresh air, moving Kate's plants from the porch to the terrace walls, pulling mine from inside the gazebo to the sunny edge of its brick floor, feeding the animals, checking the rain gauge, keeping busy. The skies were still overcast from last night's rain, but the rain had been light, producing only a tenth of an inch. So I figured the sun might come out this afternoon and the soil be dry enough by then to do some planting.

The rest of the morning I devoted to weeding and resetting the forty-five foot border of bricks along the north edge of the main vegetable garden. Not a good choice for keeping myself distracted, since Kate laid the entire brick border around the garden some twenty-five years ago. But I didn't immediately remember her creating that brick frame, for I was thinking of the spring day just a few years ago when several of my writing students came out to fix up the border from the years of rain and soil erosion that had gradually undermined it, especially along the north edge. How quickly it eroded again! Still, it was a pleasant task, and I finished it quickly, though not so swiftly as Rebecca cleaned out the big shade border where the Virginia blue bells and the pink cup daffodils and the pheasant eye narcissus and the wild single buttercups are now in bloom and the gigantic spreading leaves of the *Hosta Sieboldiana Elegans* are fully opened along with the arching leaves of the comfrey. For a moment there I was pleasantly distracted by it all.

But shortly after lunch, just as I was heading outside, the doctor called and reported that the growth did have some cancer cells in it. So next Tuesday, Kate will have the full battery of bone scans and blood scans to determine whether it has traveled anywhere else in her body. And then based on the results of the tests, the doctor will outline her various options. Kate, it seems, was expecting the bad news, for she has ever been more realistic than I am. I, as usual, was planning a celebration of the good news that never came. And even when I heard the news, I looked for the best possible outcome—that the cancer might be confined just to the growth, while Kate was facing the uncertainty itself—"I'm in limbo, man."

After the news, I tried to distract myself by spading up the annual side of the herb bed and raking it out. But working the soil hardly compared with a walk in the wilderness park, where Kate, Pip, and I suddenly came upon a hillside of wild geranium in bloom—their lavender blossoms dappling the wooded landscape like sunlight as far as the eye could see, while the sunlight itself was illuminating the flowers through the flickering leaves of the trees overhead. An impressionist scene so striking it sent me back home distracted enough to plant some curly and flat leaf parsley, two rows of nasturtium seeds, and a couple of tomato plants, a Big Beef and the fabled Brandywine. Those are the only certainties for now.

THURSDAY/MAY 18, 1995

"You're not going to fall apart on me now, are you?" Kate had a slight smile on her face when she asked me that question. I wondered what could possibly make her think I might do such a thing when I was just standing at the kitchen counter concocting Phoebe's breakfast. "Something about the look on your face, or maybe the way you were holding your shoulders, like you were about to crumble, or something." Actually, I think it was just the cold air this morning that was making me hunch up my shoulders to keep myself warm. The temperature outside was then in the mid-forties after an overnight rain that dropped another three-tenths of an inch, and I'd just come in from a chilly walk around the yard to check on the parsley and tomatoes I planted yesterday afternoon. But that little tour of the yard did set me thinking about some of the things we said to each other yesterday, the gallows humor that passed between us then, and perhaps the memory of those words had played across my face. I was thinking especially of how Kate had responded to my remark that the news would bring new life to this daybook—"You mean new death to it?" At the moment, I'd thought she was speaking mostly in jest, turning my words back on me with a twist of black humor. But later yesterday evening, I didn't think she was joking when she read my piece for the day and said that "It's beautifully written, but it sounds like an obituary, and I'm not dead yet, not by a long shot. But let's not keep focusing on it like this. There'll be enough to focus on next week after all the tests are in."

So this afternoon, after the rain passed over, and the sky cleared up, and the sun came out, and the wind died down, I focused again on the garden. A squirrel must have been digging in the potted artichoke plant, so I reset the Havahart trap under the maple tree, where a pair of the critters have been frisking with each other the past several days. Then I moved all the seedlings to their sunbathing spots and gave them a drink of water. Then seeded up a six-pack of yellow scaloppini and green zucchini. Also six-packs of three different pickling cucumbers—Cross Country, Homemade, and Liberty—so we'll be sure to have a decent crop this summer, rather than the puny pickings of the past few seasons. Enough, I hope, for Kate's bread-and-butter pickles, my Kosher dills, and fresh cucumber salads. Late in the afternoon, the soil was dry enough in the back bed for me to move another pair of tomato plants into the garden—another Big Beef and Kate's dark Russian heirloom, the Black Prince. Then after picking some spinach for a salad to go with Kate's rabbit cacciatore, I thought the day was over. But the clatter of the squirrel trap meant an after-dinner ride into the countryside. Now I hope I can catch its mate, so I can reunite them in that lovely stretch of woods with the creek running through it.

TUESDAY/MAY 23, 1995

At eight this morning, at the university hospital's oncology clinic, while I was waiting for Kate to get her blood drawn, the farmer sitting next to me was worrying about how the rain had delayed his field work. "Well, I finally got some of my beans in yesterday, but now I probably won't be able to get the rest in until next week sometime." Heavy rains last night—an inch at our place, two inches at others. And I don't have any of my beans in yet. And it's supposed to continue today and tomorrow, as I heard around eight-thirty, when I was sitting in the nuclear medicine clinic, watching the local TV news, while Kate got injected with radiated material for her bone scan. Fifteen minutes later, when I was sitting in the diagnostic radiology clinic, while Kate was getting a chest x-ray, I saw the weather report again on a different channel. "Heavy Rain." It's the big story here today, as I heard yet again on the same channel in the same clinic, just before we returned to oncology, where Kate had her blood pressure checked, and I heard another family talking about the rain. And the rain itself was falling on the rooftop pavilion, just outside the lounge and refreshment area where we went next, so Kate could get enough fluid in her to disperse the radiated material throughout her system before the bone scan could take place. After she gamely finished off two twelve-ounce cans of lime-lemon sparkling water—"Here's to radioactivity"—we then went down to the first floor cafeteria where she had two cups of tea and I noticed that the rain had stopped, at least for the moment.

And for a while some of the uncertainty also abated when we went to the nuclear radiation clinic for the bone scan itself. A high-tech procedure, complete with an animated technician, a finely calibrated body scanner, and a graphic computer display that revealed no evidence of cancer anywhere in the full-length skeletal images that flashed on the screen at the end of the scanning. The best news of the day, of the week, even though I was momentarily disarmed by the computer's display of Kate, so close to the bone, while she was also sitting on the scanner table, so fully in the skin of her own immediate existence. The technician herself was also so full of life, and her life intersected ours in so many ways—she grew up in our neighborhood, her daughter went to nursery school two doors north of us, her cousin Mike grew up in Kate's home town and was a schoolmate of Kate's brother John—that the disclosures of radiation suddenly gave way to a surprising array of happy coincidences.

But reality took hold again, when Kate finally saw her harried cancer surgeon, who removed her stitches from last week, but put off a discussion of her options until next week, because he hadn't yet seen a report of her blood scan, her chest x-ray, or even her bone scan. Uncertainty had returned, and so had the rain.

TUESDAY/MAY 30, 1995

A perfect late spring day. Low eighties—the first time this year—light breeze, sunny, and a few scattered cumulus in an otherwise clear blue sky. Parsley taking hold. Basil germinating. Nasturtium breaking ground. Snow peas blossoming. And the first head of broccoli ready for harvest. Soil still a bit cold and moist for beans, but a few more days like this and it'll be just right for planting. The only problem with this idyllic state of affairs is that nothing's ready for temperatures in the eighties—neither plants nor people. The young lettuces were already going limp by eleven this morning, when Kate and I started walking over to the hospital for appointments with her surgical oncologist and medical oncologist.

And by the time we finished our two mile walk to the hospital, we too were limp. But our leaves turned crisp and our tempers chilled after a few hours of cooling our heels in the air-conditioned hospital, waiting until twelve-thirty for a noon appointment with the surgeon, and then until two-thirty for a one o'clock appointment with the medical oncologist.

The appointments themselves were as perplexing as the weather we've been having. The surgeon upbeat about the results of the tests. No other cancer detectable anywhere in the system. The medical oncologist unconvinced by the tests. "A local recurrence in your situation indicates that it's systemic, and what to do with a woman in your situation, no one knows. There just hasn't been enough research." Suddenly I found myself thinking about the mysteries of El Niño and its paradoxical behavior. So I asked him how the tests could be negative but the cancer systemic, and he suggested that I think about a dandelion gone to seed. "Just imagine trying to find those seeds in the grass. You couldn't see them, but you'd know they were there." Never had the dandelion been so menacing a figure of speech. A sign that the medical oncologist probably likes to keep a weed-free lawn. Yet he agreed with the surgeon in opposing a bone marrow transplant, favoring instead the moderate approach of "patching along for several years." Estrogen-blocking therapy combined with a little surgery and light radiation to clean up the site of the recent tumor. The only problem is that the surgeon and the medical oncologist can't be sure the radiologists will agree to give Kate just a light dose of radiation. And Kate doesn't relish the thought of being burnt out by radiation like Madame Curie and my mother.

So we're patching along, hoping as the oncologist put it that Kate's "one of the lucky ones who has a good run." Nothing, after all, is certain. But after all that uncertainty, the definite sin of a charcoal broiled steak sure did help, as did a head of buttercrunch lettuce from the garden, sliced down the center, its leaves of growth gradually but distinctly fading from dark green to light green to yellow to the white at its core.

A rainless day—a lucky break for the neighborhood's annual spring potluck, but Kate had other things on her mind when she got up. "They're gonna cut me up again. In the same place. And I wonder if my skin'll grow back right." I assured her it would, and if her surgeon didn't think so, he'd make the incision elsewhere. As usual I was more hopeful than she. Ever hopeful—there's one in every family.

But it was "time to get cracking," as Kate put it, to get ready for the potluck at the neighborhood park. Sweep out the shelter, set up the tables, bring down the table cloths and the ice and the sliced bread and the sliced ham and the paper plates and plate holders and cups and plastic utensils. And have a good time. And we did, watching folks trickle in from noon on, from every part of the neighborhood, singles and partners and marrieds and children, some eighty people in all. Bringing cole slaw, macaroni salad, Indian rice salad, cold spaghetti salad, potato salad, lettuce salad, snow pea salad, sliced ham, lasagna, barbecued spare ribs, chicken casserole, baked chicken, spaghetti in meat sauce, brownies, chocolate cake, rhubarb crisp, carrot cake, melon mix—so many dishes I can't remember them all. And a lemonade stand, run by Nichelle and her neighbor's young daughter, to raise money for redbud trees, the Oklahoma state tree, to be planted at the park in memory of those who died in the Oklahoma City bombing. And an impromptu women's baseball game, kids against grownups. And neighbors shuffling from table to table, to share the news and the food and the good feeling of a Sunday afternoon. And wherever I went, people asking me what was eating their bean plants or tomatoes or zucchini or roses, and what to do about them. So many questions about maladies in their gardens that by mid-afternoon, when the picnic was over, I'd begun to feel somewhat like a family gardening doctor. I just wish I could solve some of my own gardening problems as well as I took care of theirs. Why some of my peppers are beginning to yellow, and what to do about the groundhog—terror to all vegetable gardeners!—that turned up in the backyard this afternoon after the potluck.

But no matter how menacing the groundhog, it couldn't offset the good feelings of the picnic and the splendid news that came later in a phone call from my brother Marshall, the doctor, telling me that he and his friend Jack, a medical oncologist, both believe that Kate's cancer is almost surely a local recurrence and not a systemic condition. "If it occurred exactly at the site of her previous cancer, why assume that it traveled through the entire system to get there? If you hear the sound of hoof beats, would you assume that you're hearing horses or zebras?" Horses, of course, which I much prefer to dandelion seeds.

THURSDAY/JUNE 8, 1995

And the weather's just as bizarre as everything else. Last night after dinner, during the last hour of daylight, the air was still so hot and heavy and humid and breezeless that I was dripping from the minute I knelt down in the garden to put in the eggplants and the second row of peppers. And the work wasn't really hard. Just digging up a large trowelful of soil, tossing in some slow release fertilizer, working it into the soil, popping in the plant, pulling the soil around it, watering it in with a transplant solution, and covering the surface with a light layer of dry earth. A few hours later, though, a cool, dry breeze started wafting in from the west, as promised, and by morning the house was so chilly that I hustled around pulling down all the windows we'd left open overnight. But the predicted overnight thunderstorm never arrived, and today has passed with only a few intermittent sprinkles. Not even enough to register a tenth of an inch in the rain gauge. And the temperature just barely made it up to sixty this afternoon, a thirty degree drop from yesterday afternoon. It felt as if we'd gone from July to April in just twenty-four hours. So I went from wearing shorts and a T-shirt yesterday to long pants, a long-sleeved shirt, and my farm jacket today. At this rate, I wonder if the weather's ever going to settle down this year.

I also wonder if Kate's condition is ever going to settle down. Last night, just before going to sleep, Kate told me that her cancer surgeon would be calling this morning to give her a lab report on the tissue he removed on Tuesday. I hadn't realized that yet another biopsy would be involved, so I suddenly went on red alert, wondering what it would mean if some more cancer cells turned up this time. Would it mean that the medical oncologist was right about its being systemic, that "the Doctor from Hell," as my brother had called him, was not so misguided as everyone had thought? And that question was still on my mind when I awoke briefly around four this morning. Just after breakfast, though, a call came through from Judy, the surgeon's nurse and research assistant, reporting that no tumors were found in the sample. But I'm still sleeping with one eye open.

The other good news is that we're supping more and more on fresh herbs and vegetables from the garden. Last night along with some chilled, poached turkey and homemade lemon mayonnaise, we had a fresh head of steamed broccoli, and a macaroni salad with minced burnet, dill, sorrel, green onion, chive blossoms, and a tarragon-tomato vinaigrette. And tonight, it was fresh thyme and parsley in the sautéed veal chop, fresh chives with the boiled new potatoes, and a fresh head of buttercrunch lettuce. No reversals in the garden, at least for the moment. And still no return of the groundhog. But I'm still sleeping with one eye open.

SATURDAY/JUNE 10, 1995

"It must be really difficult to be faced with two such different interpretations." My son, Marshall, called this morning, and I'd just finished telling him about the disagreement between Kate's cancer surgeon and the Doctor from Hell. Initially, it *was* difficult to understand how one doctor could treat her recent cancer as just a local recurrence while the other believed it to be systemic. Far worse was the hopeless future that seemed in store for Kate, according to the Doctor from Hell, who repeatedly asserted that her cancer was systemic and therefore certain to recur. "Maybe, it won't come back for four or five years. Or it could suddenly show up everywhere in the system six months from now." But once my brother explained how unlikely it would be for a cell to travel throughout Kate's entire system and return exactly to the site of her last breast cancer, I've not had any trouble weighing the merits of the doctors' radically different interpretations. Now, instead, I'm troubled by how quickly I was willing to accept the extreme diagnosis of the Doctor from Hell. Oh yes, I was initially puzzled, so I asked him how all the tests could be negative, yet the cancer be systemic. But once he began talking about the crudity of the tests and then offered me the dandelion metaphor, my skepticism was readily dispelled.

As I look back on that afternoon, I wonder why I was so quick to accept the opinion of someone I'd never met before, even though it contradicted the view of the distinguished cancer surgeon who's been taking excellent care of Kate for the past six and a half years. Partly, I think it was the unusual frankness with which the Doctor from Hell announced his dire view of things. Partly his highly articulate manner, so different from the uncomfortable behavior of the surgeon, who usually says little and explains much less. But ultimately, I think the dandelion metaphor took me in, for it spoke to me in terms I know from first-hand observation. Kate, as usual, took a more hard-nosed view of things. "Didn't you notice how I was trying to lead him on, to see how far he'd go? I've always known that it can recur, but the way he was talking just didn't make sense to me, not in terms of the evidence from the tests. And besides, he didn't have any research studies to back up what he was saying. Even he admitted that."

So, I can't help wondering why I too didn't notice the weakness of his case. I've been chiding students for years whenever they don't provide evidence for their assertions. And why didn't I tell him that his dandelion analogy was badly chosen, for the body is not like a lawn any more than a cancer cell is like a dandelion seed? Maybe, it's because the dandelion analogy did embody a germ of common sense—that some things are so small they cannot be detected even by the most sophisticated technology. But a germ of sense doesn't necessarily lead to an epidemic of truth.

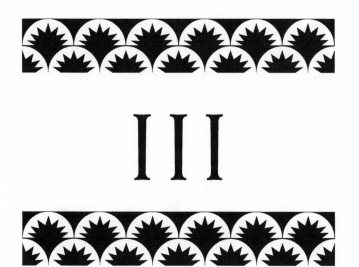

III

Henry David Thoreau

from

THE BEAN-FIELD

Meanwhile my beans, the length of whose rows, added together, was seven miles already planted, were impatient to be hoed, for the earliest had grown considerably before the latest were in the ground; indeed they were not easily to be put off. What was the meaning of this so steady and self-respecting, this small Herculean labor, I knew not. I came to love my rows, my beans, though so many more than I wanted. They attached me to the earth, and so I got strength like Antaeus. But why should I raise them? Only Heaven knows. This was my curious labor all summer—to make this portion of the earth's surface, which had yielded only cinquefoil, blackberries, johnswort, and the like, before, sweet wild fruits and pleasant flowers, produce instead this pulse. What shall I learn of beans or beans of me? I cherish them, I hoe them, early and late I have an eye to them; and this is my day's work. It is a fine broad leaf to look on. My auxiliaries are the dews and rains which water this dry soil, and what fertility is in the soil itself, which for the most part is lean and effete. My enemies are worms, cool days, and most of all woodchucks. The last have nibbled for me a quarter of an acre clean. But what right had I to oust johnswort and the rest, and break up their ancient herb garden? Soon, however, the remaining beans will be too tough for them, and go forward to meet new foes.

When I was four years old, as I well remember, I was brought from Boston to this native town, through these very woods and this field, to the pond. It is one of the oldest scenes stamped on my memory. And now to-night my flute has waked the echoes over that very water. The pines still stand here older than I; or if some have fallen, I have cooked my supper with their stumps, and a new growth is rising all around, preparing another aspect for new infant eyes. Almost the same johnswort springs from the same perennial root in this pasture, and even I have at length helped to clothe that fabulous landscape of my infant dreams, and one of the results of my presence and influence is seen in these bean leaves, corn blades, and potato vines.

I planted about two acres and a half of upland; and as it was only about fifteen years since the land was cleared, and I myself had got out two or three cords of stumps, I did not give it any manure; but in the course of the summer it appeared by the arrowheads which I turned up in hoeing, that an extinct nation had anciently dwelt here and planted corn and beans ere white men came to clear the land, and so, to some extent, had exhausted the soil for this very crop.

Before yet any woodchuck or squirrel had run across the road, or the sun had got above the shrub oaks, while all the dew was on, though the farmers warned me against it—I would you to do all your work if possible while the dew is on—I began to level the ranks of haughty weeds in my bean-field and throw dust upon their heads. Early in the morning I worked barefooted, dabbling like a plastic artist in the dewy and crumbling sand, but later in the day the sun blistered my feet. There the sun lighted me to hoe beans, pacing slowly backward and forward over that yellow gravelly upland, between the long green rows, fifteen rods, the one end terminating in a shrub oak copse where I could rest in the shade, the other in a blackberry field where the green berries deepened their tints by the time I had made another bout. Removing the weeds, putting fresh soil about the bean stems, and encouraging this weed which I had sown, making the yellow soil express its summer thought in bean leaves and blossoms rather than in worm-wood and piper and millet grass—this was my daily work. As I had little aid from horses or cattle, or hired men or boys, or improved implements of husbandry, I was much slower, and became much more intimate with my beans than usual. But labor of the hands, even when pursued to the verge of drudgery, is perhaps never the worst form of idleness. It has a constant and imperishable moral, and to the scholar it yields a classic result. A very *agricola laboriosus* was I to travellers bound westward through Lincoln and Wayland to nobody knows where; they sitting at their ease in gigs, with elbows on knees, and reins loosely hanging in festoons; I the home-staying, laborious native of the soil. But soon my homestead was out of their sight and thought. It was the only open and cultivated field for a great distance on either side of the road, so they made the most of it; and sometimes the man in the field heard more of travellers' gossip and comment than was meant for his ear: "Beans so late! peas so late!"—for I continued to plant when others had begun to hoe—the ministerial husbandman had not suspected it. "Corn, my boy, for fodder; corn for fodder." "Does he *live* there?" asks the black bonnet of the gray coat; and the hard-featured farmer reins up his grateful dobbin to inquire what you are doing where he sees no manure in the furrow, and recommends a little chip dirt, or any little waste stuff, or it may be ashes or plaster. But here were two acres and a half of furrows, and only a hoe for cart and two hands to draw it—there being an aversion to other carts and horses—and chip dirt far away. Fellow-travellers as they rattled by compared it aloud with the fields which they had passed, so that I came to know how I stood in the agricultural world. This was one field not in Mr. Colman's report. And, by the way, who estimates the value of the crop which nature yields in the still wilder fields unimproved by man? The crop of *English* hay is carefully weighed, the moisture calculated, the silicates and the potash; but in all dells and pond-holes in the woods and pastures and swamps grows a rich and various crop only unreaped by man. Mine was, as it were, the connecting link between wild and cultivated fields; as some states are civilized, and others half-civilized, and others savage or barbarous, so my field was, though not in a bad sense, a half-cultivated field. They were beans cheerfully returning to their wild and primitive state that I cultivated, and my hoe played the *Ranz des Vaches* for them.

. . . It was a singular experience that long acquaintance which I cultivated with beans, what with planting, and hoeing, and harvesting, and threshing, and picking over and selling them—the last was the hardest of all—I might add eating, for I did taste. I was determined to know beans. When they were growing, I used to hoe from five o'clock in the morning till noon, and commonly spent the rest of the day about other affairs. Consider the intimate and curious acquaintance one makes with various kinds of weeds—it will bear some iteration in the account, for there was no little iteration in the labor—disturbing their delicate organization so ruthlessly, and making such invidious distinctions with his hoe, levelling whole ranks of one species, and sedulously cultivating another. That's Roman wormwood—that's pigweed—that's sorrel—that's piper-grass—have at him, chop him up, turn his roots upward to the sun, don't let him have a fibre in the shade, if you do he'll turn himself t'other side up and be as green as a leek in two days. A long war, not with cranes, but with weeds, those Trojans who had sun and rain and dews on their side. Daily the beans saw me come to their rescue armed with a hoe, and thin the ranks of their enemies, filling up the trenches with weedy dead. Many a lusty crest waving Hector, that towered a whole foot above his crowding comrades, fell before my weapon and rolled in the dust.

. . . We are wont to forget that the sun looks on our cultivated fields and on the prairies and forests without distinction. They all reflect and absorb his rays alike, and the former make but a small part of the glorious picture which he beholds in his daily course. In his view the earth is all equally cultivated like a garden. Therefore we should receive the benefit of his light and heat with a corresponding trust and magnanimity. What though I value the seed of these beans, and harvest that in the fall of the year? This broad field which I have looked at so long looks not to me as the principal cultivator, but away from me to influences more genial to it, which water and make it green. These beans have results which are not harvested by me. Do they not grow for woodchucks partly? The ear of wheat (in Latin *spica*, obsoletely *speca*, from *spe*, hope) should not be the only hope of the husbandman; its kernel or grain (*granum*, from *gerendo*, bearing) is not all that it bears. How, then, can our harvest fail? Shall I not rejoice also at the abundance of the weeds whose seeds are the granary of the birds? It matters little comparatively whether the fields fill the farmer's barns. The true husbandman will cease from anxiety, as the squirrels manifest no concern whether the woods will bear chestnuts this year or not, and finish his labor with every day, relinquishing all claim to the produce of his fields, and sacrificing in his mind not only his first but his last fruits also.

Gene Logsdon

MY WILDERNESS

In human culture is the preservation of wildness.
                                        —Wendell Berry

1990

I used to say that it was but
a few steps from the world of my garden to the world of wild
woodland, but now I realize how that statement reflects one of the
most invidious errors we humans have been making.

It certainly is true that my garden borders woodland. It is also
true that a pronounced change in my mentality occurs when I slip
from my workaday garden into the wilder haunts of the woods. I
am transformed from Mr. MacGregor worrying about Peter Rabbit into Tarzan rallying the jungle animals against the excesses of
human civilization. Nor would I deny that my garden serves the
side of my rational mind that demands MacGregor-like order in a
chaotic world, while my woodland provides me with the wilderness that the mystic, wild side of my nature yearns for.

The error is in thinking that these contrasts represent different worlds. Vegetable gardens are perhaps more human-con-
trolled than are wild woodlands, but the difference blurs with
close scrutiny. Every effort to impose an order that would sever
the garden completely from wild nature ends in silly futility or ca-
tastrophe. One year a neighbor of mine decided that, by God, he
was going to get rid of every weed in his sweet corn patch once

and for all. He drenched the soil with atrazine above the recommended rate. No weeds for sure, but nothing else would grow there either for three years. At the other extreme, we preserve "wilderness areas" as if we could store nature away like a can of pickles to satisfy momentary cravings. I went to a wilderness area once and got trapped in a colossal traffic jam. The only wildlife I saw was elbow-to-elbow campers emitting mating calls from portable stereos.

If gardening has taught me anything, it's that we can't separate ourselves from wild nature. Even in a hydroponic greenhouse I recently visited, a cat was kept to control mice, and shipments of ladybird beetles were unleashed to eat the aphids. We live in union with a wilderness fundamentally beyond our control or we don't live long at all. We don't have the choice of moving from a human world to a nature world, but only from one footstep to another. As Theodore Roszak put it so well in *Where the Wasteland Ends* (1972):

> We forget that nature is, quite simply, the universal continuum, ourselves inextricably included; it is that which mothered us into existence, which will outsurvive us, and from which we have learned (if we still remember the lesson) our destiny. It is the mirror of our identity. Any cultural goods we produce which sunder themselves from this traditional, lively connection with the nonhuman, any thinking we do which isolates itself from, or pits itself against, the natural environment is— strictly speaking—a delusion, and a very sick one. Not only because it will lack ecological intelligence, but because, more critically still, it will lack psychological completeness. It will be ignorant of the greatest truth mankind learned from its ancient intimacy with nature: the reality of spiritual being.

I had to step back and forth from garden to woodland many times before I realized that the line between them was too fine to draw, that the "reality of spiritual being" dissolved the difference I had imagined. Amid the jungle-like fernery of the asparagus patch, for example, nature plays out dramas of eating and being eaten as wild as those that occur among the bulrushes of the woodland creek: the chipping sparrow flits from her nest in the strawberry patch to prey upon larvae of asparagus beetles with all the grisly intensity of the black rat snake snatching into its gaping mouth a field sparrow bathing at the shoreline of the creek. Wren battles wren for territorial rights to the birdhouse in the apple tree as ferociously as two bucks in the woods battling for supremacy of a deer herd.

The difference between the larvae of ladybird beetles attacking aphids on the lima beans and cheetahs attacking wildebeests on the Serengeti Plain is one of scale only. I learn to measure my progress as a gardener not by the size of my tomato harvest, but by the degree of calmness I can maintain when I abruptly meet a garter snake hunting slugs.

There is only one accurate way to describe the roiling, moiling, toiling scene of the healthy garden: *it's wild!* Hundreds, perhaps thousands, of species of bugs, birds, worms, and animals move in and out of it, all eating and being eaten. Yet most of the time, this banquet table of soil provides enough food for me, too. The real need to "protect" it comes only when nature's normalcy has been thwarted, either by its own seemingly chaotic workings or by that of humans.

An ecology-minded world would not need to protect gardens from rabbits because gardens would understand the continuum of nature and ensure the natural habits and habitats of owls, hawks, foxes, and other animals that feed on rabbits. All else failing, humans would eat their rabbits themselves, with the same gusto that they eat Big Macs. Cabbage patch and wilderness would be one. Tarzan understood gardening better than Mr. MacGregor.

I walk from one part of my property to another as through a continuous wilderness. The vegetable rows, the woods, the pasture, the creek bottom, the little grain- and hayfields are all "garden." They are all part of the Great Garden that once covered the

Earth and might cover it again. As I walk, I pass only from one realm of the Great Garden to another. The more indeterminately the borders coalesce, the more assuredly I achieve the oneness of the natural continuum. The vegetable garden, the most humanly shaped realm, becomes a kind of decontamination chamber, a place where I can slough off the fretting cares of civilization while I pull weeds—lamb's quarters, purslane, pigweed (wild amaranth), and sour grass—some of which I realize, wryly, are nearly as tasty as the salad plants I grow.

Then I step into the woods by way of a glade that also serves as backyard lawn. I leave the yard deliberately unkempt so that the mower freaks who visit me can't tell where lawn ends and wood begins. Who can say whether I should mow here or not—whether I am obeying the strictures of lawn neatness that our rural middlewestern mentality teaches? Raspberries at the woodland edge further blur the border between civilization and wilderness. Are they part of the garden or the woods? I ask the same question of the hickory nuts hovering over them.

In the woods I become a sort of high-tech Tarzan. Loincloths unfortunately are not approved of by rural middlewestern Germanic souls of propriety any more than unmowed lawns, but my belt holds a knife and more (magnifying glass and hand pruners). With binoculars around my neck, I can watch for what food, spiritual or corporeal, this wilder garden has to offer today. I find a luna moth—an endangered species in this region, where even woodland is sometimes mowed—newly emerged from its cocoon, still not ready to fly, glistening pale green and purple. I hold it in one hand and study it through the magnifying glass with the other. I am transfixed by its beauty. Of the unlimited arrangements of color and pattern that moth wings could take, why these particular ones?

I am face-to-face with mystery I cannot fathom, appearing over and over wherever I turn my eye. I begin to understand the meaning of "reality of spiritual being." Here is knowledge that science has not yet imagined, not visible to magnifying glass or the most powerful microscope. The moth flutters away. It soon will mate and lay eggs if a bird does not catch it first, and then it will die shortly, its magnificence "wasted" if not for my chance meeting with it. *Perhaps* wasted. In the realm of spiritual being, *perhaps* is the most necessary word in any language.

Leaving the woods, I enter my pasture, a miniature version of the Serengeti Plain, another mode of the Great Garden. Here, wild and domestic life mingles even more intensely than in the vegetable rows and orchard. I once sowed "improved" grasses and cloves here, believing the universities, which told me these improvements would be better for my cows and sheep than the herbage that nature grew. Nature laughed at such pride and sowed more enduring plants. In almost every case, the wilder ones have proved better for the livestock than the university-improved ones, not to mention for the birds and insects that also live there. Even the "weeds," except some of the more noxious ones introduced from Europe by pioneers who also thought they could improve the native landscape, make good grazing. If I mow occasionally, the pasture takes care of itself.

Meadowlarks sing from fenceposts, bluebirds nest in the houses I have set atop some posts, kingbirds sit on the fence wire between the posts, bobolinks burble and spin up over the fence and into the grass again, barn swallows dart at bugs rising from the grass, field sparrows crouch over nests of eggs at the base of bull thistles. Cowbirds perch on the back of the cow and the sheep, watching for flies. I rake the meadow with my binoculars and gather the whole scene into a spiritual harvest.

I pass into a third realm of the Great Garden: my fields of corn, oats, wheat, and clover hay. Red-winged blackbirds walk the cornrows, stolidly hunting cutworms. I turn over a lump of barn manure that didn't get worked into the soil at planting time and uncover two ground beetles, a species that also feeds on cutworms and wireworms. I lift another manure clump and find two more. The reason for these unworked clumps is that a killdeer had been there at planting time, and I dodged her with tractor and disk. In the wheat plot, a path of trampled stalks leading into the stand tells me that raccoons or groundhogs are probably in the field, digging burrows that the growing grain stalks already hide from view. I scowl, the Mr. MacGregor in me asserting himself.

I pass into a fourth realm of the Great Garden, the grove of trees through which the creek winds. I sit on the bridge I built across the stream, my legs dangling over the side, and gaze into the water tumbling over the rock dam the children built. The sound of water over the stones is spring's best music, next to the meadowlark's song. Along the bank, almost in the water, a wild iris blooms. It appears to have been deliberately planted there, I catch myself thinking, still needing to remind myself that nature was planting flowers long before humans and can do the job just as well.

Suddenly, a fish flies between my dangling legs. It leaps from the water under the bridge in an arc up over the dam into the upper pool. I can't believe my eyes, so I wait. Another one! At least a dozen dance over the dam as I watch. How did these common little shiners and larger suckers (as we call them) learn to leap dams built by children? There are no natural rock dams in our world of mud-bottomed creeks, far from the salmon runs of the wild Mackenzie. And yet, is the "real" wilderness any more spiritually vitalizing than this humdrum remnant left in these Ohio farmlands? If all the land were kept as part of the Great Garden, there would be little need for wilderness parks.

But all land is not kept this way. I walk into a section where, as far as my eye can see, there is nothing but plowed soil. I come here to hunt flint arrowheads and stone hammers left by the Tarzans of another era. I search a while, but the stillness, the eerie emptiness of hundreds of plowed acres stretching into the gathering dusk, overwhelms me. No barns, houses, pastures, woodlands, or fencerows are visible. I have entered a strange planet, one which man has almost succeeded in severing from the full life of nature. Ironically, the men who create these moonscapes for money use the profit to vacation in far-off wilderness areas.

I shiver from some vague fear. A vision of nature decapitated spreads before my mind's eye: a future in which this countryside is slowly but surely turned from its original Great Garden into a desert stretching between lonely roads, a no-man's-land between cities. I see whole townships and counties where a virtually limitless variety of plants, insects, animals, and humans all in their allotted niches once lived—field, pasture, woodland, farmstead, and village—now turned into empty spaces of pulverized, eroding soil producing surplus corn, rootworms, poor-quality food, and an unhealthy society. The Indians left their flints to mark the passing of their culture. I have only a hoe with a shiny handle to mark the end of mine.

I retreat back to country where the Great Garden is still remembered. A wood thrush sings as I approach my tree grove, renewing my hope. The dark vision cannot come to reality, the thrush seems to be telling me, because the continuum of wild nature is even stronger in humans than the continuum of greed. Even the agribusinessmen will understand, once the wilderness areas they escape to are all paved with traffic jams and populated with deanimalized bears eating human garbage. Then everyone will be convinced that the only "escape" is to make all the Earth over into the various realms of the Great Garden.

Judith Larner Lowry

GARDENING
AT THE SEAM

Once I spent some time at a hot springs in Mendocino County, whose accommodations included a "cool pool" for swimming, built by damming the creek on three sides with poured concrete. The fourth side of the pool was formed by the rocky base of the hill, along which flowed the creek. On the hillside, native clarkias cast a pink net through the grasses.

When, after swimming my laps, I came to pull myself up and out of the pool, I found that one hand was on concrete and one hand on native rock. Regarding the seam between the two materials, it occurred to me that this was the place where I have come to garden. At the seam between the wild and the cultivated, where they merge and mingle, the shape of one giving shape to the other.

Moving ten years ago to this small coastal town, I was entranced by the constant glimpse of ocean all over town and by the miles of protected land that surround us. My first walks into that land revealed the beauty of the coastal scrub plant community. Low mounding shrubs and sub-shrubs of all kinds of greens, grays, and gray-greens made a rich foliar tapestry, punctuated in spring and summer with the oranges, reds, blues, and golds of coastal wildflowers and flowering shrubs. I couldn't look enough. Yet, when I visited the gardens of my town, these local plants were conspicuous for their absence, as was any conversation about them. I came to see that I lived in a uniquely protected location that reflected little of the vast surrounding riches. Without quite knowing what I was doing, I began to try to work myself into this place through gardening with these plants.

My town is bordered on the north by Jack Creek, which feeds a rancher's stock pond, then wends its diminished way to the ocean. One bank of this creek has been planted with a windbreak of eucalyptus trees. Under these trees, which continually drop large, acidic leaves, little is able to grow except French broom and brambles, all shallow-rooted plants. The bank on that side is crumbling and eroding rapidly. The eucalyptus trees, forest giants, become increasingly top-heavy as their trunks shoot skyward. On the other side of the creek, the north-facing bank is covered with coastal scrub plants, a low-growing plant community which includes monkeyflower, sagebrush, coyote bush, lizard tail, mule's ear, and cow parsnip. The bank on this side is intact, verdant, complete even down to the smaller plants, such as the tiny, narrow-leaved native plantain (a larval food plant for the endangered bay checkerspot butterfly), and the spring-blooming bulb named "cat's ears" for its fuzzy white petals.

When Jack Creek empties into the ocean, the bank becomes a steep bluff. On the eucalyptus side of the bluff mouth, the tree currently nearest to the end of the bluff clings precariously for years or months, as the case may be, providing dramatic photo opportunities, then falls, taking with it a huge hunk of cliff. The beach is littered with these bleached eucalyptus trunks, resembling an elephants' graveyard. The other side of the bluff erodes at its own West Coast pace.

I saw other situations where homeowners, seeking to save their bluff-edge properties, had planted species reputed to help in erosion control. Iceplant, one such plant, installed in many places throughout California, quickly covers the ground, but it is not deep-rooted and doesn't tie the soil layers together as do the native bluff species. Indeed, its succulent leaves are so heavy, their weight can pull down sections of cliff. The salt stored in its leaves changes the chemical properties of the soil when the plants die. Walking and looking, I came to hypothesize that the group of native bluff and coastal scrub plants that hold these cliffs have just the right characteristics for the job. Their leaves filter rain to the soil in the right way, their roots dig into the cliffs in the right way, and the habitat structure they provide enables the greatest number of fauna to thrive. I began to explore the ways, both obvious and subtle, that we could benefit from the incorporation of the wild into our gardens.

So I began my own garden, juggling its creation with trips into the nearby wildlands, for seed collecting, and for idea collecting. I never drew a plan but depended on visions, gained through explorations of the surrounding wildlands. I haven't been tied to these visions but have kept open to surprises; indeed, I have come to see surprises as the highest kind of gardening experience. Gardening with our local flora has allowed me to study and live with the plants in such a way that I have discovered qualities of which I was previously unaware.

Take coyote bush, for example. On my piece of land, the only species from the coastal scrub plant community was coyote bush, which is often removed when a garden is made. We left islands of coyote bush, good places for mysterious rustlings from wildlife in the early morning. As I talked to people about coyote bush, information began to emerge. It turned out there were more coyote bush appreciators than I had thought. What had begun as a lonely conversation expanded to include many talkers, and eventually a loose association formed, dedicated to protecting and restoring habitat in our town. At first jokingly and then as a matter of course, we called ourselves "Friends of the Coyote Bush."

We learned that coyote bush is an indispensable source of nectar in the autumn, when little else provides it. Hundreds of insects take advantage of its nectar, including *Paradejeania rutillioides*, an insect critical for the control of insect pests on agricultural crops. The soil under coyote bush is rich, good for growing vegetables or for sheltering native herbaceous plants like checkerbloom or brodiaea. Its distinctive honeyed fragrance in the fall and winter locates me in this place. Some birds live their whole lives in coyote bush, finding there all they need for perching, nesting, breeding, eating, and resting. Coyote bush is enough for them. We pondered the mysteries of its many forms, from the graceful mounds, like clouds on a hillside, to the low-growing, ground-hugging form, to those individuals that unaccountably shot up to tree size. As we learned more, my friend Lea said, "It's hard to remember that I once thought that coyote bush was just . . . coyote bush."

What came to me slowly was a vision of my home nestled into the intricate earth, surrounded by those trees, shrubs, grasses, and wildflowers that at one time graced it, mammals that have slept in, eaten off, hidden in, bred in, and otherwise hung out in these plants for the last ten thousand years. The white-crowned sparrow, famous for its different dialects, has a clear, sweet whistle heard only in the area reaching from my town to a lake three miles away. The California poppy occurs in a lemon-yellow rather than a crayon-orange variety along our coast. Home was becoming more particularly defined, more specific, more tied to the details of smell, color, and form, as we searched out the clues and looked at the pieces.

While the land around my house and in my town in general can no longer be called pristine, the kind of gardening I have become interested in appears at the place where my plant choices and the general direction of the wild landscape meet, where I can work to locate myself and my garden in the ongoing evolution of life forms as they have become evident in this post-Pleistocene era, on this marine terrace, at the edge of this sea. I am increasingly eased by my association with these plants. Collecting, cleaning, and sowing their seeds, planting and transplanting them as young plants, collecting seeds from them in turn, all create a long intimacy somewhat reminiscent of, though not nearly as rich as, the complicated, layered involvement of the native Californians who used and continue to use them. When Mabel McKay, recently deceased Pomo basketweaver and doctor, heard somebody say that he had used native medicinal herbs but that they hadn't worked for him, she responded, "You don't know the songs. You have to know the right songs." With no one to teach us, we don't know the songs either. The native practice of dreaming songs about the nonhuman world seems as valuable and elusive as a piece of pure bunchgrass prairie or the truth about this land.

Our retreat hut in the garden is called the "Coyote Bush House," and its door handles are made from the hard, twisted limbs of its namesake. We use this hut for restorative naps, on a cot so situated that what you see out the open door before you fall asleep in April is the intense blue of lupines, against the creams, yellows, and golds of tidy tips, goldfields, and the lemon-yellow form of the California poppy. What you see in the winter months is coyote bush regenerating after the long time of no rain, its new leaves the freshest of greens. The structure sits low to the ground, providing a good place for guard quail to perch while watching their flock feed—their calls spring through the garden. Here, our first plant songs might be dreamed.

Eighteen years ago, when I first began working in a California native plant nursery, I wasn't sure why I was drawn to work with native plants. In the middle of a major drought, they seemed important in water conservation, though now I no longer focus on the drought-tolerant aspects of native plants. The reasons to garden with locally occurring native plants have more to do with joining in, with setting in motion interrupted processes that are unique to this place. It has to do with re-creating a garden that connects the gardener with that larger garden beyond the fence.

In that garden, many plant/animal relationships are finely tuned and easily disrupted. Certain butterflies, for example, are called "host-specific," meaning that they will lay their eggs only on one or a few different plants. When the larvae hatch, they require the kind of food that the leaves of their host plant provide and the kind of shelter that the leaf litter at the base of the plant provides. Without that particular plant, they will not survive. One example is the pipevine swallowtail, whose larvae are found only on the leaves of one of California's most beautiful native vines, *Aristolochia californica*, Dutchman's pipe. Without this plant, you won't be seeing the huge iridescent greenish black wings of *Battus philenor*. It all starts with the plants.

Gardening this way has changed me in ways I couldn't have predicted. My previous employer, Gerda, a venerable German woman whom I regard as a mentor, also has a demonstration garden of native plants, but around the house is a cutting garden, a formal rock garden, and some of the beloved plants that reflect her European ancestry. Accordingly, when I set up our demonstration garden, I followed her model, starting at the edge of the property with natives and working my way up to the house, where I half-consciously assumed I also would grow exotic plants that caught my fancy.

By the time I got to the house, which took years, I was different. What I wanted to be greeted by in the mornings was the rusty-green roughish leaves of the California hazel, its horizontal twigs slanting against the office wall. I wanted not to have to go anywhere to experience the sleek gray limbs of the California buckeye, or the deep-green leaves of the handsome coffeeberry. I wanted our fog-gray house to melt into the grays of the coastal sages. These are the friends whose seasons and graces go beyond novelty, the friends with whom I have become quite comfortable.

I want to be able to walk outside into the coastal scrub and see it jumping with those resident birds that favor it for nesting and feeding, such as the wrentit, the bushtit, and the white-crowned sparrow. Quiet makes me nervous now, reminding me of what Robert Michael Pyle calls "the extinction of experience—the loss of everyday species within our own radius of reach." He says, "When we lose the common wildlife in our immediate surroundings, we run the risk of becoming inured to nature's absences, blind to delight, and, eventually, alienated from the land."

When I hike into the surrounding wildlands, I have a purpose, a reason to be there. As well as collecting seeds, I'm seeking inspiration and information. We think we know what these plants can do, but surprises are the name of the game. Led by my friend John, who has made it the business of his retirement to know and protect this watershed, we once went deep into a coastal canyon, past marshy grasses, to a grove of Pacific wax myrtles so large that their ancient limbs created a sheltered glade, where we reclined and picnicked on its foot-deep, cinnamon-colored leaf litter. Having only seen these plants in their shrub form, we could only guess at how old these individuals were. I brought back a bit of the duff to scatter at the base of my own small wax myrtles, in case some mycorhizzal connection in the soil has enabled the spectacular growth of these plants. These treasured bits of information let us know what was once and what might be again.

In the way that our coastal creeks spread out over the land in a broad floodplain before they empty into the lagoon, so the plants in this garden and in these wild gardens have begun to spread and seep out into our lives. At the end of a performance at our community center, we threw handfuls of coyote bush seed into the audience. The shining fluffy white seeds floated and drifted and landed in people's hair, adding to the layers of memories about coyote bush. Some people grabbed at them and put them in their pockets, as though the seeds were something valuable they had never seen before. The electrician working on my house opened some buried electrical boxes to find deer mouse nests made of the brushy pappus. People stop me on the street if they have something to say about coyote bush.

One part of the garden where the seam between the domestic and the wild is particularly evident is the food garden for humans. In this area, I have planted both domestic and wild bush fruits, which include the domestic raspberry and blueberry alongside the wild huckleberry and thimbleberry. In the greens department, we have miner's lettuce, every backpacker's favorite green, side by side with domestic lettuces. The California woodland strawberry sends runners alongside Fragaria "Sequoia," asparagus beds flourish next to a plant of cow parsnip, said to have shoots that taste like asparagus. Native alliums and Bermuda onions share a bed.

In order that the smells and colors particular to this place be joined by the tastes particular to this place, twice a year I immerse myself in food preparation tasks involving our local plants. At our open houses, we offer the public roasted bay nuts, pinole made from blue wildrye, sugar cookies studded with chia seeds, miner's lettuce on cheese and crackers, manzanita berry tea, and chia seed lemonade. We may not eat like this most of the time, but the ritual acknowledgment and honoring of this aspect of our local plants has come to feel compelling enough that I find myself preparing these foods and adding to the menu every year.

Once I went to visit a friend on First Mesa on the Hopi reservation. Inquiring as to her whereabouts, I was told that she was "whitewashing the kiva." She emerged from that task with a certain virtuous glow. This glow is what I feel while roasting the seed of red maids, while shelling bay nut seeds, while roasting bunchgrass seed to make pinole. It is a mundane activity that sets the stage for important events. It is a time for honoring continuous ways, in this case, ways having to do with the plants. Like whitewashing the kiva, this food preparation is the background activity for a sacred experience, in this case, the incorporation of the molecules of local foods into our bodies.

Where you see coyote bush, you often see its partner in the coastal scrub plant community, that plant of ineffable shining silvery gray-green, California sagebrush. The smell and the color are the essence of California shrublands, both interior and coastal. A good medicine smell, a heart-easing smell. A smell with some of the sharpness common to these chaparral plants, a smell that tells us where we are, that seems to cut through grief or ennui.

I walk through the garden with Ann, who has worked here with me for seven years. She hands me a wand of pungent, palest silvered-green sagebrush and says, "Smell this." Wandering on, we stop at a large soaproot plant and look through the stems and leaves to the shadow they cast on the leaf litter at the base of the plant. We experience a certain lack of ambition. We note a strange lack of plants. Now that we have reinjected the native virus, it is, to a greater and greater degree, out of our hands. Not that there isn't plenty to do; weeds are forever, especially in a Mediterranean climate, but the balance has been tipped in the native direction. Now that the California hazel is established and thriving, we can let the rose from France next to it arch its long canes in the hazel's direction.

As the years go by and the plants develop their character, I begin to accept them at their worst. The California sagebrush, during its long summer and fall dormancy, turns a ghostly pale color, and looks, with its empty seed stalks, like it just got out of bed. But ours is not a relationship based only on looks. The wren-tit uses scrapings from its bark to make its nest, bound together with cobwebs. My partner's son Sasha cut twigs to make smudge sticks and sold them at our Christmas fair as local incense. If, as you walk through the scrub, your coat brushes the sagebrush, you become redolent with a fine fragrance, at once spicy and sweet.

Twice a year, a Pomo Indian named Milton "Bun" Lucas puts a chair between the two elderberry bushes in the garden. From there, he directs us, as we scurry about cutting shoots from the elderberry for him to turn into carved clapper sticks and flutes (musical instruments used by many Californian tribes). Our cutting goals include fostering those stems that next year will be the right width for a clapper stick or flute. Gardening can be an anxious pastime, as the demands of weeding, watering, fertilizing, and pruning accrue. I have never experienced such peaceful gardening moments as when we plan for next year's "music bush" harvest. "Cut here," says Bun, "and cut here."

Basketry materials are not as available to native Californian basketmakers as they were in the past. Basketgrass, used by a number of Californian tribes, is hard to find and often not of suitable quality. At the same time, this grass has become extremely popular in landscaping. A large, fine-textured handsome grass easily grown horticulturally, it is being planted by thousands throughout California and seems to be adaptable to many conditions; there is no reason for indigenous basketmakers to go without. This fall, I was able to offer sheaves of its beautiful pale seed stalks to a Yowlumni basketmaker.

I have talked with other indigenous Californians about plants they used to see but no longer can find, plants of cultural importance to their tribe. There is a plant gathered for its root, an elusive mention of a grass with seeds as large as wheat, a variety of wild tobacco no one has seen for a while. All these could be found and brought into the native garden. Recent anthropological theories about Indian land management indicate that, to the indigenous people of California, there was no "wilderness," but that human activities have always transformed the landscape. The distinction between the garden and the wild blurs further. The seam shifts, cracks in some places, holds more closely in others.

I have become a patron of used book stores, looking for the odd find that may illuminate some hitherto unknown aspect of this kind of landscape and these plants, of previous human interactions with them and reactions to them. The coastal plants, except perhaps the redwoods, have no John Muir. They are largely unsung. Easily removed for development or ranching, of little evident economic value, they are the underdog of plant communities. I think of myself as becoming of them. I am "of the coastal scrub."

For this kind of garden, plant lists are not taken from charts in glossy garden books. Ideas for plantings come from local floras, from hikes with naturalists into nearby undisturbed areas, from visits to botanic gardens, from the recollections of old-timers, and from the oral histories stored in our museums and libraries. They come from the diaries of early Spanish explorers, from the journals of wives of doctors living in gold-mining communities, or from the casual asides of English tourists.

This garden isn't the wild, but it looks to, and is in conversation with, the wild. It backs on, is backed up by, natural systems. The goal is that the quail in the vacant lot next to us will find in our arranged mosaic of coastal prairie, coastal scrub, and wildflower fields the forbs they need for greens, the seeds they need for protein when nesting, and the habitat structure for shelter and protection in our shrubs. The ubiquitous subclover, a plant widely sown for forage, will not be found in our garden, as it is in nearby lots, since it is now known that this plant contains chemicals that inhibit reproduction in quail. Nor will the naturalizing pyracantha, for though its berries may seem to make birds amusingly inebriated, they actually set them at risk for predation and interfere with the activities necessary for their survival. Instead, we plant toyon, the shrub for which Hollywood was named, with its bright hollylike berries at Christmas time.

With plantings of toyon, we have joined the great feeding schedule, whereby food is available at the right time for the right creature. In early summer, the buckeye blooms, sometimes for three months. Its great pendant blossoms attract the insects that nourish the protein-hungry nesting birds. Even birds that are usually vegetarian often require animal food while nesting. In midsummer, the annual and perennial seed crops come in, bee plant, poppy, miner's lettuce, clarkia. By early fall, the native honeysuckle drapes succulent red berries on trees and shrubs. Mid-fall brings the acorn and hazel harvests, and late fall sees the ripening of the madrone and toyon berries, while the coyote bush pumps out the nectar. The arrival of the rufous hummingbird is tied to the blooming of the flowering currant in January and February.

Some might say it is not truly representative of the fine art of gardening to use local natives, to use natural models. But choices have been made, plants have been arranged, an aesthetic has been developed. It embraces all I know, all I hope to know, and all I wish I knew about this set of ancient processes and associations. Some have said it is the way of a lazy gardener, but I find that horticultural challenges are many.

For example, I want to establish a stand of Indian paintbrush here, which probably grew here once but has so far not survived in my garden. Appearing in a radiant palette of apricot, scarlet, and yellow, it hosts a particular kind of aphid-eating mite. This mite lives in the flower, where it eats nectar, until a hummingbird comes along to share the nectar. At this moment, the mite runs up the hummingbird's beak and into its nostril, where it sits tight while the hummingbird flies down to Baja. As the hummingbird approaches a nectar-producing plant, the mite gets ready, rears up, and races from the nostril, down the beak, and into the flower. Since it must run so quickly, it is estimated that this creature is as fast as the fastest animal on earth, the cheetah. By establishing this flower in the garden, with its as yet elusive cultural requirements, I may be facilitating this mind-boggling nasal journey.

Some might call it xenophobic to remove or exclude non-native plants. The fact is, on all but one side of us, where coastal scrub still exists, our garden stands out startlingly from the surrounding vacant lots, filled as they are with escaped exotic plants like eucalyptus, pampas grass, passion flower vine, German ivy, and French broom. Here the native plants have become the exotics. I can justify my gardening choices with data on habitat for songbirds, butterflies, insects, voles, and lizards, with quotes from scientific journals and studies. And knowledge of the qualities of these plants seems to fill some of that cavity of longing for knowledgeable connection with our tribe, both human and other, that some of us carry around like an empty burden basket. But the truth is, some of the creatures we long to see around us may not come here at all, so isolated are we in this diminished habitat.

And too, those who say that this way of working with plants isn't really gardening might be right. Maybe my piece of land is neither the wildlands nor a garden, and maybe the activities involved aren't really gardening at all but more like inserting your-self into the long dream of this solemn, fogbound, silvered land. Though protecting, enhancing, and bringing close the coastal scrub and other native plant communities has become my busi-ness, though life is punctuated by phone calls and seed orders and scheduling, at the back somewhere always is the color of the litter made by wax myrtle leaves, and the smell of coyote bush in the rain.

Stanley Plumly

LAPSED MEADOW

Wild has its skills.
The apple grew so close to the ground
it seemed the whole tree
was thicket, crab and root—

by fall it looked
like brush among burdock and hawkweed;
looked as if brush had been piled,
for burning, at the center.

At the edges, blurred,
like failed fence, the hawthorns, by
comparison, seemed planted.
Everywhere else there was broom

grass and timothy
and wood fern and sometimes a sapling,
sometimes a run of hazel. In Ohio,
some people call it

a farmer's field, all fireweed
and thistle, a waste of nature. And true,

you could lose yourself
      in the mind of the thing,

        especially summer, in the full
sun or later, after rain and the smell
of rain—you could lose
      yourself, waist- or head-high,

        branch by leaf by branch.
There could be color, the kind that opens
and the kind that closes up,
      one for each part

        of the light; there might
be fruit, green or grounded—it was always
skin-tight, small and hard.
      There would be goldenrod

        still young or yellowing
in season, and wind enough to seed a countryside
of plows and pasture.
      But I call it crazy

        the way that apple,
in the middle of the field, dug in, part of the year
bare-knuckled, part of the year
      blossoming.

        for James Wright

EDIBLE FLOWERS, A WEED TO EAT, AND HANDSOME VEGETABLES

Gardeners, except for those mere greenskeepers who live only for their lawns, come in three basic varieties. There are those who raise only flowers and other ornamental plants. These people buy the things they eat in grocery stores. There are those who raise primarily vegetables in tidy rows in their backyard patches. When these people say "I'll be out in the garden for a while," they mean that they'll be thinning out the carrots or checking to see how the corn is coming along. The third group consists of those of us who are mixtures of the first two, purer types. We are eclectic souls who value homegrown endive and lettuce none the less for loving our delphiniums and dahlias. No statistics back me up, but I would guess that the greatest number of American gardeners fall into this mixed group, provided that we count in it those whose flowers amount to mostly marigolds interplanted among their vegetables on the theory that marigolds repel insects, and those who give 99 percent of their attention to ornamental annuals and perennials, raising a few lettuce and tomato plants in odd corners for a simple salad.

But this tidy classification breaks down for the good and simple reason that the distinctions between flowers and vegetables are far from absolute and unambiguous. The mind's tendency to tidiness sometimes creates sharper distinctions, and thus it is with the things we eat. A pig in its pen is a pig, but when it comes to the table it is pork. Within the plant kingdom, we want to say that vegetables are vegetables, flowers are flowers, and fruits are fruits—even if some vegetables, tomatoes for example, turn out to be fruits.

As for flowers, we cultivate them for ornament and delight, a feast for the eye, not the palate. But the distinction between flowers and vegetables is, again, pretty shaky. *Vegetable*, a word that has existed in culinary English for a comparatively short time (in the late eighteenth century vegetable gardens were called kitchen gardens), means any part of a herbaceous plant that is edible and palatable. Beets, carrots, turnips, and their like are all roots. Rhubarb is a stem; in fact, the leaves it bears are painfully toxic, potentially lethal because of their high concentration of oxalic acid. Okra is a seedpod. Peas and dried beans are seeds; snow peas and string beans are immature seeds encased in edible pods. Considering that almost any part of a plant may turn out to be safe and tasty to eat, depending on the plant, it's not at all surprising that some of the vegetables we commonly eat are really flowers or their buds. Broccoli past its prime shows golden yellow petals as unmistakable testimony to its floral character.

Broccoli does not stand alone. The facts of history show that our ancestors, particularly if they were Europeans, had more flowers on their daily menus than seems imaginable, and for good reason. Before the discovery of the New World, many of the staple foods of today were unknown on the other side of the Atlantic. The list includes corn, squash, pumpkins, tomatoes, and potatoes, all of which were domesticated and brought into cultivation by the native peoples of the Americas. Europeans, who only since World War II have learned that sweet corn, or maize, is not only edible but also delectable, had in former times to stock their larders with vegetables that today seem suited only for the flower garden, not the kitchen garden.

They ate violets, for example—a practice that faintly survives in the candied violets sold in gourmet shops for sprinkling on top of ice cream or decorating cakes. They also made violet syrup and violet jelly, and traditional herbal lore held that violets had important medicinal properties. A garland of violets, the Roman naturalist Pliny advised, was a sure cure for hangovers. The Romans also ate violet leaves, which in fact turn out to be rich in vitamin C.

English books on herbs from sixteenth and seventeenth centuries record many other floral foods in common consumption. One book published in 1600 states flatly that "no broths are well made without dried Marigolds," but a warning is in order here, lest someone be tempted to gather some marigold blossoms and toss them into a stockpot. The flowers we call marigolds are in the genus *Tagetes*, highly unpalatable because of their harsh odor and flavor. The old English marigold was *Calendula officinalis*, often used, wrote the great herbalist John Parkinson in 1629, in "broths and drinkes as a comforter of the heart and spirits." Roses also had a long run as flowers for both the table and the medicinal pantry. John Gerard, in the second edition of his *Herball* (1633), wrote of musk roses that "the leaves of the floures eaten in the morning, in the manner of a sallad, with oile, vinegar, and pepper, or any other way according to the appetite and pleasure of them that shall eate it, purge very notably the belly of waterish and cholericke humors, and that mightily, yet without any perill or paine at all."

Other flowers were eaten as well, or made into syrups and conserves, including the blossoms of clove pinks. Things that sound peculiar to us now had a way of turning up in "sallets" or "sallads," notably mint blossoms, peach flowers, hollyhock buds, and cowslips or primroses. Primrose salad was a special favorite well into Victorian times; the British prime minister Benjamin Disraeli is reported to have been passionate for it. I have seen eighteenth-century cookbooks with recipes for puddings made from primrose blossoms, ladyfingers, eggs, cream, and rose water.

Flower eating has made no great inroads into American life, with one historic exception, the nasturtium. Very early in the nineteenth century, Bernard McMahon wrote in *The American Gardener's Calendar*, the first truly American book on gardening, that the nasturtium "is very deserving of cultivation, as well as on account of the beauty of its large and numerous orange-colored flowers, and their use in garnishing dishes. The green berries or seeds of this plant . . . make one of the nicest pickles that can possibly be conceived; in the estimation of many, they are superior to capers." Thomas Jefferson agreed fully with McMahon. He planted many square yards of them every year at Monticello, and once, when his seed crop failed, he pleaded with a friend for whatever seeds he could spare, so that the summer salads served at his home in Virginia could be garnished with orange nasturtium blossoms and flavored by the piquant young leaves.

The idea of eating nasturtiums seems today a bit outlandish, since they are spectacularly beautiful annuals. Claude Monet delighted in growing the tall trailing or climbing sorts at Giverny, where in midsummer they climbed up turquoise arches and sprawled into gravel walks to delight the eye with their bright shades of yellow, orange, and scarlet. In the United States, the best display of nasturtiums by any reckoning occurs in March in the enclosed atrium garden of the Isabella Stewart Gardner Museum in Boston. Growing in pots in open windows with pointed Venetian arches above the first story, they hang down twenty feet or more, their succulent large round leaves jeweled with crimson orange blossoms that gleam as if afire.

The name by which these plants are commonly called sounds like botanical Latin, but it isn't. *Nasturtium*, which means "nosetwister," properly applies to *Nasturtium officinale*, the European watercress. The nasturtiums of the garden are really *Tropaeolum minor* and *T. majus*, both native to Central and South America. Gardeners merely borrowed the name of another genus altogether and used it as a common name, creating some confusion along the way. Real nasturtiums have in common with tropaeolums only one thing—a pungent-smelling and peppery-tasting foliage.

Tropaeolum, the name Carolus Linnaeus gave the genus, has its own meaning, with military overtones involving trophies captured in battle. Linnaeus thought that the round leaves, each with a slightly off-center pale dot near its middle where the veins radiate outward, looked something like shields. He also thought that the slightly cupped blossoms resembled burnished helmets. (In some of the many books on the language of flowers published in England and the United States during their vogue in the middle of the nineteenth century, a gift of nasturtiums meant "we share patriotic pride.")

It might be noted that in their enthusiasm for nasturtiums as an element of cuisine, Bernard McMahon and Thomas Jefferson were following in British footsteps. The English herbalists were uncommonly fond of this plant, which the Spanish physician Nicolás Monardes introduced to Europe in 1569. John Parkinson's *Paradisi in Sole* (1629) called the plant "larkes heeles." Parkinson claimed no medicinal properties for it but thought it of "so great beauty and sweetness withal, that my Garden of delight cannot be unfurnished of it." In *Acetaria* (1699), the first book ever devoted entirely to salads, John Evelyn recommended adding shredded nasturtium petals to greens as a way of adding a sharp and tangy note. He also advised pickling nasturtium buds for similar uses.

If any flower regains popularity as something to eat, it is likely to be the nasturtium, thanks in part to upscale gourmet vegetable catalogs like that of Shepherd's Garden Seeds, which waxes lyrical in its praise. Several varieties are offered, the most beautiful being an old strain, "Empress of India." Its crop of flowers, abundant if the plants are grown in the lean, nitrogen-poor soil they prefer, are within hailing distance of true crimson, and they are set off perfectly by leaves of a decidedly bluish shade of green.

I grow, quite unwillingly, another plant that turns out to have a distinguished history as a vegetable for eating. It is purslane (*Portulaca oleracea*). It is one of the most bothersome of summer weeds, because it seems to enjoy the rough treatment that would send less rugged plants right into weed heaven. When I pull it up, enough remains behind in the ground so that it will sprout anew, almost overnight. Furthermore, the succulent leaves and stems do not wilt when left in the hot sun, as crabgrass will. They can lie out in the open, separated from the soil and completely rootless, but still looking a bit too fat and smug, perhaps because they know a secret. After a few days, the stems make new roots, and the purslane resumes its growth as if nothing at all had happened to it. Meanwhile, being something of a demon at reproducing itself, it forms seeds, some of which germinate immediately, others of which remain dormant until the following summer. On purslane, I have long stood with Charles Dudley Warner, who in *My Summer in a Garden* (1870) said it was his most hated weed, "a fat, ground-clinging, spreading, greasy thing, and the most propagatious [it is not my fault that the word is not in the dictionary] plant I know."

My mother used to tell me to eat the okra on my plate, that it was good for me. Of late, I am getting the same advice about purslane. A recent catalog from another tiny vegetable seed company, The Cook's Garden, proposes planting purslane for food. When I got the catalog, I called Shepherd Ogden, the company's owner, and he stood by his recommendation. He offers two varieties. One, called "Green," is a selected version of the common weed, but more erect in habit and less inclined to sprawl. "Goldgelber" is even more upright, with golden leaves so thick that they resemble those of the jade plant. Both, Mr. Ogden said, made very fine eating, succulent and slightly tart in a salad.

I did a little checking in the books in my gardening library, and Ogden proved to be on the mark. Purslane has been standard culinary fare in India and Persia for some twenty centuries. According to Mary Durant's *Who Named the Daisy? Who Named the Rose?* (1976), it was praised by an early eighteenth-century New England divine, the Reverend Manasseh Cutler, as "little inferior to asparagus." Delena Tull's *A Practical Guide to Edible and Useful Plants* (1987) says that Europeans love purslane. She advises readers that after they've weeded their flower beds they should "save the purslane for the table rather than the garbage can." She calls it good raw or cooked or pickled and recommends it as a soup thickener. She offers a slight warning that its tartness comes from its oxalic acid content (about the same as spinach), so that it shouldn't be eaten to excess, especially by people who don't get enough calcium. It is quite rich in vitamin A.

I haven't gotten around yet to eating purslane, but I have it in fine supply. One of these days I'll try some. Maybe.

If some flowers turn out to have a surprising culinary history, the other side of the equation is that some vegetables are so damnably handsome that they deserve a place of honor among ornamental plants in a garden. I'll start with two that I in fact much prefer looking at to having on my plate. Eggplant is one. Cooked, it strikes me as slimy. I would argue that my long-standing negative feelings toward it are justified by its being kin to nightshade and some other deadly plants, except that so are peppers, potatoes, and tomatoes. But I am willing to admit eggplant to a garden for purely aesthetic reasons. Ordinary eggplant, with its smooth and glossy purple skin and its hint of pregnancy near full term, is beautiful to behold. I have seen it grown with great elegance and panache in twin terra-cotta planters flanking a doorway to a piazza of one of the houses in the historic district of Charleston, South Carolina—proof that the gardener who lived there understood how sublime something simple could be. As for okra, it's even slimier. The only way I will even consider eating a single bite is if it has been cut into slices, dipped into cornmeal, and then fried in bacon grease, southern style. But viewed objectively, it's an admirable plant. It bears a heavy crop of attractive yellow mallow flowers with wine-purple throats. The seedpods, once they ripen reassuringly past the point of being considered edible, are fetching things, green and fuzzy, with deep ridges running from base to tapering tip. Usually they are green, but there are maroon forms, and when the pods dry and open, they lend authority to dried winter arrangements. An okra cousin, the annual *Abelmoschos* "Manihot" reaches over three feet tall and spreads as wide. The large buttery yellow single flowers are lovely, showing up at a considerable distance. In the fall, the clusters of egg-shaped green seedpods bend toward the earth under their own weight. Covered with a soft gray down, they are extremely beautiful on a clear morning in early October when they glisten in a heavy dew.

Swiss chard, the varieties with red stems instead of green, holds its own as an accent in a flower bed. I have seen it used very simply and effectively as a long and narrow bed entirely filled with silvery dusty miller, except for individual plants at intervals of three feet. The deep green of its leaves, the luminous ruby of its upright stems, and the gray of the dusty miller all combined with quiet but telling harmony. The place was Kew Gardens—hardly some backyard vegetable patch.

Ordinary rhubarb (*Rheum rhabarbarum*), an extremely hardy perennial vegetable, commands a lot of attention when grown as a single specimen. The stems are ruby red, the bold foliage a luscious deep green, topped in late May by a foamy panicle of creamy blossoms. I first saw this splendid sight at the front entrance of Millstream, the home of the late Lincoln and Laura Louise Foster in Falls Village, Connecticut. The Fosters, beloved figures in the world of rock gardening, had such impeccable taste in plants that if they put rhubarb by their door the rest of us could know that to do so was fitting and seemly. But I am even more taken with another species of rhubarb, *Rheum palmatum* "Atropurpureum." Even the massive roots are gorgeous—substantial, somewhat woody, and cranberry red. When the first crinkled growth of leaves emerges at the crown, it is a glowing mixture of gold, lime, and scarlet. Well grown, this rhubarb can attain heights in excess of six feet, and the foliage turns a wonderfully petulant purple hue. A very suitable companion for it is another perennial vegetable, ordinary asparagus, which is tall and ferny, bearing red fruits in late summer.

My most recent discovery among vegetables is the cardoon (*Cynara cardunculus*), which is not reliably winter hardy in regions much colder than Zone 9, so I buy it as small plants from a nursery down South. I grow it primarily for its bold, long, and arching leaves, a soft gray-green on top, downy white on the underside. In late summer this six-foot plant produces great stalks of thistle-like buds that open into flowers of a soft and gentle mauve. It grows with great distinction in the Conservatory Garden in Central Park, but it first caught my eye in Dan Hinckley's garden in Kingston, Washington, where it grows near a clump of miscanthus grass with peacock feathers stuck into the leaves. The cardoons suggest power, the miscanthus brings grace, and the feathers lend iridescent color, plus an agreeable touch of whimsy. If, like Dan Hinckley, I had a few peacocks strolling my grounds, I would borrow the combination, but I'm making do by growing cardoons with bronze fennel (*Foeniculum vulgare purpureum*), another six-footer with ferny and delicate foliage. I agree with Nancy Goodwin, who says that its foliage captures the morning dew in a lovely way and that the sight of sunlight playing through the plant is unforgettable.

Maxine Kumin

AN INSIDER'S VIEW
OF THE GARDEN

How can I help but admire my ever-perseverant
unquenchable dill
that sways like an unruly crowd at a soccer match
waving its lacy banners
where garlic belongs or slyly invading a hill
of Delicata squash—
how can I help but admire such ardor? I seek it
as bees the flower's core, hummingbirds
the concocted sugar water
that lures them to the feeder in the lilacs.
I praise the springy mane
of untamed tendrils asprawl on chicken wire
promising to bring
forth peas enough to fill a pillowcase.

Some days I adore my coltish broccolis
the encauled beginnings
of their green heads sketchy incipient trees
up out of the Pleistocene.
Some days the leeks, that Buckingham-Palace patrol
and the quarter-mile of beans
—green, yellow, soy, lima, bush and pole—

demand applause. As do the dilatory parsnips
a forest of tops regal
as celery. Let me laud onion that erupts
slim as a grass stem
then spends the summer inventing its pungent tulip
and the army of brussels sprouts
extending its spoon-shaped leaves over dozens of
    armpits

that conceal what are now merely thoughts, mere nub-
    bins
needing long ripening.
But let me lament my root maggot-raddles radishes
my bony and bored red peppers
that drop their lower leaves like dancehall strippers
my cauliflowers that spit
out thimblesize heads in the heat and take beetles to
    bed.

O children, citizens, my wayward jungly dears
you are all to be celebrated
plucked, transplanted, tilled under, resurrected here
even the likes of these:
purslane, chickweed, burdock, poke, wild poppies.
For all of you, whether eaten or extirpated
I plan to spend the rest of my life on my knees.

Stanley Crawford

CROPS, WORDS, MOVIES

Cultivated crops, like words, like language, are things that glide into view out of the murkiness of the past. I think of my words as mine, but the chances are that even after fifty or sixty or seventy years of chewing on them, writing them down, word-processing them as a speaker and as a writer, I won't succeed in putting a single new one into circulation. Same with plants, with crops, as a gardener and farmer. I know that there are weeds out there waiting in line to become domesticated, or even redomesticated in the case of crops that have fallen from grace back into being weeds again. You can tell by the way they hang around the garden that they have adapted themselves to our seasonal disturbances, but I doubt I'm the one to figure out what they're good for in relation to the fashions of human existence. What we're given in words and cultivated plants has been worked over for hundreds of generations before it comes to us, and the chances of our adding much to it are very slim. What we add is illusion: each time we're born, the world looks new, is new, which gives us a strange kind of leverage against the weight of accumulated biological and cultural existence, which means for a while, off and on, now and then, under certain circumstances, we believe we are the owners or managers or the franchise operators of this world, not the other way around, and that we have invented almost everything in sight, from the words that drop so easily from our mouths to the plants we grow in our gardens.

It is possible, however, to flip over most of the terms.

I will probably never find out why a particular type of garlic chose me as its husbandman. Using the tools of rationality to figure out how crops, not identifiably articulate or rational in human terms, choose this or that farmer or gardener to grow them will not get you very far. I am reduced to saying things like: I have a certain affinity for this or that plant, and the plant responds to my caring gestures, my tendings, to my delight, my passion, my labor, to my intelligence and intuition attempting to illuminate the universe inhabited by it. There is something very obvious in this. Also something essentially mysterious, at least within a society that has a multivalent attitude toward the simpler forms of biological existence.

Twenty years ago Rose Mary and I moved to a village in a narrow valley of northern New Mexico. We had just seen the film *Easy Rider.* Its message was: Head for the Hills. The hills in question were a southern spur of the Rockies, the Sangre de Cristo Range. Several thousand people did just that. We were among them, a little too old to be hippies, though we tried. The year was 1968, that banner year in American history. Or actually 1969 by the time we got our belongings together and were able to talk our way out of an apartment lease in San Francisco. Conveniently the place had a chronic gas leak.

I don't think there's anything particularly silly about heading for the hills on the basis of a not especially good film. I went to Greece after seeing *Never on Sunday,* which, when you think about it, is a film about fringe benefits for prostitutes, though the music was lively. I wrote a couple of novels on the islands, and the last of that money was to go to buy our irrigated two-acre bottomland field in northern New Mexico. More important, I met my Australian wife, Rose Mary, on Crete, and she saved me from the perils of a life as an effete expatriate, though gained herself an expatriate's life on a farm in America. A lot of people set off across the prairies in wagons a hundred-and-some years ago on the basis of even less reliable information. Most Native Americans will argue that Columbus should have waited for the movie. And who could have been more deluded than the Conquistadors?

Anyway, that in brief was how we made our way from the island of Crete via Dublin and San Francisco to a lovely little mountain valley in northern New Mexico where we would soon begin making mud bricks for the house we would eventually build with our own hands. And by then we would have two small kids in tow.

Each year, of course, we grew a garden, and each year it got bigger. One spring, 1971 or 1972, a friend brought by a bucketful of plants freshly dug up from an apple orchard a few miles down the road. They were garlic plants. He thought I might like to try them in my vegetable garden. I hadn't had much luck with the bulbs I was buying at the feed store or through mail-order catalogs. I was beginning to think you couldn't grow garlic at sixty-five hundred feet where the winter temperatures had recently dropped to a record-breaking forty below zero Fahrenheit.

One of the things that gardening does for you is to allow you to bring into the world of exchange a wealth of cheap biodegradable goods of unsurpassable quality. All but pathologically stingy gardeners are generous with whatever they grow. This has nothing to do with wealth, the other kind of wealth, which is early schooled against the dangers of generosity. It has to do with natural abundance, with the seeming ease with which plants and trees bear, compared to the onerous labor required to craft anything by hand.

From the point of view of the plant, the bounty is a survival tactic. We live amid vast seas of the sperm and ova of the plant world. We help manage the flood, spread it, distribute it, nurture it, and consume it. Trading seeds and plants is something we almost instinctively do. We've been doing it for thousands of years. The plants I grow in my garden and fields originated in Europe, South America, Africa, Asia, and they were brought here consciously by human hands. Humankind has been in effect a force of nature helping distribute plants throughout the planet. The garlic plants that my friend dug up in his orchard, and which grow in the wetter spots of countless small orchards in northern New Mexico, may well be the descendants of plants brought up from Mexico, brought over from Spain, along with fruit tree grafting stock, by the same Spanish colonists who were transporting corn, chile, squash, beans, potatoes, and tomatoes in the opposite direction. My friend moved them only two miles farther away from their probable place of origin in Central Asia. A journey of ten thousand miles ends with the last step.

It was spring. The plants were young and bulbless, perhaps six inches tall, rather like leeks. I planted them. Neither he nor I knew that garlic does not like to be transplanted. The results were not particularly impressive. However, I did take notice of the fact that these vigorous young plants, even though they became much less so after I planted them, had at least once been thriving enough to inspire a friend to dig them up and bring them over. They had still looked good in the bucket.

By midsummer the somewhat sickly plants produced only small bulbs. But by fall I must have noticed out of the corner of my eye that the bulbs I missed digging up were sprouting pairs of rich green leaves. This was an interesting though confusing phenomenon. The various plant encyclopedias I consulted claimed that garlic should be planted in the spring "as early as the ground can be worked." The advice seemed to be ill-founded, or else I was one of those slothful gardeners who did not want to be out in the March winds preparing my garden. Or else the experience of gardeners in radically different climates had been falsely generalized. Or, more likely, one of those inexplicable fissures had opened up between those who farm for a living and thus must know such things, and those who compose idyllic articles for gardening magazines and encyclopedias.

A second messenger arrived bearing a bowl of garlic seed tops, or bulbils, as plucked from garlic growing wild in an apple orchard up the road. I broke up the clusters and planted the bulbils the following spring, a couple of rows a hundred feet long each. I had visions by then of suddenly possessing a lot of garlic. And by then our garden was getting up toward half an acre and we were selling produce in the summer at the farmers' markets in Taos, a thirty-mile drive to the north. The bulbils, the largest the size of a grain of corn, produced a slip of a plant of no more than four leaves that vaguely resembled young wheat or rye and grew no more than a foot high, if that. In July they stopped growing. Then the folded leaves, never very broad in the first place, wilted and died back. I dug up a few plants. They had produced a bulb, but a very small one, rounder than the inverted heart shape of your normal garlic bulb. Further, these tiny bulbs that ran in size from a dime to a quarter had no clove divisions. They were solid garlic flesh. Much later I learned that they were called "rounds."

What to do with rounds? Most of them were too small to sell, too small even to dig up and throw away. Dead end, I thought. I left my couple of rows of rounds in place, neglected them, maybe even tilled under the weeds at one point late in the summer.

In September of most years the Gulf Coast hurricanes shunt masses of warm moist air up over the Sangre de Cristo Range that collide with the drier, cooler air that tends to inhabit the area. The result can be great roiling stacks of thunderheads leading to cloudburst, deluge. The moisture from the fall storms signals the myriad seeds of cool-weather annual and perennial grasses that the time has come to germinate and sprout, root and reclaim the land. It is also a signal to garlic which, as I was about to become aware, shares the same cycle.

The summer-dormant bulbils that had grown into rounds sprouted again in late September. They sprouted just like cloves. They produced a pair of wide folded leaves, lightly tinged with red their first days into the air. The implication was that a grain-sized bulbil, given an extra season in the ground to produce a clove-sized round, would eventually grow into a normal-sized garlic bulb with the usual number of clove divisions. Not surprising, of course, when you come to think of it. That's the sort of thing seeds usually do.

Bulbils are sprouted, but their leaves were as in the spring much finer, thinner, more like those of grasses. Over these couple of years in my haphazard experiments with growing garlic, quite a few bulbs and bulbils and rounds got scattered around the place. In fact I have probably learned as much or more about the life of garlic by observing the behavior of plants that have escaped my control than the ones I have planted. I pretended not to pay a lot of attention to the renegades at first, to the bulbs that got dropped or broken in the shed, raked out into the garden, swept into ditches.

As an educated man it took me many years to figure out a few facts of life, the main one being that the truth did not always announce itself by means of the written word.

The fact of the matter may be that by the time the written words do finally arrive, with all the usual bureaucratic delays, the truth has been sitting around waiting on the edges, in the ditches, by the side of the road, for the longest time.

Sara Stein

WE DON'T
GARDEN RIGHT

I'm writing this for a modest reason. I want to change the whole suburban landscape. I want to walk into any roadside nursery and see wild roses. I want every landscaper to know their local berries like they know the alphabet. I want wildflower societies to treasure native grass like they treasure the flowers that grow in it. I want growers to see trees as woodlands, shrubs as hedgerows, perennials as meadows. I want professionals not just to landscape with native plants, but to landscape with native ecosystems.

And if I seem to have left out ordinary homeowners—the backyard gardeners, the ones who get to mow the lawn—I want more from you than from anyone. Because you're the ones who own the land.

That's a strange thing, to own the land. Because the perception of ownership isn't shared by any of the creatures who live on it, or live from it, or cross over it. You own the plants, but not the relationships by which their roots are nourished, or their flowers are pollinated, or their seeds are dispersed. You own the dirt, but not the living systems that maintain it. Yet ownership gives you license to harm all these things that don't belong to you.

The way we've landscaped our suburbs is harmful, and I'll tell you why by telling you the story of my own piece of land. About 16 years ago, my husband and I bought a few acres of neglected New England farmland. By neglected, I mean that nothing had been done to it for maybe 20 years. So the woods were choked with brush, the meadow was tangled in vines, and you couldn't even see the pond through the brambles.

We were too busy with the house at first to do any clearing. So for a few years we enjoyed what came with the thorns and tangles. We saw pheasants and grouse. There were all sorts of small animals—mostly common ones like woodchucks. But we saw foxes trotting through; and sometimes we heard owls. There were plenty of grasshoppers in the tall grass, and the pond was full of frogs. I remember how the ladybugs used to overwinter in the window frames and crawl out by the hundreds in the spring.

But finally, we got around to clearing. We cleaned the woods of underbrush, cut down junipers and cherries, tore out the vines, and mowed nearly the whole place to lawn. Then we planted it in typical suburban style—the same as you see everywhere all across the country—and of course we kept it neat: sheared, mowed, raked, and deadheaded.

But the fact is that we groomed the life out of our land, because what we cleared away were those animals' food and shelter, and what we substituted for it offered nothing to eat and no place to hide. In the space of a few years, we managed to make our land uninhabitable to nearly all the creatures that had shared it.

I might not have noticed if it hadn't happened so fast. For the first few springs the place was filled with birds. Then we whacked down the junipers. The next spring there were hardly any birds. So of course I noticed right away; what took a lot longer was to take the blame.

I'd been interested in biology all my life, but it was as though what I knew about the natural world was in one compartment in my brain, and gardening was in another.

What finally connected the two were memories of childhood. Thinking back, I realized that even the liveliness we'd enjoyed at first wasn't much compared to how things used to be. When I was a kid, vanishing species like box turtles and luna moths were still fairly common. Even 20 years ago, no one thought of buying ladybugs in cans. Today, kids are growing up on grass without grasshoppers.

What's happened in those 50 years between my childhood and theirs is a wholesale change in the landscape: from fields to lawns, from thickets to foundation plantings, from woods to specimen trees.

The loss of wildlife that's accompanied that change says very clearly that there's something wrong with how we treat the land. We don't garden right. The style of landscape we prefer is not a good one. The reason we have to buy ladybugs in cans is that our own have starved to death.

By the time I came to my senses, the grouse and pheasants were gone. So were the owl and the small mammals that had been its food. The fox had left. Even the woodchuck had moved away. I began to list the missing. They included ladybugs, fireflies, grasshoppers, butterflies, even newts and toads.

On the other hand, we had some things we hadn't had before.

We had bags and bags of fertilizers in the shed. A pile of mulch behind the garage. And in the garage a tractor, a mower, a weed whacker, a leaf blower, and a couple of backpack sprayers. We had pests and the dozen pesticides needed to control them. We had a sprinkler system. Also a lawn company. And an arborist.

And we had more work than it was fun to do.

That got me to thinking. Why was it that this land that got along just fine without us when it was wild couldn't get along without us anymore? It seemed to me that since everything had happened all at once, there must be some connection between the loss of animals and this new helplessness.

So I sat down with a bunch of books on ecology to see what I could see, and the first thing I saw was that by wiping out tons of food—heaps of grapes, blackberries, rose hips; seeds and grain and nectar—we'd drained the fuel from our land. Food is what runs ecosystems, so one reason we have to put so much energy into maintaining our land is that it lacks the energy to run itself.

Put simply, if you want birds to eat your pests in June, you have to feed them berries in September.

But the answer to my question wasn't just a matter of calories. It was as though we'd put a pretzel stand where there used to be a supermarket. You can't run a supermarket on just bread, and you can't run an ecosystem on just lawn. We've all heard of biodiversity. What diversity comes down to is lots of different kinds of food for lots of different kinds of customers that together support the whole enterprise. Lawns and foundation plantings are a lot simpler than the wild landscapes they replace. And for an ecosystem, being simple is the same as being simple-minded.

Let's say we simplify our society by removing a few kinds of people, like carpenters or doctors. With each removal, we lose the knowledge that kind of person had, and the more kinds we remove, the more helpless our society becomes.

It's the same in natural communities. Each species has some bit of know-how that no other species has. Removing any plant or animal excises that portion of intelligence, and leaves the land more stupid.

An example is what my husband and I did just by mowing down the rushes around our pond. You don't think of rushes as having high IQs, but just by being able to grow at the water's edge, they provide habitat for dragonflies and frogs. So by cutting out that apparently minor talent, we also damaged the considerably greater intelligence involved in controlling the mosquito population.

I was pretty shocked by some of the things I learned. When we bag leaves and put them out with the trash, we're also throwing out next summer's generation of moths and butterflies that overwinter in leaf litter, and if we do that year after year, we eventually wipe out the wildflowers those moths and butterflies pollinate. And with those flowers' seeds goes a major food source for the ants that do more to turn and aerate soil than all the gardeners in the world.

You see, the whole system's wired together, like in the movie 2001. And what we've done to our land is what was done to Hal: We've pulled its circuits.

I'm not stretching a point here, either: Remember what Hal

was responsible for before he went haywire? He took care of the environmental systems on the ship. That's exactly what land is supposed to do when it's properly connected.

It's supposed to cool us in the summer and cut the winter wind. It's supposed to conserve water and make the soil richer. It's supposed to support all those animals that, in turn, control pests, pollinate flowers, plant seeds, decay litter, and recycle nutrients. These are all services that any piece of land can do—and do better, and do cheaper, than I can with all that junk in my garage.

So this isn't just a question of bringing butterflies into the garden. Restoring the ecology of suburban land is an act of environmental conservation every bit as important as preserving wilderness. And it is a viable alternative: Where you can't preserve, you can replant.

That's what we've been doing, and that's what I want you to do. Replanting is the most amazing adventure you can ever undertake, because it's like re-educating the land, or recovering lost data. The grass makes grain, the flowers make nectar, the bushes make fruit, and back come the animals, and away goes all that life-support equipment that seemed so necessary before.

I won't say that natural systems can be put back together as quickly as they were taken apart, or as easily. I don't say that they can ever again be just like they used to be. In these 40 years, the land has been subdivided over and over again, so the scale is much smaller than it's ever been before. Back when I was a kid, you could just neglect a corner, and it would come up raspberries and roses. Now neglected places come up weeds.

Still, there's a lot of damage we can undo. If lawns replaced fields, at least some of that lawn can be restored to meadow. We don't have to be stuck in this rut of rhododendrons. There's a crew of berries waiting to be reassembled into thickets. And if all we have left are stands of trees, we can make them into woods again. Even on the smallest scale—I mean a yard of less than an eighth of an acre—we can plant a landscape that's similar enough to wild examples that the land will get to work again.

By similar to wild examples, I mean of course that the emphasis should be on native plants, especially ones from our own region. I'm not fanatical on this subject; but I am practical. I don't like spraying and feeding and watering and staking, and I know a Black-eyed Susan doesn't need me to do anything but stick it in the ground.

But these new landscapes aren't just for our own convenience. Local plants are what local animals expect—and vice versa. Our birds expect dogwood fruits to be bite-size and oily; Chinese dogwoods have big, sugary fruits; they expect them to be dispersed by monkeys. So the tree is disappointed, and so are the birds, and that's why you don't see Chinese dogwoods popping up in the woods. Distant natives aren't wired in, either. Blue columbines from the Rockies won't work in the East, for example. Columbines here are pollinated by hummingbirds, but our hummingbirds expect them to be red.

Another thing that's happened in these 50 years is that plants that were common once—and columbine's a good example—now survive only in remnant, isolated populations. Columbine just drops its seeds; it could take a century just to move across a subdivision. So the third reason for choosing natives is that many won't come back unless we reintroduce them. Two of the species in our meadow are nearly extinct in our state—and not because they're fragile or hard to grow, but because their habitat is gone—ripped out, mowed down.

So the most important thing I mean by "similar to wild examples" is putting plants back where they belong, with their usual companions in the kind of place they're used to. That means azaleas in the woods, not on the lawn. And meadow flowers with meadow grasses, not stuck in a bed all by themselves.

It means learning to appreciate plants for their place within the community. No matter how exciting this or that individual might be—or how dull or common—what's most exciting is how the land comes to life again when they're all brought back together.

I look out my kitchen window over a dividing line of sorts: To one side, the lawn, just lying there looking green. To the other side, the meadow with its butterflies, dragonflies, grasshoppers, and finches. Even at night, you turn in that direction to hear the crickets or see the fireflies. That's where the swallows fly in summer. That's where the fox hunts in winter. And in the fall, when the dogwood thicket's fruiting and the meadow's going to seed, birds feast there all day long, while the lawn stays empty.

Birds are a good indicator of a healthy landscape. Their disappearance was my first clue that we'd done something wrong. Their reappearance was my first evidence that we were getting it right. If I needed any additional proof, I got it last fall when I went to a conference at a corporate park. There were acres and acres of lovely grounds, but the only birds around were a couple of crows. When I drove up my own driveway at the end of the day, flocks of robins, juncoes, and cedar waxwings flew up all over.

I guess birds must have terrific eyesight to have found our speck of natural vegetation. That's all it is—a speck, an ark. And if it's an ark, it's stranded in a sea of other people's lawns. So are the butterflies that depend on the milkweed that's been cut down. And the bullfrogs that can't live along mowed shores.

And the bluebirds.

The bluebirds were like that childhood story, about a boy and girl who go looking for the Bluebird of Happiness, only to find it in their own backyard. We couldn't see the bluebirds because we were looking at the land the wrong way. As though we owned not just the deed to it, but the right to its abuse. As soon as we gave it back what we had taken, there they were—first a male, then one wife—and then another—and by summer's end, quite a crew of youngsters.

Every year we watch those youngsters fledge and fly away, and every spring we worry about how they're getting on, because we know they're looking for suitable real estate to raise their own families—and we don't have room for them.

You do. You grow the plants; you plan the yards; you own the land. You are allowed to harm, but you don't have to. You are equally allowed to help.

I hope you choose to.

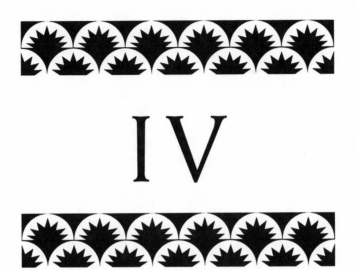

IV

LEARNING TO WORK

I liked to go with my mothers to the cornfields in planting time, when the spring sun was shining and the birds singing in the tree tops. How good it seemed to be out under the open sky, after the long months in our winter camp! A cottonwood tree stood at a turn of the road to our field. Every season a pair of magpies built their nest in it. They were saucy birds and scolded us roundly when we passed. How I used to laugh at their wicked scoldings!

I am afraid I did not help my mothers much. Like any young girl, I liked better to watch the birds than to work. Sometimes I chased away the crows. Our corn indeed had many enemies, and we had to watch that they did not get our crop. Magpies and crows destroyed much of the young corn. Crows were fond of pulling up the plants when they were a half inch or an inch high. Spotted gophers dug up the roots of the young corn, to nibble the soft seed.

When our field was all planted, Red Blossom used to go back and replant any hills that the birds had destroyed. Where she found a plant missing, she dug a little hole with her hand and dropped in a seed, or I dropped it in for her.

It was hard work, stooping to plant in the hot sun, and Red Blossom never liked having to go over the field a second time. "Those bad crows," she would groan, "they make us much trouble."

My grandmother Turtle made scarecrows to frighten away the birds. In the middle of the field she drove two sticks for legs, and bound two other sticks to them for arms; on the top, she fastened a ball of cast-away skins for a head. She belted an old robe about the figure to make it look like a man. Such a scarecrow looked wicked! Indeed I was almost afraid of it myself. But the bad crows, seeing the scarecrow never moved from its place, soon lost their fear, and came back.

In the months of midsummer, the crows did not give us much trouble; but, as the moon of Cherries drew near, they became worse than ever. The corn had now begun to ear, and crows and blackbirds came in flocks to peck open the green ears for the soft kernels. Many families now built stages in their fields, where the girls and young women of the household came to sit and sing as they watched that crows and other thieves did not steal the ripening grain.

We cared for our corn in those days, as we would care for a child; for we Indian people loved our fields as mothers love their children. We thought that the corn plants had souls, as children have souls, and that the growing corn liked to hear us sing, as children like to hear their mothers sing to them. Nor did we want the birds to come and steal our corn, after the hard work of planting and hoeing. Horses, too, might break into the field, or boys might steal the green ears and go off and roast them.

A watchers' stage was not hard to build. Four posts, forked at the tops, upheld beams, on which was laid a floor of puncheons, or split small logs, at the height of the full grown corn. The floor was about four feet long by three wide, roomy enough for two girls to sit together comfortably. Often a soft robe was spread on the floor. A ladder made of the trunk of a tree rested against the stage. The ladder had three steps.

A tree was often left standing in the field, to shade the watchers' stage. These poles could be shifted with the sun.

Girls began to go on the watchers' stage when about ten or twelve years of age, and many kept up the custom after they were grown up and married. Older women, working in the field and stopping to rest, often went on the stage and sang.

There was a watchers' stage in my mothers' field, where my sister, Cold Medicine, and I sat and sang; and in the two weeks of the ripening season we were singing most of the time. We looked upon watching our field as a kind of lark. We liked to sing, and now and then between songs we stood up to see if horses had broken into the field or if any boys were about. Boys of nine or ten years of age were quite troublesome. They liked to steal the green ears to roast by a fire in the woods.

I think Cold Medicine and I were rather glad to catch a boy stealing our corn, especially if he was a clan cousin, for then we could call him all the bad names we wished. "You bad, bad boy," we would cry. "You thief—stealing away from your own relatives! *Nah, nah*—go away." This was enough; no boy stayed after such a scolding.

Most of the songs we sang were love-boy songs, as we called them; but not all were. One that we younger girls were fond of singing—girls, that is, of about twelve years of age—was like this:

> You bad boys, you are all alike!
> Your bow is like a bent basket hoop;
> Your arrows are fit only to shoot into the air;
> You poor boys, you must run on the prairie barefoot,
>   because you have no moccasins!

This song we sang to tease the boys who came to hunt birds in the near-by woods. Small boys went bird hunting nearly every day. The birds that a boy snared or shot he gave to his grandparents to roast in the lodge fire; for, with their well-worn teeth, old people could no longer chew our hard, dried buffalo meat.

Here is another song; but, that you may understand it, I will explain to you what *eekupa* means. A girl loved by another girl as her own sister was called her *eekupa*. I think your word "chum," as you explain it, has nearly the same meaning. This is the song:

> "My *eekupa*, what do you wish to see?" you said to me.
> What I wish to see is the corn silk peeping out of the
>   growing ear;
> But what you wish to see is that naughty young man
>   coming!

Here is a song that older girls sang to tease young men of the Dog Society who happened to be going by:

You young man of the Dog Society, you said to me,
"When I go east with a war party, you will hear news of
    me how brave I am!"
I have heard news of you;
When the fight was on, you ran and hid;
And you still think you are a brave young man!
Behold, you have joined the Dog Society;
But I call you just plain *dog!*

Songs that we sang on the watchers' stage we called *meedaheeka*, or gardeners' songs. I have said that many of them were love-boy songs, and were intended to tease. We called a girl's sweetheart her love-boy. All girls, we know, like to tease their sweethearts.

At one side of our field Turtle had made a booth, diamond willows thrust in the ground in a circle, with leafy tops bent over and tied together. In this booth, my sister and I, with our mothers and old Turtle, cooked our meals. We started a fire in the booth as soon as we got to the field, and ate our breakfast often at sunrise. Our food we had brought with us, usually buffalo meat, fresh or dried. Fresh meat we laid on the coals to broil. Dried meat we thrust on a stick and held over the fire to toast.

Sometimes we brought a clay cooking pot, and boiled squashes. We were fond of squashes and ate many of them. We sometimes boiled green corn and beans. My sister and I shelled the corn from the cob. We shelled the beans or boiled them in the pod. My grandmother poured the mess in a wooden bowl, and we ate with spoons which she made from squash stems. She would split a stem with her knife and put in a little stick to hold the split open.

I do not think anything can taste sweeter than a mess of fresh corn and beans, in the cool morning air, when the birds are twittering and the sun is just peeping over the tree tops.

SWEET CORN

Sweet corn was our family's weakness. We were prepared to resist atheistic Communism, immoral Hollywood, hard liquor, gambling and dancing, smoking, fornication, but if Satan had come around with sweet corn, we at least would have listened to what he had to sell. We might not have bought it but we would've had him in and given him a cup of coffee. It was not amazing to learn in eighth-grade science that corn is sexual, each plant containing both genders, male tassel and female flower, propagating in our garden after dark. Sweet corn was so delicious, what could have produced it except sex? Sunday after church, when the pot roast was done and the potatoes were boiled and mashed and a pot of water was boiling—only then would Dad run out with a bushel basket and pick thirty ears of corn. We shucked it clean in five seconds per ear and popped it in the pot for a few minutes. A quick prayer, a little butter and salt, and that is as good as it gets. People have searched the world over for something better and didn't find it because it's not there. There's nothing better, not even sex. People have wanted sex to be as good as sweet corn and have worked hard to improve it, and afterward they lay together in the dark, and said, "Det var dejligt." ("That was so wonderful.") "Ja, det var." "Men det var ikke saa godt som frisk mais." ("But it wasn't as good as fresh sweet corn.") "Ney."

Thomas Fox Averill

TO GROW

CORN

I don't know why I did it, or what they thought, but the summer of my fourth-grade year I asked my parents for some of our Kansas back yard so that I might grow corn. They gave me a small plot, no bigger than the area rug in my bedroom, and bought me seed. I dug the earth as deep as I could, read the directions on the seed packet, planted the shriveled kernels of seed corn, and waited.

There is no tradition in my family for vegetable gardening. Yes, my mother always grew a profusion of hollyhocks, bachelor buttons and her favorite flower, daisies. And my father, who loves roses, still cultivates the many bushes that surround their home. When we first moved to Topeka, Kansas, in 1953, our split-level house was built on prairie; few trees provided shade. My parents planted a slim arc of weeping willow in the front yard, and it grew up to bend its thin branches down, perfect for whistles and whips. But I was first with vegetables.

Corn is a dramatic plant, a good choice for the first thing to grow. Many other plants—lettuce, carrots, dill—break tentatively through the earth towards sky, their first slips of green like a mist, like a fungus, like mold clutching the earth. Not corn. Suddenly one morning my corn was sprouted, with leaves as broad as the green tailfeathers of my parakeet, Paul Bunyan, had they drifted down and stuck into the ground. In the next sixty days, my corn grew sixty inches, sometimes at a rate of more than an inch a day.

I have been told that farmers can actually hear corn grow, hear it slipping up through its joints, its firm waxy leaves creaking out from the stalk, the stalk itself thrusting up with the sound of a hesitant periscope. I never heard my corn grow, but its progress was exciting. I measured that progress with my own small body: knee high, belly high, chest, then shoulder, then head high. It tasseled, with hair blonder than mine. When I weeded around the stalks, pollen fell on my arms. Wiped into the skin, it left small marks, like tiny pieces of crayon: yellow, mustard, ocher.

In a Kansas August, corn can drink incredible amounts. I sat near the small patch with the garden hose in my hand, filling the cracks in the parched earth, keeping the corn the brightest of greens.

And then the ears. One, then two, sometimes three per stalk. Perhaps I had only twenty stalks, but I was rich with potential harvest. Again, growth was remarkable: from pencil stubs to cigars to full-sized ears the shape of a torch, the corn pushed and swelled inside the husks. The silk at the tip of the ear turned coarse, then browned. Day by day, I felt the corn, kernel by fat kernel, until I grew impatient.

My mother put my corn on our dinner menu. She readied a huge pot of boiling water, then helped me pick my ready ears. We husked them, the thick, tough layers littering the garden, the silk everywhere, the bright yellow kernels of exposed corn glowing in the evening sun. And we ate. The six of us in my family ate the corn. We held it up as though toasting each other with it. We lavished it with butter and salt. We made our way up and down the ears, smiling and talking. We demanded more, and more, until all of it was eaten, until our faces glistened with butter, until our teeth were littered with corn flecks, until everyone was full of congratulations for "Tommy's corn." And, because memory has such a keen edge, I have never had better corn, nor been prouder of an accomplishment as a gardener.

GREEN BEANS

In the summer of 1971, I moved into a one-hundred-year-old farmhouse ten miles southwest of Lawrence, Kansas. I was twenty-two years old, and ready to begin graduate studies at the University of Kansas. I was also ready to garden in more space than my usual small patch of back yard.

The Freeman place had been abandoned for several years, and I had to search for what previous occupants had used as garden plot. As on many abandoned places in Kansas, the evidence of gardening was there. Along a fence line just south of the outhouse I found tall shoots of lacy asparagus, three feet high and already going to little red balls of seed. I located a soft rectangle, maybe twenty by sixty feet, next to that fence, and knew it was garden when I found fragments of the rags someone had torn into strips to tie tomato plants to the large stakes I eventually discovered in the nearby empty barn. On the far edge of the rectangle, choked in weeds, rhubarb waited for breathing room; strawberries, their tiny whitestar blossoms shaded by pokeweed and bindweed, by stalks of sunflower and jimsonweed, asked only for their share of sun; a growth of winter onions, tangled and crowded, rioting for space, promised immediate flavor in salads, soups and stews, insisted on what they could do, how far they could go, if only given the chance. And so I dug the soil around the perennials, burned the middle, roto-tilled, hoed, and planted summer crops: tomato, corn, squash, melon, okra, pepper, and green beans.

That fall I had a fine crop, but not enough to carry me very far into the winter. A new idea in gardening took hold of me: the next spring I would plant so much crop that, frozen, or buried, or dried, or pickled, or canned, I would eat my vegetables the year around. Thus began what I still think of as the year of the green bean.

Remember, I was not a very experienced gardener. But I was young, and hardworking, and especially ambitious in the spring of 1972, the beginning of the green-bean year. Besides the garden plot I had discovered, there were new ones to be made. The biggest of those was a half-acre that had been the corral: a fenced area where horses and cows had wandered in and out of the two barns. This packed earth was overgrown in the woodiest weeds, everything from the hollow jimsonweed and wild sunflower to the more pernicious cedar sprout, sumac, Virginia creeper, and poison ivy. I cleared it with a corn knife and then a scythe, then burned it. I planted pound after pound of potato. I sowed the tiny black seeds of carrots and the spiked seeds of beets in early spring. Then, in early summer, when the soil was warm to the touch throughout the night, I planted row after row after row of green beans.

Years of horse and cattle droppings enriched the soil, but that earth was hard-packed, and the hoe sprang back at first as I cultivated between my rows of beans, working against the proliferation of weeds whose seeds always come to life in the ground of a new garden plot. Green beans are hardy plants, thrusting up with springy resistance, their leaves broadening, their stalks thickening, their small white flowers blossoming, falling off and soon replaced with the tiniest snap of a bean, shaped like the crescent of an early moon. Then the beans lengthen very quickly, so quickly that, like corn, you might almost believe a sensitive ear could hear it.

I didn't know how many beans I'd get from ten rows, each row twenty feet long. I was raising chickens at the same time, and I bought chicken feed in fifty-pound sacks. By July, I spent my Saturday mornings picking nothing but beans: two or three feed sacks full each picking. I spent Saturday afternoon washing them, snapping off the ends, pressure cooking them in sterile jars, and waiting for the canning lids to depress. Saturday nights I lifted jar after jar onto the kitchen and dining room shelves I had built with my housemates: we wanted to see the fruits of our labor.

And so July, and August, and September passed, our shelves filling with jar after jar of green beans, enough to eat, I soon realized, for several years. This profusion was joined by mason jars of tomatoes, pickled peppers, beets, pickled okra, carrots, corn, even sauerkraut. In late summer, we dug a deep pit, about six feet in diameter, in the old corral garden. We lined it with straw, laid in our three-hundred-pound potato crop, topped it with straw, and then earth. From a small hole in the middle, plugged with straw, we could reach in and find potatoes all through the freezing winter. And, in December, in the spirit of doing for ourselves, we fermented mead in old Vess quart soda bottles; we placed them next to green beans to age. They would help us celebrate the holiday season. Everything—jars lined up on the shelves, potato mound waiting in the corral garden, bottles of mead, bags of drying onions hanging from the ceiling of the side porch—told us that we had worked hard, and well, and would eat abundantly through the winter.

One cold December Saturday, an old Chevrolet chugged down the slightly graveled road that went by the farmhouse. It pulled into the dirt of the drive. A small man in a cheap suit climbed out, reached for his black briefcase, and headed to our door. His suit shone in the sun like the body of a housefly. I met him on the porch in dirty overalls, asked him his business.

"It's not business, it's pleasure," he said. He set his briefcase on the cement porch floor and pulled out a brochure. "It's the pleasure of bringing folks like you, who live out in the country, all the groceries you have to drive to town for." He handed me the colorful brochure. "All at very competitive prices. With free delivery, too."

I should have told him I wasn't interested. Should have sent him packing. Should not have invited him in. But I did. I was vain, and, before I turned down his offer, I wanted to show off how few groceries we'd need that winter. I wanted to show him row after row of jar after jar of green beans.

So he came in and sat at the table, surrounded by the fruits of our labor. My two roommates gathered with us. We let him make his pitch. We nodded, and smiled at each other, and rolled our eyes. We let all our hours of work—planting, hoeing, picking, washing, sterilizing jars, pressure cooking, stacking—make us smug as we listened to this eager man extol the virtues of his frozen pizza and peas, Wonder bread and hush puppies, canned tuna and tamales. He had the same pride in his larder, it turned out, as we did. And, forty-five minutes into his enthusiastic spiel, we began to wonder when, and then *if*, he was going to stop.

Then he did stop. Because there was an explosion. A few chunks of glass flew through the room like shrapnel. We were sprayed with thick liquid. We looked at each other, shocked, pale, fearful. Then we looked above our heads, in one corner of the room, to see which of the mead bottles had exploded, leaving the walls and table sticky with fermented honey.

In my relief I began to laugh. But the young food salesman was not laughing. He was the only one who had been wounded. A thin line of blood had puckered up on his hand, the one that held the brochure. He stared at the blood, then rushed to pack his briefcase. He stood up. "I don't think you're serious customers," he said, and then he was gone.

I remember thinking that I was, at least, a serious gardener. And now someone who had to get serious about cleaning up a quickly drying mead mess.

"If it's going to ferment till it breaks the bottles," said one of my roommates, "I think we better drink it up as soon as we can." He put on some gloves, went to the shelf and pulled down a bottle. He used a church key to pop off the top, and poured us each a glass.

So we cleaned mead, and drank mead. By the time we'd finished our second bottle, we were hungry, and I said, "We're trying the mead, let's try everything else." And so we made a huge vegetable soup with one mason jar of each thing we'd preserved, and we added potatoes from the mound and onions from the porch, and we ate and we drank until we couldn't move. Because we didn't need to move. We had all we needed, surrounding us, on our shelves.

PEANUTS

Before I was finished with graduate school, before I left the Freeman place, I wanted to grow all the vegetables I'd read about but had never gardened: like kohlrabi, brussels sprouts, bok choy. And peanuts.

Especially peanuts. Some people insisted they wouldn't do well in Kansas, that they needed a longer, warmer growing season. But Kansas can vary from year to year: the first hard frost can come anywhere from early September to late November. So I took a chance, ordered seed peanuts, and planted two thirty-foot rows in the same corral garden where I'd learned to restrain my enthusiasm for green beans.

Peanuts are grown in small mounds, or hills. They leaf into tender plants that look like a cross between shamrocks and soybeans. As they grow, they produce root tendrils that need to be covered with soil: so, the mound around them grows, too. The very tips of these root tendrils will make the pod, or shell: late in the season, if you dig one up, a fully formed peanut shell, the size of a child's finger, will be ready for the nut. But it will be empty. In one of those miracles of plant life, sometimes within a mere several-day period, the peanut plant withers in its late season and suddenly decides to put all of its energy into the seed. Peanut shells can go from hollow to bursting in less than a week.

I was very interested in when that week might be, because I was in the process of moving away from the Freeman place. I had married the January before, and my wife and I had decided that our lives might be more convenient with running water (only a pump on the Freeman place, and only an outhouse, too) and a consistent heat supply (we'd warmed ourselves by the sweat of our brows, the wood we cut and split and kept burning in two woodstoves). The Freemans had given us permission, after we moved, to come back weekends through the fall to harvest whatever might be left in the garden. That meant we could watch our peanuts through the growing season.

Which, fortunately, was a long, warm season. Or maybe that wasn't so fortunate. Because the Freemans were fixing up the place so that one of their relatives could move in. We'd told some neighbors down the road, young people like ourselves, that they might come down and forage whatever was ripe.

One day in late September, Glenn Freeman gave me a call. "We scared up those hippies down the road. They were in your garden, stealing everything they could carry."

"I told them they could," I said. "It'll just go to waste."

"Well, I don't like people wandering onto my property."

I promised Glenn I'd talk to the neighbors the following weekend, when Jeffrey Ann and I hoped to harvest our peanut crop.

And I did, on the way to the garden. When we arrived at the Freeman place, the Freemans were there, working inside. I walked onto the front porch. I stopped. Resting against the front door jamb, just four feet in front of me, was a rifle.

"Glenn?" I called.

He came to the door, looked at me, then at the rifle in the doorway. He didn't say a word.

"I talked to the neighbors. They won't be down again. Meant to tell you, too, to take whatever you want. We just don't have time to harvest everything this year."

"We have our own garden in town," said Glenn.

The peanuts were still hollow, and we picked a few half-ripe tomatoes, some winter squash, the last of the okra, and left.

The next week, we went back for the peanuts. But there *were* no peanuts, just two rows of freshly dug mounds. We were stunned, thinking of our neighbors, or drive-by poachers—then the Freemans. Glenn was the likeliest thief, and so we drove to his house in town. We pulled into the drive, past the house, toward their garage. Glenn's pickup truck, gun rack empty, was parked there.

Sure enough, the peanuts hung from their tops in a fringe all around the Freeman's back porch. I pulled a shell from its shriveled root, cracked it open. A plump nut rested inside. Glenn Freeman, who had no doubt heard us pull in, appeared at his back door.

"These are *our* peanuts," I said. "We were just out at the farm."

"Well, they're my peanuts, now," he said. "You don't live there anymore."

"But you said we could harvest the rest of the garden."

"And you said I could have whatever ripened up," Glenn reminded me. "Said you didn't have time for it all. We thought last week was your last time out there."

"We wanted our peanuts," I said. "The rest doesn't matter. The peanuts do matter."

"It's late October. You've been off the place two months now. You're not paying rent."

"I want the peanuts, Glenn," I said. I reached up and began to pull down peanut plants.

I had no idea what Glenn Freeman would do. I remembered the gun on the porch on the farm. I balanced my fear against all the work of planting, creating hills, watering with bucket after bucket of cold well water, all the waiting for ripeness as the plant transformed into something edible. I took one armful of peanut plants to my truck, and went back for another.

"I've never grown peanuts before," I said. "I want this first crop."

"Leave me a couple of plants, will you?" he asked.

I looked at him, incredulous, bolder now that I knew he would not stop me, that nothing would stop me.

"I went to the work of digging them out," he said.

I nodded in agreement. He stood, arms folded over his chest, on the porch. I left him a generous number of plants.

Just before I climbed in my truck, he walked out into his driveway. "They're good plants," he said. "You were lucky. Be sure to hang them up, let them dry all the way."

"I will," I said. "And I'll eat them. Every one of them."

"So will I," he said. "Peanuts are my favorite."

"Hey," I said, "thanks for digging them for me." And that was the last thing I ever said to Glenn Freeman, on whose place I had grown so many vegetables, grown as a gardener, grown.

HABAÑEROS

These days I grow in smaller plots, what my wife calls "envelopes." Our old house is shaded by huge ash trees in the south yard. Sweet gum and silver maples grow on the parking west of the house, and elms line the north parking. It's taken several years to discover where a small patch of ground might find enough sun to produce a crop: lettuce, beets, radishes, carrots, spinach and chard, a few small rows of each in the spring; then tomatoes and basil in the summer. And peppers, too.

My wife is the expert tomato planter. I cultivate the basil, and the peppers. But not just any kind of pepper: only those not easily found in the store. My favorite to grow is the habañero, the hottest of all the peppers in the world. Very close in kind to the goat pepper and the Scotch Bonnet, the habañero can be five times hotter than the jalapeno pepper. It has a sweet heat, a fire in the mouth that burns intensely but rapidly, and mellows more quickly than the jalapeno.

Of all the peppers I've grown, it is loveliest in its plant. It starts with a profusion of leaves, as though to shade whatever might grow under it. I've always had short bushes, maybe two feet tall, shaped like little umbrellas. And under the canopy, tiny white blossoms come and go rapidly, turning to the smallest green balls. These grow rapidly until they look like green lanterns, an inch long at most. As they open, they turn a bright orange, like little suns ready to set.

When they set in the mouth, you feel as though you have, indeed, swallowed the sun, a sun that might refuse to continue setting, might continue to burn all night in your mouth, and your throat, and your belly. Then it mellows into its sweet dusky taste and you want the sun again.

Much is made of peppers these days. The variety available in supermarkets grows every year. Catalogues offer fresh peppers, dried peppers, pickled peppers, powdered peppers, smoked peppers, pepper sauces, pepper jelly, pepper candy. Newspaper articles trumpet the virtue of capsicum as stimulator of endorphins, or as topical painkiller. Most often, the appeal is directed at men, for eating peppers and being a man, being macho, have come to be synonymous. One catalogue I received in the mail offered: "Island Heat," "Scorned Woman," "The Hot Box," "Arizona Gunslinger," "Hawaiian Passion," "Satan's Revenge," "Melinda's XXX," "Six-Pack From Hell," "Beaver Extra Hot," and "I Am On Fire—Ready to Die." The description of that last one read: "Please note that this product is not simply rated XXX. Nick ten Velde feels that it warrants an XXXX rating."

I truly like hot and spicy foods, the tongue-burning hot sauces, devilish barbecue marinades, jerked chicken, curries and chili-pickled garlic. And I suppose I understand marketing in general enough to understand the not-so-subliminal connection being made between tantalizing the taste buds and sexual pleasure, between tasting the new and exotic and the wicked sin of biting the first apple in the Garden of Eden, between swilling down hot salsa and throwing down shots of whiskey like a cowboy in a frontier saloon. But I don't feel macho when cultivating my habañeros in a small envelope just to the east of my ash tree. Instead, I feel connected.

As I garden, I grow. A relationship with any patch of earth, with any ancient and honorable plant, with any dream of eating what has been nurtured through dream, care and sweat, is, finally, a relationship with the self. For me, from the time I was ten and suddenly felt the impulse to make corn grow in the prairie of my suburban back yard, gardening has been one of the grounding experiences of my life, has defined who I am on this earth. As I tend the lives of plants, I tend my own life. I take pride in them, and in myself. I surround myself with them. I work for them, and fight for them. I grow. The whole process is so simple, I realize, that it must be sacred.

TSIL

The sacrament often comes in the eating. And the cooking precedes the eating. Recently, I've been studying those foodstuffs indigenous to the Western Hemisphere, and creating recipes that use "Pre-Columbian-New World-American-Indigenous-Western Hemisphere" ingredients only. Because all those names between the hyphens seem too ethno- or Euro-centric, I'm partial to the TSIL, which is the name for the Hopi Kachina who, in a foot race, stuffs hot peppers in the mouths of the runners he overtakes. Because of my love for chilies, I've borrowed the word TSIL, and used it to mean all the plants and animals indigenous to the Western Hemisphere: the foods Europeans knew nothing about before 1492, when Columbus sailed the ocean blue. After all, the whole wide world has been stuffing hot peppers in our mouths ever since.

Many TSIL foods are essential parts of our diets, are common in our pantries, refrigerators, larders. I have written about four favorites: corn, beans, peanuts, and chilies. Add to those: potatoes, tomatoes, squash, vanilla, avocados, chocolate. Or the less publicized: berries (strawberry, blackberry, gooseberry, raspberry, cranberry); nuts (pinon, pecan, black walnut, cashew, peanut); fruits (pawpaw, guava, tomatillo, pineapple); meats (buffalo and turkey, but also Gulf shrimp and all kinds of fish); in short, everything from the roots of Yucca cactus and Jerusalem artichokes to the Great Plains sage and Mexican oregano to spice them up.

In my gardening and cooking and eating, I am exploring an American world of tastes, textures, combinations. I learn both the common and exotic. And my relationship with all these plants has become a way of cultivating my mind, of making connections, of trying to understand my connection with those Native American people who had my best interests in mind so many years ago as they gathered greens and herbs, as they sorted the seed of corn, as they saved the best beans and dried them and secured them in a sacred place, as they learned the cycle of the peanut, one of the easiest nuts to crack, or as they grew peppers for spice, for medicine, for color, for the power of capsicum oil to kill the bacteria in the stomach.

My interest has taken me into a new language: Spanish. *Sí, es el idioma de los conquistadores*, but that tongue best describes much of what was known of the New World. My interest has taken me to Mexico, where I have learned to cook those things which combine all worlds.

CHICKEN TINGA,

for example:

Shredded meat of that Old World bird
Rice from the orient cooked in the chicken broth
Sauce of:
"xi-tomate" (the Aztec word we still use for that fruit without fruit's sweet-
     ness, that vegetable without a vegetable's firmness and texture, that
     kin to the deadly nightshade) tomato
chipotle peppers (smoked red jalapenos)
limes
garlic and onion, my favorites from the Old World

¡Que delicioso!

And my interest has taken me into new and interesting ways of preparing food. I entered a holiday recipe competition sponsored by my local newspaper. To celebrate Columbus Day, I suggested to the editors that we honor Native Americans and Native America by cooking exclusively with pre-Columbian ingredients. I enclosed my recipe for Black Bean Gooseberry Enchiladas, to be served with "New World" Guacamole. To my great surprise, I won ten dollars, a certificate, and saw my recipe published.

People reacted strangely to Black Bean and Gooseberry Enchiladas. Some indulged me with kindly stares.

"Saw your recipe in the paper," said others. "It looked interesting, but hard to make."

"What?" others said. "Black beans and what?"

"Gooseberries," I said. "If you can't find them fresh, you buy them canned in the supermarket. And these enchiladas are really good," I insisted.

They nodded in the kind of assent that does not mean agreement: it means an unwillingness to argue.

I'd like to share the recipe, because, for me, cultivating, harvesting, cooking, and eating are all different ways of thinking about food. But first, a note. Some of the cooking techniques are European, no doubt. This is *not* an authentic recipe from any particular time and place. When I ask you to quickly heat corn tortillas in corn oil, I know that Native Americans did not process oil as we do today. I am aware that this recipe could not have been enjoyed by anyone in the "New World" in 1491. Nowhere in the Western Hemisphere could this list of ingredients have been gathered in the same place at the same time. And, yes, the dish requires a fair amount of what cookbooks often call "preparation time." Many people who prepare meals seem to resent the time involved. I do myself, on certain days. Contemporary America seems increasingly attracted to "fast" food, with "kwik" preparation time. In my experience, fast food tends to be eaten quickly, and with little enjoyment. I know, because I eat it myself.

But on many days, many evenings, the pleasure of being in the kitchen, slowly preparing food, is unsurpassed. It is akin to the pleasure of gardening. The time spent is doubly rewarded. The pleasure in the garden, growing, and the pleasure in the kitchen during preparation are matched by the pleasure in the food and the meal itself. The care and feeding of our human community bind us with place, with time, with tradition. When we lose our sense of place, of history, of tradition, we ourselves are lost. As for the care and feeding of our friends, our families, our communities, we cannot afford to resent it, belittle it, or try to minimize it. Instead, we must cultivate it, taste it, and grow.

BLACK BEAN AND
GOOSEBERRY ENCHILADAS

One cup black beans, dry
One chili anchos (dried)
One can (16 oz.) gooseberries (or two cups fresh)
*One dozen corn tortillas (preferably blue)
*Corn oil
Four large red tomatoes
One tablespoon medium-hot chili powder
Salt
Three ripe avocados
Two medium yellow tomatoes
**Three big fresh jalapeno peppers
***Two tablespoons sage vinegar (crumble sage, preferably from Ameri-
*   can sagebrush, in vinegar and let sit overnight or longer)*

Cook black beans in water with the dried chili anchos until they
are tender. Add drained, slightly rinsed gooseberries, in an
amount equal to black beans.

Make enchilada sauce by buzzing the four large red tomatoes in a
blender. Put them in a saucepan with the chili powder and two of
the jalapenos, cut into fine pieces. Cook for at least an hour, until
sauce thickens.

Quickly heat corn tortillas in hot corn oil, but do not cook to
crispness. Dip tortillas in enchilada sauce, lay flat, and spoon on
two tablespoons of the black bean and gooseberry mixture. Roll
up to make a tube. Set on plate. When all twelve tortillas are on
plate, cut in half and push out to the edges of the plate to form a
circle.

Make a guacamole from the avocados, yellow tomatoes, sage vinegar, and remaining jalapeno pepper, everything chopped fine

and mixed together. Put guacamole in the space you created in the middle of the plate. Spoon guacamole onto enchiladas.

*Corn is incredibly adaptable, so much so that it is the foundation for many of our twentieth-century products, both food (corn starch, corn oil, and corn syrup are ubiquitous in supermarket selections) and nonfood (toothpaste, adhesives, and cosmetics). No part of our lives remains untouched by corn, and no plant was more important to the Native Americans of North and Central America, to whom it was the staple of their existence, both physical and spiritual.

**For less heat, cut out the membranes that hold the seeds—they hold most of the capsicum oil that gives the chilies their heat—and do it with gloves on. If you don't wear gloves, then you must be sure not to touch your eyes or other sensitive body parts through the rest of the evening. And don't touch anyone else's, either.

***Nothing beats the pungency of the sage of the Great Plains. Old World sage is often packaged in the leaf or ground into powder. I pick sage from the Flint Hills of Kansas, put it in an old wine bottle with half a dozen arbol chilies, and cover it with vinegar. This both preserves it and allows me to control its flavor, since coming across a leaf of Kansas sage in a dish can make you forget anything else.

Gary Nabhan

INVISIBLE EROSION: THE RISE AND FALL OF NATIVE FARMING

I

We're beyond the end of a long runway, at the bottom of a dry irrigation ditch. Just a few hundred yards away, a jet lifts up off the ground and thunders over our heads. My three-year-old daughter's hands fly up to cover her ears, and she hunches over in fear. Horrified by the deafening noise of the aircraft above her, she looks around for shelter. But the ditch bottom is largely barren clay, dried and cracked. The few saltbushes nearby are whipped violently by the tailwinds of the jet. Failing to find any cover that will muffle the roar, she cries out to be held, and runs toward me down the ditch.

Fish as large as my daughter once swam down this prehistoric Hohokam Canal. The canal itself is among the largest built in pre-Columbian North America. Among the fish it formerly carried was *Xyrauchen texanus,* the humpback sucker, reaching up to a yard in length and weighing thirteen pounds. Humpbacks were once common throughout the Salt and Gila watersheds in central Arizona; they frequented the main ditches of the River Pima Indians, who came after the Hohokam. Today, elderly Pima men can still describe with some flair this fish, which they call *o'omuni:* "It has a yellow belly [and] looks like trout, more or less, but the back is high, the tail thin, and it comes down like this . . . " they say, shaping with their hands the low spot between the hump and the tail. For Sylvester Matthias, its actions are also well remembered: "*O'omuni* behave like carp, not [like those which move] in schools. They are fast, and stay on the side where the river is cutting under the bank, so they can go under it and hide. And they are *slippery*. . . ."

As late as 1949, these suckers were being caught in commercial quantities in the Salt—up to six tons in a single spawning season. Even then, the humpback was declining because of dams that blocked their movements and that created temperatures below reservoirs too cold for spawning. During the last few decades, elderly Pima farmers express surprise if they even spot a single sucker while draining their ditches. Exotic fish, introduced into the reservoirs on the Gila and Salt, prey upon them. Biologist W. L. Minckley has shown that the humpback sucker was becoming scarce in the Salt and Gila rivers by the 1950s, and in the Colorado by the 1960s: "As with the Colorado squawfish, this unique animal is now extirpated in the Gila River basin, where it formerly occupied all large streams." Only recent reintroduction efforts have kept it from permanently vanishing from the Colorado, Gila, and Salt for good.

The only one I have seen alive was in an outdoor museum, where it hovered in front of an underwater window, staring back at the tourists who stared at it. Its mouth slowly opened and closed while it vacuumed the pond floor, and its grayish dorsal fin swept back and forth atop a bony, olive-colored hump. This one was younger than the few wild-born humpbacks left in the rivers. As Minckley has quipped, the viability of the humpback sucker population remaining in natural habitats is comparable to that in the nearby retirement community of Sun City, Arizona: "Most are too old to reproduce."

Why, I wondered, did a fish become imperiled after it had survived harvesting by streamside desert dwellers for centuries? Minckley has identified the humpback and five other large fish from the prehistoric Hohokam village of Snaketown on the Gila. Although never abundant in Hohokam sites, Minckley believes they were easily accessible to irrigation farmers in both prehistoric and early historic times: "Diversion of water and drying of a canal segment made them simple prey to man and other animals."

When the Spaniards first contacted the River Pima culture in the 1690s, they described this tribe as subsisting on "the innumerable fish that abound in the river," a diet *supplemented* with maize and beans. Is it a coincidence that the many varieties of maize and beans formerly grown by the Pima were lost from their diet at about the time that the fish began to vanish?

I think not. Over the last decade, I have sporadically assisted my former teacher, Amadeo Rea, with his life work of documenting the changes in the economy and habitat of the River Pima. In the process, I have become convinced that both cultivated and wild food resources were imperiled whenever the cultural landscape radically changed along the Gila and Salt rivers. These changes initiated the abandonment of some traditional Pima crops long before improved, modern crop varieties could have been introduced to supersede them. Like the Hohokam before them, the Pima lost everything whenever they lost control of the river that fed their canals. When the river was kept from recharging floodplain habitats with moisture and nutrients, both wild and domesticated resources would decrease in frequency and in productivity. Wildlife would also become scarce. The drying of a river and the ditches it fed would trigger the drying-up of gene pools.

Compared to the soil erosion evident on stretches of the downcut channel of the Gila River, such genetic erosion is relatively imperceptible. Few of us have the foresight to catch the fall of genes from a single crop, let alone recognize the impending collapse of whole farming communities as it begins to occur. If we do, we are initially hard-pressed to associate these losses with their ultimate causes.

Today it is hard to imagine how either the Hohokam or Pima ways of farming worked. Only six of the 1750 miles of Hohokam canals in metropolitan Phoenix remain intact, the rest having been eroded, bulldozed, and built upon over the last century. After digging and sampling two miles of backhoed trenches across Hohokam canals, archaeologist Bruce Masse recovered only three pollen grains of a single domesticated plant: maize.

Inspection of a grain of pollen through the ocular lens of a microscope hardly offers a profound sense of the former agricultural grandeur of a region. Over much of the continent, where fields once flashed green with a dozen native crops, palynologists find a few pollen grains of domesticated plants per gallon of soil. Where prehistoric women prepared succotash day after day, archaeologists are lucky to discover more than a handful of desiccated corncobs and squash rinds. Where vibrant farming cultures nurtured fields for generations, the soil is now covered by offices, feedlots, slaughterhouses, subdivisions, and shopping centers.

To recover a sense of what native farming once was, we must cultivate our imaginations—allow pollen grains to bloom, becoming mixed fields. The asphalt, metal, blood, and manure of the last few centuries must be stripped away, exposing fertile soils once again. Seven thousand years of plant culture, buried beneath our feet, must be unearthed. America before Columbus was not a wasteland, nor an untouched wilderness. It held home ground for farmers; vast territory for hunter-gatherers; and places where farming and foraging fused themselves into the same cultures. To feel at home here, to learn from our predecessors on this continent, each of us must kneel on the ground, put an ear to the earth, and listen.

I I

In the 1530s, the lost party of Alvar Núñez Cabeza de Vaca arrived at an Indian village on a large river somewhere in Texas; there, they were greeted by an odd sound:

At sunset, we reached a hundred Indian huts and, as we approached, the people came out to receive us, shouting frightfully, and slapping their thighs. They carried perforated gourds . . . which are ceremonial objects of great importance. They use them only at dances, or as medicine, to cure, and nobody dares touch them but themselves. They claim that those gourds have healing virtues, and that they come from Heaven, not being found in that country; nor do they know where they came from, except that the rivers carry them down when they rise and overflow the land. . . .

Gourds such as those may have been the first plants cultivated north of Mexico. Around seven thousand years ago they apparently were grown in small gardens in southern Illinois, as the archaeological reconstructions of David and Nancy Asch have demonstrated. And yet, this crop, in and of itself, hardly changed the diet of Eastern Woodland hunter-gatherers. They continued to rely on hickory nuts, walnuts, and groundnut tubers as their staples for many more centuries. Nonetheless, gourd cultivation may have begun the process of seed selection, saving, and sowing that has involved more than two hundred and thirty generations of Native Americans north of Mexico. The gourds that Cabeza de Vaca saw were recognized as a gift—something peculiar in the plant kingdom, and something fitting human needs.

We do not know what species of gourd the Indians danced with that day, four hundred and fifty years ago. But archaeologists have recovered from ancient Woodland sites in Illinois both the bottlegourd, *Lagenaria*, and *Cucurbita pepo*, the same species as the wildly colored ornamental gourds and jack-o'-lantern pumpkins found in fruit markets at Halloween time. In early prehistoric times, *pepo* fruits were undoubtedly smaller, with harder rinds. These gourds could have provided bowls and canteens to people who lacked pottery, or supplied greasy seeds to mix with other vegetable foods.

The early gourds grown along the Illinois River may not have been native that far north in the Mississippi watershed. Although egg-shaped *pepos* are sometimes found today on riverbanks from Illinois through Missouri to Texas, they are usually thought to be escapees from recent cultivation. Some geneticists and archaeologists speculate that gourds originally were traded northward, possibly from Tamaulipas (just south of Texas), where truly wild relatives of these gourds persist to this day. Other scholars, such as Charles Heiser, leave open the option that gourds may have been independently domesticated in the Eastern Woodlands and in central Mexico.

Regardless of their place of origin, cultivated gourds and related squashes have undergone considerable evolution in North America. Over seven millennia of growing in what is now the United States, *Cucurbita pepo* did indeed become native to the northern soil. Thanks to Native American horticulturists, squashes and gourds floresced into numerous folk varieties not found anywhere else in the world. It was once thought that the entire vegetable repertoire of early North American gardeners was imported, part and parcel, from Mesoamerica. Although it still serves certain geopoliticians to claim that North America borrowed all its crops from other lands, this notion finally has bitten the dust. Much earlier than the arrival of Mexican corn varieties about 1500 years ago, Eastern Woodland horticulturists domesticated several seed plants on their own, such as sumpweed, giant ragweed, and sunflower. Combine these natives with later introductions of common beans, bottlegourds, tobacco, and goosefoot, and Eastern Woodland farmers had a wide array of crops in use by 1000 A.D.

One of the domesticates native to North America is the sumpweed or marshelder. Known to scientists as *Iva annua*, this sunflower analog was found in association with humans in the Mississippi watershed nine thousand years ago. By 4000 B.C., this oily seeded annual was intentionally cultivated and in widespread use throughout the lower Midwest. And, with cultural selection over the following two thousand years, its seeds show impressive size increases. Knotweed, maygrass, little barley, giant ragweed, Jerusalem artichokes, and sunflower may have become common garden plants in the Eastern deciduous forest zones, although the latter was the only food crop that emerged as a domesticate fully distinct from its wild ancestor.

Some scholars guess that the success of the domesticated sunflower may be what led to the demise of the sumpweed crop. In fact, sumpweed cultivation not only declined in late prehistoric times, but the Indian-selected variety ultimately became extinct. Around the time of the first European contact, large-seeded sumpweeds dropped out of sight. In 1972, when archaeobotanist Richard Yarnell described *Iva annua* variety *macrocarpa* as "an extinct American cultigen," he added these speculative remarks:

> It is possible that sumpweed cultivation developed earlier and had the initial advantage of being well adapted to the wetter climate of the Eastern Woodlands. It may be that sunflowers ultimately outdistanced sumpweed in productivity and totally displaced it as an oil source toward the middle of the second millennium A.D. Both plants apparently were displaced as major food sources by corn, perhaps by the latter half of the first millennium A.D.

Sunflower achenes (seeds enclosed in shells) were about twice the size of sumpweed achenes, and so sunflowers may have been favored over sumpweeds for that reason. But why did the two crops continue to coexist in the same fields for thousands of years before one fell by the wayside? And while the sunflower was displaced later by corn as a major staple, why did it not disappear as a cultigen as well?

As ethnobotanist Richard Ford has observed, sumpweed actually continued to be grown "in the central Midwest until historic contact [with Europeans]." Yarnell alludes to its presence in Ozark caves as late as 1430, and does not rule out a terminal date of 1670 A.D. Was sumpweed made obsolete by the sunflower in prehistoric times, or did it rapidly vanish when Europeans began to vanquish the East? Wasn't native farming altogether disrupted elsewhere by European-introduced diseases, pests, weeds, and competing crops? If sumpweed persisted as a minor crop until after the European arrival on this continent, how would it have fared when local farmers were being decimated by new illnesses, and the landscape was being changed in innumerable ways?

I don't know for certain why sumpweed achenes aren't eaten anymore, for the details of its demise are lacking. But one thing is clear. Today, the pool of genes left from domesticated sumpweeds is as dry as a Hohokam Canal.

I I I

What can't be learned from the sumpweed story in America's heartland is amply evident in the desert where the Hohokam canals once brought water to sixteen species of desert crops. Here, it is possible to relate the waning of many prehistorically cultivated plants of particular periods of environmental stress or social upheaval, and sometimes to ultimate causes.

Along the Gila and Salt floodplains of central Arizona, twenty-five hundred years of crop history have been tracked by some of the finest ethnobotanists who have worked in the New World: Edward Palmer, Edward Castetter, Hugh Cutler, Vorsila Bohrer, Jonathan Sauer, Amadeo Rea, Charles Miksicek, Suzanne Fish, Robert Gasser, Adrianne Rankin, and Jannifer Gish. A remarkably complete sequence of crop introductions and extinctions can be pulled together from these scholars' identifications of excavated plant macrofossils, pollen, interpretations of historic documents, and collections of oral histories. They record radical changes in the biotic diversity of a land described in 1975 as "good for all kinds of seeds and plantings." Today, the floodplains of the middle Gila and the Salt harbor a paucity of crops, and far fewer wild plants and animals than ever before.

To reconstruct where the Hohokam crops came from and where they went, we must travel back before canals of any size were constructed along the Gila and Salt rivers: to a period prior to the florescence of the Hohokam.

Maize became a significant foodstuff in southern Arizona in Late Archaic times, between 1000 and 700 B.C., during a period when floodplain soils were naturally accumulating rather than downcutting into gully-like arroyos. The earliest corns in the Southwest, a flinty chapalote and reventador popcorn, are no longer found in the United States, although I've collected both from Indian farmers just a few hundred miles south into Mexico. But the other race of maize that arrived in the Gila and Salt valleys early on—the floury eight-rowed sixty-day corn—persists until this day. These corns may have initiated crop production adjacent to the Gila and Salt rivers, where shallow ditches diverted runoff or streamflows into small fields cleared on the lower floodplains.

Between 300 B.C. and the time of Christ, a small group of native horticulturists began to utilize a set of technologies previously unknown in the Gila–Salt region. Labelled the Hohokam by archaeologists this century, this prehistoric culture began producing pottery, textiles, stone and ceramic sculpture, and houses in a distinctive, sophisticated manner. Their canals of water diverted from springs, marshes, and rivers allowed for a greater intensity of crop production than what rainfed or runoff farming might provide in a desert region. Through the end of the Pioneer Period between 600 and 700 A.D., they gradually added several minor crops to their cornfields: common beans, cotton, agaves, and little barley. At the same time, they continued to rely upon a wide variety of wild foods, such as mesquite, cacti, and winter annuals. Some of these wild foods, such as greens, became more intensively harvested from ditchbanks and fields.

During the next two periods of Hohokam culture, the Colonial and the Sedentary, these "backwater farmers" spread into a wide variety of environments across fourteen thousand square miles of southern Arizona. Archaeologist Dave Doyel observes that from 600 to 1100 A.D., "The Hohokam underwent a time of population growth, regional expansion, and developing complexity in their material products. . . . Settlements in the central region, such as Snaketown, also continued to grow, approaching [240 acres] in area and populations of approximately one thousand people. . . . Large canal systems serving multiple villages became common. . . . Some of these ancient ditches, excavated by the Hohokam from hard desert soils with nothing more than pointed wood sticks, measure over five [yards] wide and three [yards] deep."

Finding their way into the Hohokam larder were new crops from the south such as tepary beans, limas, tobaccos, and squashes. Around 1000 A.D., when a warmer, wetter period began, ethnobiologist Charles Miksicek believes that climatic conditions became more favorable for Mesoamerican domesticated crops. Two grain amaranth species became prominent, and tropical jack beans made a brief appearance in the region. There is tantalizing evidence that a Mesoamerican goosefoot may have also been introduced, here and in the Ozarks and Great Plains. The little barley plant's grains show signs of incipient domestication after 1000 A.D. The spectrum of crops available to the Hohokam had radiated into a rainbow of seed colors. A thousand years ago, the Hohokam had the most diverse crop complex of any culture living in what is now the United States.

But this cultural flowering, and the moisture that allowed its growth, was of short duration. Around 1150 A.D., a drought may have starved the fields fed by river-diversion canals, and there are increasing signs of the build-up of salinity in Hohokam fields. By this time, some of the canals had been consolidated into more extensive irrigation systems. Because so vast a canal network had been built over an eighteen-mile stretch of the Salt River, farmers could easily deplete the river of its entire water supply during months of low flow. A breakup and period of social disequilibrium among the Salt River Hohokam between 1050 and 1200 A.D. may have been aggravated by this water crisis. About that time, Snaketown was abandoned; pottery and other cultural remains dating from the Late Sedentary Period are altogether lacking from that large settlement on the Gila.

As more people migrated to the well-watered reaches of the Salt from surrounding drought-stressed areas, huge new canals were constructed that connected several older irrigation areas. Still, water conflicts and times of scarcity must have arisen. Mesoamerican crops such as amaranths and jack beans dropped out of the prehistoric archaeological record of the region.

"But why?" I recently asked Charlie Miksicek, as we went over mounds of his carefully gathered data on the kitchen table of his Tucson home. He paused for a moment, and then answered: "I think climate has a lot to do with it, but so does cultural upheaval. After 1150, the people there don't behave like the earlier Hohokam. They were retreating from some of their older villages, leaving things behind. . . . "

Archaeologist Dave Doyel's analysis echoes the same feeling. It was not a time when people simply dropped a few moisture-loving crops, reorganized their canal systems, and went on again without mishap. The greater population concentrations clustered on the Salt and the Gila led to what some call "subsistence stress," and what others refer to as "unregulated competition for water." Downstream villages were disadvantaged. Bruce Masse sees "the dissolution of a regional system of water management and . . . resultant abuses of the water supply upstream."

But the movement toward longer, larger canals in communities concentrated upstream may have led to greater vulnerability. Dendrochronologist Don Graybill has integrated tree ring analysis of climate change with archaeological interpretations of the Salt River environment in the fourteenth century. His reconstructions of rainfall and river water availability for the Salt River watershed rough out a disturbing picture: "From 1300 to 1350, a period of decreasing streamflow occurred that was nothing like what the sedentary Hohokam had experienced before," Graybill explained to me. The watershed dried out, and perhaps lost a considerable density of its plant cover. "Then," Don went on to say, "there were several extremely wet years: 1354, 1356, and 1358. A high spike in streamflow. A wet period after a long dry one. The conditions through the mid-1350s were the kind that could have resulted in very major damage to canal intakes down in the valley."

If the land was barren and brittle enough from the long drought, such wet years could have carried monstrous floods off the uplands in the watershed above the Hohokam farming villages. These floods may have cut the river channel below the level of the canal intakes, or washed them away altogether. By the time another devastating flood occurred in 1382, much of the irrigation systems on the Salt had likely been abandoned, and human populations had begun to relocate themselves. Although many Hohokam archaeologists still maintain that the Hohokam disappearance occurred one or two centuries later, few disagree that the growth of this civilization had been curtailed by the 1350s. Dave Doyel feels that these natural disasters were among the forces that ultimately "stressed the Hohokam system."

Already overspecialized and hyperdependent on their huge canals, the Hohokam began abandoning their riverine farming villages, canal systems, and ceremonial centers. Between 1350 and 1400, the Salt and Gila valleys were depopulated. The agaves and native barley patches that had been plentiful were gone by the time the first European observers set foot in this region. Eleven of the sixteen prehistoric crops somehow hung on, persisting into historic times, but they too may have suffered from varietal erosion during the Hohokam collapse.

Hohokam. It is derived from the Piman term *Huhugam O'odham,* "the people who have vanished," or "exhausted people." In Pima legend, they were on this earth before the Pima emerged. They began to disappear into a hole in the ground when Coyote said something to them that kept them from vanishing altogether. They are known to us today by their rock art, their large ruins, and their widely scattered pottery shards. We know which of their crops were lost, and how pottery designs rich in images of aquatic birds were never to be made again. What we'll never know is how the last Hohokam farmers felt when they abandoned their fields along the canals.

I V

"The green of those Pima fields spread along the river for many miles in the old days," recalled the River Pima leader, George Webb, from his home in Gila Crossing. But that was in the time "when there was plenty of water. Now the river is an empty bed full of sand. . . . Where everything used to be green, there were acres of dust, miles of dust, and the Pima Indians were suddenly desperately poor."

In those words, George Webb telescoped the history of the last three hundred years in his homeland, the former home of the Hohokam. During those three centuries, the Pima have lost at least seven crop species that were introduced to the Southwest prehistorically. Seven native varieties of five New World species survive precariously today, in the dooryard gardens and small fields of the River Pima: sixty-day corn, white and brown teparies, mottled limas, narrow-seeded bottlegourds, and striped cushaw squash.

It was not only the native crops of "subsistence farmers" that died of thirst. The Pima's once-thriving export economy based on Spanish-introduced wheat faltered also. In *Once a River*, Amadeo Rea has recorded twenty-nine species of birds that were extirpated in Pima country over the last century, and he counts another dozen bird species that dramatically declined because of habitat deterioration there. Fish, like the humpbacks, and river-loving mammals were left high and dry. And as Rea has since discovered, the number of wild plant resources lost from the Gila floodplain was of an even greater magnitude.

Without these resources, the life of the *Akimel O'odham*, "River People," changed radically over the last one hundred twenty years. Yet as Henry Dobyns has suggested in his ethnohistory essay, "Who Killed the Gila?", the erosional processes that disrupted agricultural landscapes on the Gila River floodplain were set in motion by the Spanish much earlier. The Spanish introduction of European diseases and livestock triggered changes in the intensity of management of the Gila floodplain. Along one stretch of the Gila, Rea has recorded that the number of River Pima *rancheria* settlements fell from thirty to just three in the first century after Spanish contact, presumably because of the depopulation caused by smallpox and other pandemics. Unable to manage the Gila floodplain with the intensity of labor that they had previously, the River Pima perhaps more readily converted croplands that had been abandoned to pasture for newly arrived livestock. By the mid-nineteenth century, cattle populations in the Gila watershed had overgrazed the vegetation to the degree that hydrological conditions were severely altered.

Well in advance of the Civil War, overgrazing as well as woodcutting and beaver trapping in the Upper Gila began to change gentler streamflows to flashfloods capable of eroding out the floodplain fields of the Pima. Yet there was a time lag before these disturbances actually began to disrupt the agricultural environments tended by the Pima. During drought and flood sequences much like those that wreaked havoc during Hohokam times, the repercussions of many environmental disturbances became concentrated on the middle Gila floodplain, where most Pima farms were located. Arroyo cutting and aquifer draining were initiated as early as mid-century, but accelerated by the 1870s.

Then, in 1867, an additional sort of pestilence fell upon the River Pima of the middle Gila and the adjacent Salt. That year, Jack Swilling, an entrepreneurial alcoholic and morphine addict with vision enough to notice the old Hohokam canals, organized his Anglo neighbors to divert water out of the Salt River above the

Pima villages. He began to "reclaim the desert," an effort continued today by the massive Salt River Project.

Upstream from most of the Pima villages on the Gila, other recent arrivals to the desert opened up large canals during the drought in the early summer months of 1870. These Anglos poured onto their fields an excess of irrigation without returning their tailwater to the river for others to use. By 1873, three hundred Pima and Maricopa Indians left the Gila for good, hoping that in a new settlement upstream from Phoenix they would avoid such conflicts. The situation did indeed become far worse on the Gila, because settlers in Florence began to expand their new farming colony upstream. Ethnohistorian Edward Spicer wrote that, "By 1887 the irrigation canal constructed to take water out of the Gila River utilized the whole flow. No water reached any of the Pima fields downstream."

Only where the Pima could rely on the tributary flows from the Salt or the Santa Cruz was any native farming still possible. Fields that once held a mix of crops were left too dry to support anything but the hardiest of weeds. What happened, then, to the seedstocks usually saved in Pima storage baskets and pots? Did they remain in storage, unplanted, until they lost their viability? Were they sold off to those who still had water? Were the grains and beans eaten up as food supplies dwindled?

V

In the 1750s, when missionary Juan Nentvig visited the depopulated Pima, he claimed that "so much cotton is raised and so wanting in covetousness is the husbandman that after the crop is gathered in, more remains in the fields than is to be had for a harvest here in Sonora." By 1873, this fiber crop was already declining. When botanists finally collected a few samples just after the turn of the century, they claimed that it had all but died out completely. In 1901, Frank Russell claimed that there was so little cotton that there was not enough in Pima villages to finish making even one piece of cloth on a small loom. He added that "the Pimas no longer spin and weave; the art is dying with the passing of the older generation."

Although Egyptian cotton production began in central Arizona in 1908, it did not directly replace the fine-fibered native cotton. The aboriginal Pima cotton was nearly extinct when modern "Pima" cotton was selected from a single superior plant of the Egyptian species in 1910. The Pima cotton in our clothes today was not commercially produced until 1916. By that time, the only remaining authentic collection of aboriginal Pima cotton was restricted to plant breeders' collections in agricultural field stations.

The last remaining grain amaranth apparently perished between 1870 and 1890. Varieties of common beans, squashes, and a small grain called *kof*—perhaps a relic goosefoot surviving from prehistoric times—ceased to exist even in hand-watered kitchen gardens. Foods that had been mentioned in the Pima creation myth were never again grown, prepared, or eaten after 1900.

Following the turn of the century, the remaining wet places on the reservation dried up. Cultivated acreage decreased to less than a third of what it once was. From 1898 to 1904, droughts and upstream diversion of water by Anglos kept the Pima from producing any crops at all. Groundwater pumping was soon initiated. It quickly depleted remaining springs and seeps near farmlands. Mesquite and cottonwood forests died as the water table dropped below the reach of their roots. In their stead, the exotic salt cedar took hold.

Men such as George Webb were forced out of farming in the 1930s due to lack of irrigation water, even though the San Carlos Irrigation Project promised them a return to better days.

"When the dam was completed there would be plenty of water," Webb remembered. "And there was. For about five years. Then the water began to run short again. After another five years, it stopped altogether."

It was that time that Johnny Cash sang about in the ballad of the Pima Indian hero at Iwo Jima, Ira Hayes: "Down the ditches of a thousand years, the waters grew their crops / Until the White Man stole their water rights, and the sparkling waters stopped / Then Ira's folks grew hungry, their land grew crops of weeds / When the war came he volunteered, forgot the White Man's greed."

The year when the Webb and the Hayes families had to abandon their fields, Edward Castetter and Willis Bell began field-work on Pima agriculture. They caught the tail end of garden cultivation of two native tobaccos, and most if not all of the native common beans. Mottled limas had been absent from Pima market-places for two decades, but were then reintroduced by the USDA station at Sacaton, the headquarters for the Gila River Indian Community. However, the Indians who had access to San Carlos Project water were required to grow alfalfa and barley rather than their traditional crops, as part of a government-promoted soil building program.

The amount of farmed land on the Gila River Reservation increased in the late 1930s, but this was due to the addition of the Agency farm controlled by the Bureau of Indian Affairs, using some twelve thousand acres of unallotted reservation lands. Take away this acreage, and Pima families were farming less land for themselves in the thirties than they were at the time of the Civil War. And, because of the earlier constraints put on them by a BIA-enforced allotment program, Indian farmers had less land to work with. Between 1914 and 1921, each member of the Pima tribe had been allotted just ten acres of arable land. Twenty years later, the progeny of those tribal members were having to divide up that land. Today, some of the original allotments must be split among a hundred or so descendants.

For those who had only a few acres at their disposal, and no credit or equipment with which to develop them, it was easier to turn to wage work. Many Pima families left their whittled-down farmsteads to pick cotton for Anglos in the Casa Grande Valley to the south of the reservation, never to return to family farming again.

Another, far more debilitating kind of allotment program had happened on most Indian reservations, one that the River Pima had successfully resisted. This allotment program, initiated by the 1887 Dawes Act, is considered by many historians to have begun the decline of Indian farming in most parts of the United States.

Economic historian Leonard Carlson has documented the failure of Dawes Act allotments, which presumed to encourage Indians to initiate family-based farming enterprises, by means of a land development scheme superficially similar to the Homestead Act. In many areas, white settlers were also allowed to purchase unallotted Indian lands that had formerly been held in trust for the entire tribal community. In an argument that thinly disguised their motive, real estate developers asserted that "protecting Indian ownership of unused land would encourage idleness." Provided with economically industrious Anglo neighbors, the Indians would be more rapidly assimilated into the dominant society.

In one year alone, 1891, the Indian Commissioner Thomas Morgan sold off one seventh of all the Indian lands in the United States to white settlers, some 17,400,000 acres. Other kinds of ownership transfers were common during this period as well. All told, from the 1887 implementation of the Dawes Act to the termination of allotments and sales of Indian territories in 1934, some 84,000,000 acres of land passed out of Indian hands. This amounted to 60 percent of all the land that had been held in trust or through treaties on behalf of Native American peoples when the Dawes Act was passed.

Much of the arable land that Native Americans had formerly utilized for farming, hunting, and gathering was thus usurped by others. Where supplemental water was essential to avoid crop failure, Indians often found irrigation projects biased toward their non-Indian neighbors. Once their land and water were taken away, it is no wonder that Indian farming declined, and with it went much of the remaining native crop diversity.

Nevertheless, most Indian people remained close to the land, even though many of their families were suffering from both a declining cash income and a deteriorating resource base. In 1910, 95 percent of the Native Americans in the United States lived in rural areas. This percentage dropped only to 90 percent in 1930, and 78 percent in 1960. During the era of the Dawes Act, its proponents claimed that allotments would encourage more Indian farming. However, the percentage of the Indian population employed in agriculture declined from 74.7 percent in 1910 to 64.5 percent in 1930.

Perhaps some sociologists would claim that this decline was not catastrophic; after all, it simply mirrored the move of the general American population away from the farm. During the same period, the overall farm population of the United States slid from 34.9 percent to 24.9 percent of the total population.

Many Native American farmers, however, were irrevocably losing control of croplands that had been in their families since long before the arrival of Europeans. In 1910, about 22,000 Indians worked their own farms while another 26,500 served as farm laborers. By 1950, despite considerable growth of Indian populations, the number of Indian farmers had dropped to 14,300, and their farm labor force to 14,100. By 1982, only forty-seven hundred Native Americans were full owners of farms, another seventeen hundred were part owners, and seven hundred fifty were tenant-operators. In total, about seven thousand Native Americans are managing farms at present. Less than five hundred of these Indian farms nationwide grow any sizeable mixture of crops, including vegetables, staple grains, and beans for self-consumption. Of course, not even all of these farms focus on traditional crops native to their region.

These data from census statistics contrast sharply with the inflated numbers from USDA and BIA reports promoting "new initiatives" to help Indian farmers. For instance, the USDA today claims participation in its programs by fifty thousand Native American agriculturists—more Indian farmers than the Census

Bureau has counted since the turn of the century! A BIA work group on Native American agriculture recently boasted that thirty-three thousand individuals and tribal enterprises are involved in farming or ranching on Indian reservations, utilizing nearly fifty million acres of land. Those figures seem impressive until it is realized how little of it must be anything more than introduced forage and livestock production.

How much of that "Native American farming" effort draws upon crop resources traditionally utilized by the cultures involved? Neither the USDA nor the BIA bureaucrats track the actual use of native crops. To be sure, these agencies have hardly ever promoted those resources either.

In fact, several years ago, USDA policymakers published a statement of their legacy entitled, "The Lack of Native Crops in the United States." In 1979, and again in 1984, the official USDA policy statement on plant genetic resource conservation began with this preposterous assertion:

> If American consumers were asked to live on food from crops native to the United States, they would probably be shocked that their diet was limited to sunflower seeds, cranberries, blueberries, pecans, and not much else. . . . Tobacco would be available, but they would have no cotton. . . . [The] resources that support our domestic food and fiber production [today] are imported.

In a meeting with USDA officials, Kent Whealy of the Seed Savers Exchange pointed out why so many of our plant genetic resources are indeed imported from developing countries: "There has never been a systematic, large-scale search for [crop] plants *within* the United States; the USDA has always done its explorations outside the United States."

Further, USDA policy claims that *in situ* conservation of crops—which could be done by providing incentives to native farmers to keep growing their remaining traditional varieties—is too unstable, risky, and ineffective, and therefore beyond the scope of its plant preservation concerns. The only real policy that our Department of Agriculture has for the native crop legacy of our country is "a policy of neglect."

V I I

Fortunately, tribal governments no longer believe fatalistically that this must be their policy as well. Among the Iroquois, the Sioux, the Mississippi band of the Anishanabey, San Juan Pueblo, the Winnebago, the Tohono O'odham, the Navajo, and other tribes, there have emerged community or tribal projects to conserve and revive native crops as cottage industries for their rural-based tribal members. On both reservations where the Pima live, they have initiated tribally supported farm efforts to increase the supplies of traditional crop plants.

Perhaps the most appealing of these efforts has been the Agricultural Resources Project of the Salt River Indian Community. A few years ago, a survey of tribal members indicated that it was hard to obtain the native foods they favored. And of more than sixty families contacted, only four said that they were currently growing native crops.

The community obtained foundation assistance to design a project that would provide nutritious foods as well as new sources of income to its Pima and Maricopa members. Three young Native Americans came on as the project staff: Darren Washington, Angie Silversmith, and Berkley Chough. On five acres of land, they experimented with six commercial vegetable varieties, as well as twenty-five traditional desert crops provided to them by Native Seeds/SEARCH.

As NS/S contact Kevin Dahl recalled from his conversations with Angie and Berkley, "When bugs became a problem, they overwhelmed the commercial vegetables while hardly touching the native varieties. Not all the native crops were a success, however. . . . [But] it was the Gila Pima corn, Pima cushaw squash, Papago sugar cane, and Papago dipper gourds that flourished. [And] Tepary beans proved to be an outstanding success."

These crops have been grown twice and sold to community members, who expressed great interest in them. On a reservation where more than three quarters of the farmable land has been rented out to Anglo lessees for decades, the Pima and Maricopa have newly demonstrated the value of crops from their own tribal legacies. However, the future of the Agricultural Resources Project remains uncertain; foundation assistance has terminated, and it is up to the tribal government and community to reinitiate plantings without outside support.

From the renewed interest generated by this project, the Salt River Indian Community helped Scottsdale Community College sponsor a conference called "Native American Agriculture—A Critical Resource" in October, 1987. In its position statement, the conference coordinators reminded participants that even today, "Indian land and its potential agricultural use are in danger of being lost. The most important economic resource available to the American Indian is the land and its agricultural potential. Properly using agricultural land within Indian reservations is one of the greatest challenges now confronting Indian people and tribes."

Out of the conference came a proposal for an American Indian Agricultural Resource Center. To be located less than fifteen miles from the old Hohokam canals on the Salt River, this center would search for ways to ensure that tribal farmlands will be "wisely utilized and preserved for future generations." In light of what has already been lost, this proposal seems a century late. Yet the little seed and land that remain are valuable enough that the Pima wish to guarantee their survival. The feeling that something still precious remains also pervades the Park of the Four Waters, where remnants of some eighteen prehistoric irrigation canals run parallel to a modern one heading off toward downtown Phoenix. No matter that less than a hundredth of the original reach of Hohokam canals remains intact. No matter that dirt bikers use the eroding crest of the canal bank as a jump course. No matter that jets fly overhead every few minutes, obliterating any silent respect for the past that one tries to muster. Those ditches are monuments.

It does not require much quiet contemplation to be awestruck by what went before us. The Hohokam canals humble us as do the Mayan pyramids, the Sistine Chapel, or the Great Wall of China. If those who are involved in historic preservation wish to celebrate a great engineering feat from the pre-Columbian agricultural heritage of North America, let them provide greater protection for these canals.

But let us remember that centuries ago, this irrigation system provided grain and beans and fish for the bellies of people. It would be a hollow kind of historic preservation if sixty-day flour corn, tepary beans, and humpback suckers became extinct while the earthen walls of the ancient ditch were preserved as public monuments. Let us not overlook the monumental contributions of the crops far more ancient than the European discovery of this continent, foods that still have the power to nourish us. We must keep them alive.

Gene Logsdon

THE FUTURE:
MORE FARMERS,
NOT FEWER

Although the percentage of Americans engaged in farming has been decreasing steadily since the ink was hardly dry on the signing of the Louisiana Purchase (from 90 percent of the population then to 2.5 percent today) and has been decreasing in actual numbers since 1916, the one continuous viewpoint I have heard in my fifty years among farmers is that the number of farmers can't go any lower. I have personally known all the editors of the prestigious *Farm Journal* except the first, who started the magazine 110 years ago and, at some point in their careers, every one of these astute gentlemen opined editorially or privately that the decline of the farm population was about to bottom out. Even Wheeler McMillen, who in the thirties wrote a book titled *Too Many Farmers* (thereby earning himself the undying enmity of small farmers everywhere), thought that the right number to get down to was about 9 million, more than four times what we have today. And of the 2.2 million remaining (or whatever the number is this week), only about 700,000 contribute significantly to the commercial food market. All of which at least means I am in good company when I continue the naive tradition of optimism in the face of statistical and economic reality and declare without batting an eye that the family farm is not dead, and that, far from continuing to decrease, farms and farmers are on the increase.

Although megafarms will continue to be an important part of

the food production business, I don't think the future belongs to them at all, despite the predictions of wishful-thinking agribusiness interests. The real action is going to occur in the comparatively small-scale food production systems now sprouting up everywhere, and in those that have handily survived the economic crunch of the eighties. In short, there is no better time than right now for dedicated young people, determined to own and operate their own businesses, to make it in agriculture.

I can give three reasons for my prediction that the number of food and fiber producers ("food and fiber producer" is the only definition of farmer that works) is about to increase. One: historically, in all the past civilizations I have studied, the denser the population becomes, the smaller and more numerous the farms become. Two: financially, the economies of scale that apparently rule manufacturing do not really apply to any sustainable kind of food production; when you count all the costs, it is cheaper to raise a zucchini in your garden than on your megafarm. And three: socially, people are beginning to understand they really are what they eat and are demanding quality food, which megafarms can't supply.

New attitudes toward food are not only increasing the number of farms but, more importantly, are bringing a new kind of farmer to the land—a farmer with roots in urban culture, not traditional rural culture. While commercial agriculture stolidly continues to pile up government-subsidized mountains of surplus hybrid corn and hard red wheat, these new farmer-entrepreneurs bend an ear to the marketplace and produce the food consumers want. They are often called specialty farmers, but they are more apt to refer to themselves as "guerrilla marketers"—they strike where the big boys aren't looking, and they come in a variety that is mind-boggling. The *New York Times* food writer, Marian Burros, noting that "there's not a New Englander or farmer in the lot," recently listed such disparate new farm products in New England as goat cheese, farm-raised oysters, hand-pressed cider, hydroponic spinach, stone-ground flours and meals from locally grown organic grains, baby lambs for the hoity-toity restaurants of New York and Boston, pheasant and other once-wild game such as buffalo, and dairy sheep producing Roquefort cheese.

All across America, hundreds of small sheep flocks have come into existence in the last ten years to supply wool directly to the bustling cottage hand-spinning and -weaving industry. Angora goat farms have become almost common, even in the corn and soybean wastelands of the Midwest. A feedlot in Nebraska now raises ostriches, some of which bring $22,000 a pair. In Michigan, Juliet Sprouse told me last year that female llamas she and her husband raise on their thirty-five acres had skyrocketed in price from $1,500 six years ago to $10,000 now. New Jersey vegetable farmers, taking a cue from the West Coast, are learning to market squash flowers as well as squash fruit for food. Catfish farms thrive in the South as consumers learn how good a humble, down-home fish can taste when raised in unpolluted water. Crayfish farms are on the upswing in the South, too, and very likely, if humans persist in using their rivers and oceans as a sewage-disposal system, *all* fish and seafood will eventually be raised on domesticated "farms."

Samuel and Louise Kayman are good examples of specialty farmers developing new markets. In 1983 they began making high-quality yogurt from their herd of Jersey cows at Stonyfield Farm near Wilton, New Hampshire. (Sam had quit his job in the defense industry in the sixties.) Their market exploded and they could not keep up with demand. The Kaymans sold their cows and concentrated on the yogurt; they bought Jersey milk from surrounding farmers, even paying them a premium over the outrageous price the tax-funded dinosaur government-subsidy program allows farmers in the conventional market. They brought in Gary Hirshberg from New Alchemy Institute to provide financial and overall management. By 1988 they had hit $3 million in sales and moved into a new half-million-dollar plant away from the farm. "Significant profit is still in the future," says Hirshberg, "but there's a tremendous nonmonetary reward we gain from customer satisfaction. We get hundreds of letters from people who love our yogurt, and that's very important to us. We also provide a better profit picture for the farmers who sell milk to us, which is part of our overall goal of revitalizing rural areas. When we succeed at those goals, there's an intellectual payoff more valuable than money."

Those words are a fairly accurate modern translation of the traditional farmer's reverence for and stewardship of the soil entrusted to him. I heard the same echoes from Jay North, who, with his wife, Pamela (and now forty employees), grows about a million dollars' worth of edible flowers and herbs a year—not bad for a thirty-seven-acre farm, even in California. Admitting he didn't have a computer yet, Jay explained. "If I computerized this business, I probably wouldn't need as many employees and I wouldn't like that. The success of this business depends a lot on a sensitive relationship between humans and the land. We would rather employ people than machines." North's background? Previously he was a hairdresser.

Thus a historic shift takes place. The Vergilian ecology and careful husbandry of the traditional yeoman farmer that gave way to the all-consuming dreadnought of agribusiness economics now reappear in the unlikely form of the ex-urban farmer. Fleeing industrialism, this new farmer is characterized, writes Marian Burros in the *New York Times*, "by an environmental awareness often influenced by the 1960s counterculture movement: a desire to be free of the constraints of the crowded city and nine-to-five jobs and a belief that success can be achieved by working fourteen-to-sixteen-hour days." Jefferson's agrarian dream returns in modern guise.

So many specialty farms are starting up that it is hard to keep track of the number of new growers. Jay North complains that there are almost too many, driving the price of baby vegetables, salad greens, edible flowers, and other high-value crops down to where he fears the profit will go out of them (the old Wheeler Mc-Millen syndrome). He guesses the number in his area has gone from about four to thirty in the last couple of years.

California's *Farmer-to-Consumer Directory* lists about a thousand certified roadside farm marketers. The foods offered include everything from baby beans to nasturtium blossoms to feijoa (pineapple guava). The *Directory* also lists one hundred farmers' markets and twenty-two regional "Farm Trail" organizations that promote their members' locations and products. The story is the same in New England. While nationwide more than a million farms were lost in the last twenty years, and while more than a million people have left the land since 1980, Massachusetts, of all places, gained over 500 farms since 1978. Maine, despite a very bleak picture in its commercial potato fields, gained over 400. In the Midwest, Minnesota gained 2,000 farms in the latest census and Wisconsin 1,000. Georgia and Florida gained 1,000 each, too.

However, I discount census numbers, up or down. By census definition, a farm is an establishment from which $1,000 or more of agricultural products are sold during the year. There are thousands of homesteads where nothing is sold, but which produce over $1,000 worth of food, including thousands of the more than 30 million gardens in this country. In 1983, some imaginative statistician figured out that the total value of food raised in American gardens exceeded the profit in all of commercial agriculture that year.

It is my contention that gardens are the incubators of the new farm ecology. In Berkeley, California, a city "farm" of one-third acre grosses more than $300,000 in salad vegetables for Konakai Farms. An article in the Salem, Oregon, *Capitol Press* of August 19, 1988, tells about Neil Lawrence's three-quarter-acre "farm" from which he says he makes a living raising high-priced vegetables.

Mark Musick, who now works as a buyer for Larry's Market, a local supermarket chain (and who deserves the title of Guru of the Guerrilla Marketers), works hard as a liaison between the store and garden farmers, some of whom hitherto were too small to interest supermarkets. Just to list a few of the foods he deals in makes the palate quiver in keen anticipation: exotic pepper varieties from Krueger Pepper Gardens in the Yakima Valley; wild blue huckleberries, harvested by Yakima Indian families; yellow finn potatoes and romanesco broccoli from Dungeness Organic Produce; several varieties of red, white, and blue potatoes; Spanish Roja garlic; nettles (along with a recipe for cream-of-nettle soup from Chef Karl Beckley in Seattle); boletus mushrooms and cattail corn from Mike Maki, who has leased 40,000 acres of forestland for commercial foraging of wild foods (making his one of the largest "farm" operations in the world); shungiku and baby bok choy from a co-op of six Laotian refugee farmers called the Indochinese Farm Project. Musick was a longtime farmer at Pragtree Farms, the home of Tilth Publications, north of Seattle, where he helped spearhead the new interest in unique foods, especially salads, as a way to make small farms both ecologically sane and economically profitable. Pragtree's "Impromptu Salad," which contains twenty or more different herbs, salad vegetables, and edible flowers mixed together, costs twenty-eight dollars a pound before packaging and, since being featured in *Harrowsmith* magazine, has become nationally renowned. "Before, we were grossing $3,000 an acre on five acres of conventional vegetables. But cabbage at twenty-five cents a pound just didn't pay. What we were able to do by switching to lightweight, high-value specialties like salad vegetables, herbs, and edible flowers was reduce farmland from five to one-half acre, sell both tractors, hand-dig the plots, and still make the same amount of money."

Nor is the new yeomanry confined to the far-out East and West coasts. In New Mexico, Richard Deertrack has made a success of selling traditional blue corn flour by mail—from the crop grown by his fellow Pueblo Indians. In southern Indiana I watched a remarkable friend, Ed Fackler, struggle for years to establish a commercial organic fruit orchard. He had previously worked for the railroad. For anyone aspiring to the ranks of ex-urban yeomanry, he would make a good model, and I can tell you his secret in four words—intelligence plus pure mule-headedness. In time, he mastered everything known about organic orcharding and finally concluded, after eleven years, that he couldn't raise fruit that way in his humid southern Indiana location. But rather than give up his high environmental ideals, he worked out an orchard agronomy that uses only a small portion of the toxic sprays conventional orchardists regularly douse their trees with. He started a mail-order nursery, emphasizing trees and varieties that perform well in his locale. He also started selling richly flavored old and unusual varieties of apples and other fruits to the Louisville market. The Louisville *Courier Journal* did a story on his unusual apples last year, and he sold out completely in ten days, at premium prices. "People went ape over these different kinds of apples," he said. "We had customers from as far away as Bowling Green, Kentucky, and central Illinois. One broker drove down from Cincinnati to set up next year's purchase of 200 bushels of Scarlet Gala apples and all the Asian pears we could furnish. At the same time, growers nationwide were taking a beating on standard apple varieties, which were in oversupply because, in my opinion, they have poor fruit quality." Fackler says that he began to pay special attention to the Gala apple, now his favorite, when he noticed that his little daughter would invariably pass up the other 500 or so varieties in his experimental orchard to feast under the Gala tree.

Parker Bosley, of Parker's Restaurant in Cleveland, Ohio (closed because of fire in 1991), has played the same role in Cleveland that other innovative chefs like Wolfgang Puck and Karl Beckley have on the West Coast. He went directly to the farms and told them what he wanted and how he wanted it—and that he was willing to pay for it. He established what *Ohio* magazine calls "an old farmboys' network," reminiscent of Mark Musick's program. Bosley's network supplies him with, among other things, rabbits and ducks from Ashland County and lambs from Portage County. Two women from Cleveland Heights grow blue oyster mushrooms in their garage for him. He buys veal from Geauga County, berries from Lorain County, and thick Guernsey cream from Wayne County. During the growing season he uses all-local produce and pays premium prices for it.

Obviously, people who eat edible flowers or pay twenty-eight dollars a pound for salad greens are not eating just to live. But in a deeper sense, that is perhaps exactly what they are doing, since these foods are almost always raised without pesticides. After years of hearing from conventional agribusiness that consumers would not pay for quality food or (heaven help us) organic food, quite the opposite is suddenly true. This is new. For years the image of the "good" little housekeeper was bargain-hunting Mom, trundling off to the grocery store to take advantage of every coupon, every sale, every loss leader offered. Virtue as a good shopper consisted of finding the cheapest food in town. Now, more and more, food is seen as an enhancer of health or beauty or status, as having not only intrinsic health value but also recreational value like beer and whiskey. While it is true that the keen edge of demand comes from the social levels that have lots of disposable income, people in general are deciding good food is worth paying a little more for.

Whether "organic" or simply free of pesticide residue, or just plain fresh and flavorful, the specialty crops from the new farms are also deemed by consumers to taste better. "It's not just status-seeking yuppies influencing the market," says Jay North. "Our main customers are women between the ages of forty-five and sixty-five who really know their foods." Gary Hirshberg, at Stony-field Farm, points out that quality foods are not necessarily so expensive, either. "Not at the retail level. Our yogurt is only about five cents a cup more than the common brands."

At this point, I wish the reader could turn quickly to the first chapter of Jane Jacobs' brilliant 1969 book, *The Economy of Cities.* Jacobs' thesis is that civilization did not necessarily proceed, by orderly evolution, from a hunting and gathering stage, to domestic farming, to villages, to towns, and, finally, to cities. She argues, instead, that cities actually preceded a genuine agricultural economy. "Cities are not built on a rural economic base. . . . Quite the reverse is true. Rural economies, including agricultural work, are directly built on city economies and city work." Just as alfalfa was grown in French gardens for a century before it became a commercial farm crop, as Jacobs notes, so too can we observe the same process with salad greens, herbs, and edible flowers today. It is cities that have created the market from these new products. Restaurants with innovative chefs inspired the new farmers. Their farms are extensions of the city, willed by the city. And therein lies the reason they must be taken seriously.

The animal rights movement also springs purely from city culture, which is one reason why conventional farmers oppose it so vehemently. Yet if the moderate mainstream of animal rightism prevails—that is, if society still wants to eat meat but insists that animals be treated more humanely and raised more naturally than is now the case in large confinement factories—the result will be good for farmers. It will mean that more of them will be able to derive a decent living from husbandry rather than the condition that now prevails, wherein fewer and fewer megafarms raise more and more of the poultry and pork with methods that depend increasingly on drugs and chemicals. The meat will cost more money perhaps, but it will be worth more, and the new consumer is obviously willing to pay. It is very likely that the huge animal factory complexes will eventually be phased out for no other reason than because, like landfills, nobody wants to live near them. Meanwhile, the state of Vermont has now passed a law whereby traditional family dairy farms will be paid so much per pound of milk produced just to stay in operation. Urban society wants the beauty of the open space that farms provide to remain on the landscape. Even twenty years ago, such an attitude would have seemed highly unlikely.

If my argument for a future of more farms and farmers rested solely on the specialty farms, I would not advance it with so little fear and trepidation. But there is another kind of farming, another kind of guerrilla marketing that, in concert with what I have been describing, makes more permanent something that looks like only a fashionable, momentary trend. To describe this kind of farming, I need only to look out my window across the Upper Sandusky neighborhood I have watched for fifty years and which has always told me the future of farming, when I was paying attention. Next door to me, a couple and their two school-age children recently started milking eight cows on two acres, the sort of spare-time endeavor the universities tell their ag students is not profitable. Fortunately, my neighbor did not go to college and does not know he can't make money milking cows on two acres, so he does it anyway. He wants to be a "real" farmer but fate has not put into his hands the kind of money it takes to own a "real" farm. So he operates a tile drainage business by day and milks his cows by night. He says he comes out in the black most of the time because he has no huge investment in farm land and machinery, and because he can take advantage of the propensity of megafarms to overproduce corn. For eight cows, he can buy feed cheaper than raise it. But as with all real farmers I know, he *really* milks cows because it is something the whole family can do together, something his children can earn wages and learn responsibility from. And, at the bottom line, he just *likes* to do it.

If I swivel my head in a slightly different direction, I see my own barn through the trees, where Betsy and her new calf are presently penned. They represent, among other things, a successful experiment I thought I had pioneered in the production of low-fat, low-cholesterol beef, only to find that my friend Oren Long, a Kansas rancher, had already perfected the method and was selling all the organic baby beef he could raise to supermarkets, who displayed it right alongside the conventional meat showcases—even at three times the price of conventional meat. His beef tests lower in calories and cholesterol than chicken, and he says the taste is unbeatable, a claim I believe, because my own beef, raised similarly, is absolutely delicious. Organic baby beef, as Oren and I produce it, comes from a calf slaughtered at about 700 pounds and seven months of age (conventional beef goes to market at 1,000 to 1,200 pounds and nearly two years old).

These calves grow mostly on mothers' milk and good pasture, along with some grain in the last two months but, in my experience, if the calf is getting a lot of rich milk from its mother, it won't each much grain. No antibiotics. No drugs. No protein supplement. The calves do not get fat, so the meat is not marbled as in prime beef and does not have the heavy, tallowy aftertaste of prime beef.

Consumers have been so responsive to this kind of beef when made aware of it that large feedlots are now trying to reproduce it. It is my contention, and Oren's even more so, that this kind of organic beef (he calls his Lite Beef) *can't* be raised on a large scale. It demands too much personal attention, a steady supply of good pasture, and a mother cow that is a cross between dairy and beef breeds—he uses Jersey-Angus, I use Guernsey-Angus. Says Oren, who's in his sixties, "I'm getting too old to do this much work. There's opportunity here for young small farmers with a flair for salesmanship." The implications are enormous. If beef feeders followed this method, pasture, not corn, would become the chief food in beef production, negating the need for thousands of acres of soil-eroding corn and providing consumers with what they want: low-cholesterol, low-fat red meat.

My neighbor across the road is a plant manager and farms eighty acres. Next to him in one direction is a mechanic who farms eighty acres. In the other direction, yet another part-timer, a carpenter with eighty acres who has just built a new barn. Across the road from him is a retired farmer whose son farms the land as a part-timer. They sell eggs from free-range hens, just as I do. His clientele say they enjoy driving out to his farm and so the cost of transporting the eggs is absorbed by customer satisfaction.

In another nearby neighborhood are five small farms almost

adjacent to each other that are owned or rented by small farmers very familiar to me. Two are relatively new operations started by men who formerly had other occupations. The wife of one of them has her own small business, which she conducts out of the house. A third farmer carries on a machinery-repair business along with his farming. A fourth recently rented additional land after a megafarmer got into financial difficulties and had to give the land contract back to the original owner. This renter also has another business. The fifth farmer has always farmed only his family's 200-acre homestead, dividing the income with his brother and sisters, and, contrary to what the farm magazines assert about such arrangements, has done just fine financially, even in these "bad" years of the eighties. The pattern emerging before my eyes tells me that good, conservative, conventional farming is not in trouble at all, because small farmers either avoid indebtedness or have another source of income upon which to draw. Not only will these farms be around as long as their owners live (and then, very likely pass on to offspring), they give every indication of being on the increase. My own brother, for example, using money from another small business to purchase land, has in these so-called hard times realized his dream to become a full-fledged farmer. My niece and her husband recently bought a small farm with their savings. They are in their twenties. Bidding against them were not big farmers, but other young couples like them. In the whole area west of my place, centering around the village of Kirby, there is a long-standing tradition of combining farming with another job or business—I could fill this page with the names of families doing it. Nor is it at all surprising; a study of how farms got started in the Midwest shows that among the pioneering families, farmers invariably depended on cash from another job or business to establish themselves on the land.

What is so intriguing about these small farms is that because many of them carry a relatively small debt load (interest payments are the highest cost per acre on most Midwest farm operations that have expanded greatly in the last twenty years), they can actually raise food cheaper than the megafarms can. The Amish, of course, are the best example of this phenomenon, but many other small farmers practice similar economies. If not horses, they use old tractors and machinery they repair themselves, have no hired labor to pay, and often share labor and machinery with each other.

In addition to these small commercial farmers, there are also those of us who come to be called "hobby farmers," although we resent the label—believe me, what I do is no hobby, it's a way of life. But my thirty acres produce only about $3,000 in food and wood per year, hardly a commercial enterprise. If I look at my immediate neighborhood of several thousand acres, I can count about twelve part-time commercial farmers, four "hobby farmers," one full-time family dairy farm, and three very large cash-grain operations. I also count four recent failures, all larger commercial enterprises. I rest my case here: none of the small farms have been forced out by economics.

DAISIES

Go ahead: say what you're thinking. The garden
is not the real world. Machines
are the real world. Say frankly what any fool
could read in your face: it makes sense
to avoid us, to resist
nostalgia. It is
not modern enough, the sound the wind makes
stirring a meadow of daisies: the mind
cannot shine following it. And the mind
wants to shine, plainly, as
machines shine, and not
grow deep, as, for example, roots. It is very touching,
all the same, to see you cautiously
approaching the meadow's border in early morning,
when no one could possibly
be watching you. The longer you stand at the edge,
the more nervous you seem. No one wants to hear
impressions of the natural world: you will be
laughed at again; scorn will be piled on you.
As for what you're actually
hearing this morning: think twice
before you tell anyone what was said in this field
and by whom.

Cathrine Sneed

CATHRINE SNEED
TALKS ABOUT
HER WORK WITH
PRISONERS
AND GARDENS

Hello. I always love to talk to people about what we're doing in San Francisco because hearing about it gives people ideas about what can happen in places other than San Francisco.

I have spent a lot of time in jail myself—as a counselor to women serving time there. It was my job to try to help these women find ways to do something with their lives other than what they had been doing. Most of them were in jail for drug use, drug possession, drug sales. Most of them had been and were prostitutes, and most of them had children. These women *wanted* to believe me when I told them there was something else they could do with their lives, but the reality was that they didn't have any education. In San Francisco, we test everyone that comes in our jail. The median reading level is fourth grade, fifth grade, sixth grade. Most of the people in our jail have never had jobs. And so as much as these women wanted to say, "Yeah, Cathy, we believe what you're saying, we *can* do something else with our lives," the reality was grim.

After several years working closely with these women, and despairing about their situation, I learned that I had gotten a serious kidney disease. I was twenty-eight and I had two little kids, and it was a shock when the doctor said, "Well, it doesn't look good. You're not responding to drugs and you can either stay here in the hospital and die or you can go home and die." Just before my doctor came up with that statement, a good friend of mine had given me *The Grapes of Wrath*. I read it, and what struck me was this—Steinbeck is saying that to be really alive, these people felt that they must be connected with the soil, with the earth. I grew up in Newark, New Jersey, and I had not had much connection with the earth. Now, lying in the hospital, it occurred to me that since San Francisco's jail stands right on what was, in the 1930s, a 145-acre farm, it made good sense to bring prisoners outside of the jail buildings, onto the land, and try to grow things again.

I was fortunate, because I was supposed to kick the bucket any minute, and when my dear friend, Michael Hennessey, our sheriff, visited me in the hospital he said, "Yeah, Cathy, if you want to take them outside and garden, fine. Why don't you do that?" He said this thinking that I was going to kick the bucket, but that in the meantime I would feel good. Well, I didn't die, and when I got out of the hospital, I set out with four prisoners onto the old farm. I wish you could have seen their faces when they said, "We're going to do *what* here?" I said, "Well, first of all, we have to start by cleaning up this mess."

And so we started cleaning up. For twenty years, the sheriff's department had used the old farm as a storage area and it took us three years to clean up the mess. We did it without tools, without wheelbarrows. The jail gardeners literally tore down old buildings with their hands. They didn't have jackets or rain gear. They had their T-shirts and their thin jail clothes and little thong shoes to clip-clop around in. What began to touch me was that I started to see these people care about something for the first time. I started to see them *care* that we were slowly cleaning up this mess, and *care* that I was so excited about it. And then I saw *them* get excited. From that point on we began to grow things.

One of the first people who came out into the garden with me was a man I'll never forget. His name is Forrest. Forrest was about forty-five then, with a criminal history that spanned three decades. He had ten arrests for assault with a deadly weapon, probably fifteen arrests for drunk driving, and related things. Not a nice guy. And yet Forrest came out with me, busted his butt to clean up this old dump, this old farm. Soon, a wonderful horticulture therapist named Arlene Hamilton joined us. We started to grow herbs. We started slowly, with only $300 from the sheriff and his friends to buy a few things, and maybe ten gardeners in 1984. Today, 160 prisoners go out every day to an eight-acre garden. It is fenced for the deer, because we have lots of deer. We have tools now and we grow an amazing amount of food that we give to the soup kitchens, and to projects that feed seniors, the homeless, and people too sick with AIDS to feed themselves. A lot of people ask me, "Why do you *give* the food away?" We give the food away because it is important for the prisoners to have an opportunity to feel good about themselves.

People ask me, "What is it about gardening—getting your hands in the earth—that makes the connection with these people? Why couldn't it be getting them on a computer? What do you think is so good about the gardening?" Well, in fact it is important to say that gardening isn't for everyone, but growing things does give many people a sense of power. When the prisoners see a garbage dump turn into a garden and know that Alice Waters wants vegetables that are growing there, they get a sense of power. They made it happen with their hands! And also it is the experience of living things, green things, beauty, Mother Nature. This reminds me of something Wendell Berry said in *The Unsettling of America*. He talks about how, in America, anything done with your hands is looked down on. I looked at the community I'm working with, and I think, "What's missing is nature and beauty, the beauty that can be made with our hands." I say to these guys, "Look, you guys, let's weed the baby lettuces, and then let's watch what happens. They're going to grow more, they'll be better. And people will pay top organic dollar for them." Growing things is a metaphor. I also say to them, "If we don't put chemicals on this stuff that we're growing, people are going to pay more for it. It's the same for you.

If you don't put heroin into your arm, you are going to be better off. Your family will be better off." The experience of growing works in terms of healing, of my counseling. I can *show* them what I'm talking about. Many, many people here in the jail are substance dependent. One thing the garden shows them is how much better life is without chemicals. You can take chemicals and put them in the garden and get fast results, but look what it does to the soil.

My concern with farm programs in the jail is—well, I'm sure you all saw that movie with Paul Newman, *Cool Hand Luke*, in which prisoners were *forced* to do agricultural labor in chain gangs. I mean, there have been jail farms forever, and it is very, very important that our jail people have a *choice*. Either you can work in the farm and grow food for the soup kitchen, *or* you can go to computer class, *or* the literacy class. There has to be a choice. It's very, very important that you give people who have hurt people, who have killed people, an opportunity to be able to look in the mirror and say, "God, I can do something good."

People in our country do want solutions, and I have seen many, many people like Forrest go from all those long convictions to being a kick-ass radish grower. Now he is the first person to come up to you in the garden. At first, it is kind of menacing, because he looks kind of menacing. He's got tattoos everywhere, but what he wants to do is give you a bouquet of flowers, because he is very proud of the flowers. That is transformation. This program makes people who have no hope have hope, which is a tremendously powerful thing. It is working with these green things that gives them a sense of life. And most of them have never had it from anywhere else. Another prisoner, named Danny, said to me, "I'd like to go work on a farm for somebody. And I want to be dedicated to the farm like I am here. I was like a dead tree when I first came here. And I've seen what watering does: if you water the tree and feed it nice, it grows up and it has fruit. I don't want to go back to the streets and just hang around, and waste, and die." And these women—who are almost all in here for prostitution—are *strong* women. Do you know how hard it is to stand on a street corner every night for hours, in the cold, with practically no clothes on? *Strong women,* only on the wrong path.

I want to tell you something, because not many people like you get an opportunity to visit a jail—jails are bleak places. Our jail is so bleak, despite our beautiful garden, that I always wonder—*How can we keep people in this horrible situation in horrible cages, and then expect them to come back and be normal nice people, living with everyone?* That's not going to happen. The people I work with are the kind of people who, when you see them, you cross the street because they are scary people. But this garden program helps people understand that they aren't just scary, they are part of a community. They leave our jails all over the country and they come back and live in our communities, they ride the bus with us.

For many years I felt it was wonderful that we had this garden, that we were feeding people, that people's lives were changing. But it is frustrating to realize that for most of the people in our jail, being in the garden program is better than their lives at home—*better* than living on the street, than living in hotels for homeless, than living in projects. It was devastating for me to realize that for many of these people, the garden program was the best experience of their adult lives, of their whole lives. At the end of their sentence, many people came up to me and said, "Cathy, I don't want to go, I want to stay here." In fact some of them ended up back in jail just because they wanted to be back in our garden. But most of them returned to selling their bodies and drugs because no one would hire them to do anything else. So I realized we needed another program to help them continue the experiences they had in our garden, but outside the jail.

I often bring people from the community to the jail to see what we are doing. One day, a local businessperson came, a man named Elliot Hoffman who has a large bakery named Just Desserts. He looked around and he said, "You know, I need so many strawberries. You could grow strawberries and I could buy them from you." Personally, I was hoping that this man would say, "Hey, I'll give you a check. You can buy tools." But he kept saying, "No, no, I would really like to buy strawberries from you." So he invited me out to his bakery in Hunter's Point. Behind his bakery was this old garbage dump, about a half an acre. And he said, "You could bring the people here and you could grow a lot of strawberries." I kept looking at this garbage dump and thinking to myself, "You know, I have enough to do here at the *jail*, I would really just like a check from this person."

Fortunately for us all, Elliot persisted, and finally after a couple of hours, when it became clear to me that he wasn't going to give me a check, we decided to start a post-release program for people leaving the jail. Today, people can leave our jail program and come to this half-acre garden and continue to grow food that we sell to Chez Panisse, which is a very fancy, wonderful restaurant in Berkeley run by Alice Waters. We also sell a lot of fruit to Just Desserts and we are involving other businesses. We're talking with The Body Shop, we're talking with Esprit. We're talking with any business that will listen about spreading this idea. We call this place in Hunter's Point "The Garden Project." After a while, Elliot got to know our people and hired some of them. Of course, that first guy Elliot hired disappeared with the Just Desserts truck. He had just gone to cruise his neighborhood and he didn't think anything about it because he had never had a job before. Elliot didn't get scared by that, and he has hired more people from our program for his bakery.

When we first started The Garden Project, the land belonged to a certain huge corporation. I said to them, "Well look, you guys, you have a garbage dump in this poor neighborhood. Let us help you clean it up; we'll grow things on it, and your property won't be a wreck anymore." The huge corporation said to me, "Look, lady, we're not a charity. Give us $500,000 for the land." It seemed to me there was no way I was going to give them a dime. And so we climbed over their fence and made a garden. Now, this is felony trespassing, and remember on my little business card it says, "Special Assistant to the Sheriff." So I said to the sheriff, I said, "Michael, this huge corporation says I need $500,000 and what I'd like to do is clean up their dump and start a garden." Michael said, "Do it. And don't forget that not only are they going to have to put *you* in jail, they're going to have to put *me* in jail." I always encourage people to say *no* to anybody who says it can't be done.

What we have throughout this country are poor people and vacant land. I grew up in Newark, New Jersey, and when I left, twenty years ago, there were acres and acres of land where buildings were burnt down in the riots after Martin Luther King died. Now, instead of having people standing out on the corner, they could instead be growing fruit that Ben & Jerry's says they'll buy. They could do that in Newark; they could do that in Denver. What we're doing is finding ways to connect nature and people.

I go from feeling very hopeful to feeling extremely sad in my work. I feel very sad when I go to our jail and see so many African-American men, so many Spanish-speaking men and women who do not have a future, who do not have any hope. And, it's discouraging when I hear cops say, "Well, that's all they want," or when I hear people say, "They can make more money selling crack." That's so false. The people out there selling drugs for the most part are making barely enough to buy the crack they are using. They are on a path that is destructive—for all of us. Crime affects all of us, every day, and it's important that we start looking at what's happening in our country. We are producing millions of people who have no hope, who have nothing to lose and if you have nothing to lose, you're a dangerous, dangerous person. What happened in Los Angeles is what happens when many, many people feel that they don't matter, that they don't count. The sadness that I feel about these human situations, and I'm sure all of us feel, in some way numbs us. It makes us feel that it might be easier to protect the spotted owl or to protect land. With land, you know, you can buy it up and make sure that no one builds on it. But to help people to change, it doesn't take a year. It takes many years, many other people.

When I was asked to speak here [at the Aspen Design Conference] I thought, oh, what am I going to say to these people?

They cannot know what I'm doing. But then I realized that you are the people who are *designing* our communities. And I feel very hopeful that with your understanding and all your expertise, you can start designing an America that *includes* the men and women that I work with, the men and women who fill our jails. You know, California spends many millions of dollars building jails, and fewer millions of dollars educating children. It costs $25,000 a year to keep a person in a cage. They could go to Harvard! They could go a lot of places. What I see in our project is what happens when government, business, and community people join together. I'm asking you to help to redesign a new world. When I tell my students, "I went to Aspen and to Harvard and told the people what we're doing here in the garden and they listened and they *cared*," my students know that it means that they *count*, that there's hope. They hold their heads up a little, and they think, "God, we matter. We count."

When I told the San Francisco Unified School District that Alice Waters at Chez Panisse wants to buy all the vegetables we can grow, they said, "Well, we have land all over and we're spending to clear the weeds, so why don't you do something with it?" That's good, that's good. We can grow a lot of radishes for Alice on what used to be school district land. The Department of Forestry is also spending a lot of money trying to safeguard our forests. Now, the Angeles Forest is not so far from South-Central Los Angeles, so I said to them, "Let's pay the people that are standing around the streets in South-Central Los Angeles to plant trees. Let's pay them to maintain the trees." What we are talking about is putting people and the environment together. It starts with us saying, "We can do better," because we *can* do better.

Last Friday, I spoke at the funeral of Donnell, a man who was in my garden program four years ago. He had just turned eighteen. This man could not tell time. He could not read. So I asked Smith & Hawken, which is a fancy tool company, to hire this young man when he left our program in the jail, and they did. But after two months of him coming to work late, and a few times of him stealing clothes that they were trying to sell, they said, "Cathy, we really want to help your project, but, you know, this guy isn't working." I understood when they let him go. But when they did, he went back to the Sunnydale projects, back to selling drugs. He was killed by a young man with whom he had had an argument. The young man came back after the argument and blew his head off. This happens every day.

Donnell was one of those young men who did not want to leave our jail, the garden. He said, "Cathy, I don't want to go back out there. Can I stay here?" I said, "Donnell, you *cannot* stay in jail. It's, it's illegal!" Donnell said to me, "Cathy, you know a lot of people. You can pull some strings. The sheriff's your friend. Please ask the sheriff to let me stay here." I asked Sheriff Hennessey, who's a wonderful, wonderful man, "Michael, can we let Donnell stay? He's afraid to go back." Michael said, "Cathy, it *is* illegal, and our jail is overcrowded. People are sleeping on the floor. We can't keep Donnell in the jail." When I was talking at his funeral, I was aware that most of the people attending were young men, and most of the young men knew who I was, and it was not because they heard me on National Public Radio or read about me in The *New York Times*. Anywhere I go in San Francisco people come up to me and say, "Oh, I know you." If they're African-American, I know they know me from the jail. Something's very wrong.

People say, "You seem so passionate about this. It seems like more than a job to you. What keeps you going?" What keeps me going is that the young men and women in our jail look very much like the young men and young women who live in my house—my children, my nieces and nephews. If you look at statistics, I know that my daughter and son don't have a future. We are talking about reconstruction, redirecting, rebuilding. We are talking about hope and solutions. I look at these lupines and trees on the stage with us today, and I think—We could be paying somebody to be watering these plants. The somebodies could be people like the people in my program. When I see vacant lots and garbage dumps, I know who would love to have the opportunity to clean them up. We need to see that, despite the enormous obstacles these young women and men face, they are remaking their lives.

The people who have said "This makes sense" come from all over. I got a letter not so long ago from California's attorney general. I have to say I was afraid to open the envelope; I thought maybe I was being indicted. The attorney general wrote to me to say, "Cathy, what you're doing is a model for law enforcement, throughout this state. It is an inspiration to law enforcement and I'm sending information about it to all the attorney generals' offices in the state, and I am going to *make* them come visit you." And so many people hear of our program and we are getting more support and requests to help begin similar programs.

Last summer, we got a contract to plant trees for San Francisco. Since then we've planted over 2,000 trees in the city. The people planting trees are called The Tree Corps and are getting eight dollars an hour to plant trees. They used to be crack sellers. They used to sell crack to pregnant mothers, to their own mothers. Now they're selling hope because when they're out there planting trees in Hunter's Point and in The Mission, people look at them and say, "Wait a minute. I don't have to sell crack. I can do something else 'cause if my uncle and my cousin and my brother can plant trees, I can plant trees." I have a *waiting* list of people who want to plant trees, and wherever we go, people follow us. This one young man came, and he said, "Cathy, I'm sorry to come to you like this." He had an Uzi under his little jacket and crack in the pockets. He said, "I'm sorry to come to you like this, but I don't want to do this. I want to plant trees." I want to be able to give him an opportunity to plant trees because we need trees. You *have* heard of global warming?

Planting trees is super work and, for me, the most powerful thing is when you consider that the person doing it used to be selling drugs, hurting other people, and is now trying to figure out whether the tree pit is deep enough. When you give people an alternative to throwing their lives away, most people choose that. And I will never forget my first day when The Tree Corps and I began working with John, the Department of Public Works employee who was first assigned to work with us. His co-workers were teasing him, but John just puffed out his chest and said, "Wait a minute, these people are just like you. They are going to learn a skill." And then John proceeded to teach our students as much as he knew—and he has been a tree trimmer and planter for twenty years. But what he really taught our students is that people care. And that you can learn Latin names if you want to. It was a powerful relationship. John has since been transferred and we are doing it on our own. Now that The Tree Corps reflects the people in the neighborhood, people know that this tree in the ground means that their uncle, or brother, or sister has a job and so they protect the tree, whereas before they often cut it down. It is not weird, but quite wonderful.

One of our planters is Rumaldo. He is about fifty-three years old and he has been to jail six times. Rumaldo has four grown children and now he brings his children around and says, "I planted that tree," and then he tells them the Latin name for the tree and what the tree needs and he puffs out his chest and he doesn't hurt people anymore. Because he is too tired to—he is out planting trees. But it is a long, constant struggle. I got a message the other day from a man named Burl who was with us for about six months. When he started working with The Tree Corps, he had just overcome his crack addiction. He came to work every day but he had nowhere to live and was living in his car, and he got back on the street and readdicted. I got a message the other day that he was asking whether or not I was too mad at him to consider allowing him to rejoin the program. And of course I am not too mad at him.

Wendell Berry

THE PLEASURES
OF EATING

Many times, after I have finished a lecture on the decline of American farming and rural life, someone in the audience has asked, "What can city people do?"

"Eat responsibly," I have usually answered. Of course, I have tried to explain what I meant by that, but afterwards I have invariably felt that there was more to be said than I had been able to say. Now I would like to attempt a better explanation. I begin with the proposition that eating is an agricultural act. Eating ends the annual drama of the food economy that begins with planting and birth. Most eaters, however, are no longer aware that this is true. They think of food as an agricultural product, perhaps, but they do not think of themselves as participants in agriculture. They think of themselves as "consumers." If they think beyond that, they recognize that they are passive consumers. They buy what they want—or what they have been persuaded to want—within the limits of what they can get. They pay, mostly without protest, what they are charged. And they mostly ignore certain critical questions about the quality and the cost of what they are sold: How fresh is it? How pure or clean is it, how free of dangerous chemicals? How far was it transported, and what did transportation add to the cost? How much did manufacturing or packaging or advertising add to the cost? When the food product has been manufactured or "processed" or "precooked," how has that affected its quality or price or nutritional value?

Most urban shoppers would tell you that food is produced on

farms. But most of them do not know what farms, or what kinds of farms, or where the farms are, or what knowledge or skill are involved in farming. They apparently have little doubt that farms will continue to produce, but they do not know how or over what obstacles. For them, then, food is pretty much an abstract idea—something they do not know or imagine—until it appears on the grocery shelf or on the table.

The specialization of production induces specialization of consumption. Patrons of the entertainment industry, for example, entertain themselves less and less and have become more and more passively dependent on commercial suppliers. This is certainly true also of patrons of the food industry, who have tended more and more to be mere consumers—passive, uncritical, and dependent. Indeed, this sort of consumption may be said to be one of the chief goals of industrial production. The food industrialists have by now persuaded millions of consumers to prefer food that is already prepared. They will grow, deliver, and cook your food for you and (just like your mother) beg you to eat it. That they do not yet offer to insert it, prechewed, into your mouth is only because they have found no profitable way to do so. We may rest assured that they would be glad to find such a way. The ideal industrial food consumer would be strapped to a table with a tube running from the food factory directly into his or her stomach.

Perhaps I exaggerate, but not by much. The industrial eater is, in fact, one who does not know that eating is an agricultural act, who no longer knows or imagines the connections between eating and the land, and who is therefore necessarily passive and uncritical—in short, a victim. When food, in the minds of eaters, is no longer associated with farming and with the land, then the eaters are suffering a kind of cultural amnesia that is misleading and dangerous. The current version of the "dream home" of the future involves "effortless" shopping from a list of available goods on a television monitor and heating precooked food by remote control. Of course, this implies, and depends on, a perfect ignorance of the history of the food that is consumed. It requires that the citizenry should give up their hereditary and sensible aversion to buying a pig in a poke. It wishes to make the selling of pigs in pokes an honorable and glamorous activity. The dreamer in this dream home will perforce know nothing about the kind of quality of this food, or where it came from, or how it was produced and prepared, or what ingredients, additives, and residues it contains—unless, that is, the dreamer undertakes a close and constant study of the food industry, in which case he or she might as well wake up and play an active and responsible part in the economy of food.

There is, then, a politics of food that, like any politics, involves our freedom. We still (sometimes) remember that we cannot be free if our minds and voices are controlled by someone else. But we have neglected to understand that we cannot be free if our food and its sources are controlled by someone else. The condition of the passive consumer of food is not a democratic condition. One reason to eat responsibly is to live free.

But if there is a food politics, there are also a food aesthetics and a food ethics, neither of which is dissociated from politics. Like industrial sex, industrial eating has become a degraded, poor, and paltry thing. Our kitchens and other eating places more and more resemble filling stations, as our homes more and more resemble motels. "Life is not very interesting," we seem to have decided. "Let its satisfactions be minimal, perfunctory, and fast." We hurry through our meals to go to work and hurry through our work in order to "recreate" ourselves in the evenings and on weekends and vacations. And then we hurry, with the greatest possible speed and noise and violence, through our recreation—for what? To eat the billionth hamburger at some fast-food joint hell-bent on increasing the "quality" of our life? And all this is carried out in a remarkable obliviousness to the causes and effects, the possibilities and the purposes, of the life of the body in this world.

One will find this obliviousness represented in virgin purity in the advertisements of the food industry, in which food wears as much makeup as the actors. If one gained one's whole knowledge of food from these advertisements (as some presumably do), one would not know that the various edibles were ever living creatures, or that they all come from the soil, or that they were produced by work. The passive American consumer, sitting down to a meal of pre-prepared or fast food, confronts a platter covered with inert, anonymous substances that have been processed, dyed, breaded, sauced, gravied, ground, pulped, strained, blended, prettified, and sanitized beyond resemblance to any part of any creature that ever lived. The products of nature and agriculture have been made, to all appearances, the products of industry. Both eater and eaten are thus in exile from biological reality. And the result is a kind of solitude, unprecedented in human experience, in which the eater may think of eating as, first, a purely commercial transaction between him and a supplier and then as a purely appetitive transaction between him and his food.

And this peculiar specialization of the act of eating is, again, of obvious benefit to the food industry, which has good reasons to obscure the connection between food and farming. It would not do for the consumer to know that the hamburger she is eating came from a steer who spent much of his life standing deep in his own excrement in a feedlot, helping to pollute the local streams, or that the calf that yielded the veal cutlet on her plate spent its life in a box in which it did not have room to turn around. And, though her sympathy for the slaw might be less tender, she should not be encouraged to meditate on the hygienic and biological implications of mile-square fields of cabbage, for vegetables grown in huge monocultures are dependent on toxic chemicals—just as animals in close confinement are dependent on antibiotics and other drugs.

The consumer, that is to say, must be kept from discovering that, in the food industry—as in any other industry—the overriding concerns are not quality and health, but volume and price. For decades now the entire industrial food economy, from the large farms and feedlots to the chains of supermarkets and fast-food restaurants, has been obsessed with volume. It has relentlessly increased scale in order to increase volume in order (presumably) to reduce costs. But as scale increases, diversity declines; as diversity declines, so does health; as health declines, the dependence on drugs and chemicals necessarily increases. As capital replaces labor, it does so by substituting machines, drugs, and chemicals for human workers and for the natural health and fertility of the soil. The food is produced by any means or any shortcut that will increase profits. And the business of the cosmeticians of advertising is to persuade the consumer that food so produced is good, tasty, healthful, and a guarantee of marital fidelity and long life.

It is possible, then, to be liberated from the husbandry and wifery of the old household food economy. But one can be thus liberated only by entering a trap (unless one sees ignorance and helplessness as the signs of privilege, as many people apparently do). The trap is the ideal of industrialism: a walled city surrounded by valves that let merchandise in but no consciousness out. How does one escape this trap? Only voluntarily, the same way that one went in: by restoring one's consciousness of what is involved in eating; by reclaiming responsibility for one's own part in the food economy. One might begin with the illuminating principle of Sir Albert Howard's *The Soil and Health*, that we should understand "the whole problem of health in soil, plant, animal, and man as one great subject." Eaters, that is, must understand that eating takes place inescapably in the world, that it is inescapably an agricultural act, and that how we eat determines, to a considerable extent, how the world is used. This is a simple way of describing a relationship that is inexpressibly complex. To eat responsibly is to understand and enact, so far as one can, this complex relationship. What can one do? Here is a list, probably not definitive:

1. Participate in food production to the extent that you can. If you have a yard or even just a porch box or a pot in a sunny window, grow something to eat in it. Make a little compost of your kitchen scraps and use it for fertilizer. Only by growing some food for yourself can you become acquainted with the beautiful energy

cycle that revolves from soil to seed to flower to fruit to food to offal to decay, and around again. You will be fully responsible for any food that you grow for yourself, and you will know all about it. You will appreciate it fully, having known it all its life.

2. Prepare your own food. This means reviving in your own mind and life the arts of kitchen and household. This should enable you to eat more cheaply, and it will give you a measure of "quality control": you will have some reliable knowledge of what has been added to the food you eat.

3. Learn the origins of the food you buy, and buy the food that is produced closest to your home. The idea that every locality should be, as much as possible, the source of its own food makes several kinds of sense. The locally produced food supply is the most secure, the freshest, and the easiest for local consumers to know about and to influence.

4. Whenever possible, deal directly with a local farmer, gardener, or orchardist. All the reasons listed for the previous suggestion apply here. In addition, by such dealing you eliminate the whole pack of merchants, transporters, processors, packagers, and advertisers who thrive at the expense of both producers and consumers.

5. Learn, in self-defense, as much as you can of the economy and technology of industrial food production. What is added to food that is not food, and what do you pay for these additions?

6. Learn what is involved in the *best* farming and gardening.

7. Learn as much as you can, by direct observation and experience if possible, of the life histories of the food species.

The last suggestion seems particularly important to me. Many people are now as much estranged from the lives of domestic plants and animals (except for flowers and dogs and cats) as they are from the lives of the wild ones. This is regrettable, for these domestic creatures are in diverse ways attractive; there is much pleasure in knowing them. And farming, animal husbandry, horticulture, and gardening, at their best, are complex and comely arts; there is much pleasure in knowing them, too.

It follows that there is great *dis*pleasure in knowing about a food economy that degrades and abuses those arts and those plants and animals and the soil from which they come. For anyone who does know something of the modern history of food, eating away from home can be a chore. My own inclination is to eat seafood instead of red meat or poultry when I am traveling. Though I am by no means a vegetarian, I dislike the thought that some animal has been made miserable in order to feed me. If I am going to eat meat, I want it to be from an animal that has lived a pleasant, uncrowded life outdoors, on bountiful pasture, with good water nearby and trees for shade. And I am getting almost as fussy about food plants. I like to eat vegetables and fruits that I know have lived happily and healthily in good soil, not the products of the huge, bechemicaled factory-fields that I have seen, for example, in the Central Valley of California. The industrial farm is said to have been patterned on the factory production line. In practice, it looks more like a concentration camp.

The pleasure of eating should be an *extensive* pleasure, not that of the mere gourmet. People who know the garden in which their vegetables have grown and know that the garden is healthy will remember the beauty of the growing plants, perhaps in the dewy first light of morning when gardens are at their best. Such a memory involves itself with the food and is one of the pleasures of eating. The knowledge of the good health of the garden relieves and frees and comforts the eater. The same goes for eating meat. The thought of the good pasture and of the calf contentedly grazing flavors the steak. Some, I know, will think it bloodthirsty or worse to eat a fellow creature you have known all its life. On the contrary, I think it means that you eat with understanding and with gratitude. A significant part of the pleasure of eating is in one's accurate consciousness of the lives and the world from which food comes. The pleasure of eating, then, may be the best available standard of our health. And this pleasure, I think, is pretty fully available to the urban consumer who will make the necessary effort.

I mentioned earlier the politics, aesthetics, and ethics of food. But to speak of the pleasure of eating is to go beyond those categories. Eating with the fullest pleasure—pleasure, that is, that does not depend on ignorance—is perhaps the profoundest enactment of our connection with the world. In this pleasure we experience and celebrate our dependence and our gratitude, for we are living from mystery, from creatures we did not make and powers we cannot comprehend. When I think of the meaning of food, I always remember these lines by the poet William Carlos Williams, which seem to me merely honest:

> There is nothing to eat,
>   seek it where you will,
>   but the body of the Lord.
> The blessed plants
>   and the sea, yield it
>   to the imagination
> intact.

COPYRIGHT ACKNOWLEDGMENTS

Excerpt from "General Advice," from *Garden-Making*, by L. H. Bailey, published by Grosset and Dunlap, 1808.

"Two Gardens," by Michael Pollan, from *Second Nature* by Michael Pollan. Copyright © 1991 by Michael Pollan. Used by permission of Grove/Atlantic, Inc.

Excerpt from *In My Father's Garden*. Copyright © 1995 by Lee May. Reprinted by permission of the Longstreet Press.

"Tomato," from *Antarctic Traveler*, by Katha Pollitt. Copyright © 1981 by Katha Pollitt. Reprinted by permission of Alfred A. Knopf, Inc.

"Woman's Place," from *Green Thoughts*, by Eleanor Perenyi. Copyright © 1981 by Eleanor Perenyi. Reprinted by permission of Random House, Inc.

"The Garden," by Kathleen Norris, reprinted by permission of The Putnam Publishing Group/Riverhead Books, from *The Cloister Walk* by Kathleen Norris. Copyright © 1966 by Kathleen Norris.

"Touch Me," from *Passing Through: The Later Poems New and Selected* by Stanley Kunitz. Copyright © 1995 by Stanley Kunitz. Reprinted by permission of W. W. Norton & Company, Inc.

"What Goes Wrong," from *The Other Side/El Otro Lado*. Copyright © 1995 by Julia Alvarez. Published by Dutton, a division of Penguin USA. First published in Mirabella, May 1995.

"Seed Saving," excerpted from *Plain and Pleasant Talk about Fruits, Flowers, and Farming*, published by Perby and Jackson, 1859.

"Did I Say?" from *Odd Mercy: Poems* by Gerald Stern. Copyright © 1995 by Gerald Stern. Reprinted by permission of W. W. Norton & Company, Inc.

"Cultivating Diversity," excerpted from *Groundwork: A Gardener's Ecology*. Text copyright © 1994 by Roger B. Swain. Reprinted by permission of Houghton Mifflin Company. All rights reserved.

"Succession," reprinted from *Parsnips in the Snow: Talks with Midwest Gardeners*, by Jane Staw and Mary Swander. Copyright © 1990 by the University of Iowa Press. By permission of the University of Iowa Press.

"August," by Jane Smiley, from *Ordinary Love and Good Will*, by Jane Smiley. Copyright © 1989 by Jane Smiley. Reprinted by permission of Alfred A. Knopf, Inc.

"For the Sake of Seeds," by Boyce Rensberger. Copyright © 1992, *The Washington Post*. Reprinted with permission.

"Near the Center of the Earth," by Barbara Robinette Moss. Copyright © 1997 by Barbara Robinette Moss. Used by permission of the author.

Excerpt from *My Vegetable Love: Journal of a Growing Season*. Copyright © 1996 by Carl H. Klaus. Reprinted by permission of Houghton Mifflin Company. All rights reserved.

"The Bean-Field," from *Walden*, by Henry David Thoreau, Houghton Mifflin Company, 1929 edition.

"My Wilderness," from *At Nature's Pace*, by Gene Logsdon. Copyright © 1994 by Gene Logsdon. Reprinted by permission of Pantheon Books, a division of Random House, Inc.

"Gardening at the Seam," by Judith Larner Lowry. First published in *Orion* magazine, Summer 1994, copyright © 1994 by The Orion Society.

"Lapsed Meadow," from *Summer Celestial*, by Stanley Plumly. Copyright © 1983 by Stanley Plumly. First published by The Ecco Press in 1983. Reprinted by permission.

"Edible Flowers, a Weed to Eat, and Handsome Vegetables," from *The Gardener's Eye and Other Essays*, by Allen Lacy. Copyright © 1992 by Allen Lacy. Reprinted by permission of Henry Holt and Co., Inc.

"An Insider's View of the Garden," from *Connecting the Dots*, by Maxine Kumin. Copyright © 1995 by Maxine Kumin. Reprinted by permission of W. W. Norton & Company, Inc.

"Crops, Words, Movies," from *A Garlic Testament*, by Stanley Crawford. Copyright © 1992 by Stanley Crawford. Reprinted by permission of HarperCollins Publishers, Inc.

"We Don't Garden Right," copyright © 1997 by Sara Stein. Used by permisison of the author.

"Learning to Work," from *Waheenee: An Indian Girl's Story*, edited by Gilbert L. Wilson with an introduction by Jeffery R. Hanson. Published by the University of Nebraska Press.

"Sweet Corn," excerpted from "A Letter to Copenhagen" in *Leaving Home*, by Garrison Keillor. Copyright © 1987 by Garrison Keillor. Used by permission of Viking Penguin, a division of Penguin Books USA Inc.

"To Grow," by Thomas Fox Averill, copyright © 1997 by Thomas Fox Averill. Used by permission of the author.

"Invisible Erosion: The Rise and Fall of Native Farming" from *Enduring Seeds: Native American Agriculture and Wild Plant Conservation*, by Gary Nabhan. Copyright © 1989 by Gary Nabhan. Reprinted by permission of North Point Press, a division of Farrar, Straus & Giroux, Inc.

"The Future: More Farmers, Not Fewer," from *At Nature's Pace*, by Gene Logsdon. Copyright © 1994 by Gene Logsdon. Reprinted by permission of Pantheon Books, a division of Random House, Inc.

"Daisies," from *The Wild Iris* by Louise Glück. Copyright © 1992 by Louise Glück. First published by The Ecco Press in 1992. Reprinted by permission.

"Cathrine Sneed Talks About Her Work with Prisoners and Gardens," by Cathrine Sneed. Previously published as "These Green Things" in *Orion* Magazine, Summer 1994, copyright © 1994 by The Orion Society.

"The Pleasures of Eating" from *What Are People For?* by Wendell Berry. Copyright © 1990 by Wendell Berry. Reprinted by permission of North Point Press, a division of Farrar, Straus & Giroux, Inc.

ABOUT THE EDITOR

Mary Swander is the author of *Out of This World: A Woman's Life Among the Amish*, three volumes of poetry, and a musical. She has received numerous honors, including a Whiting Award and the Carl Sandburg Literary Award from the Chicago Public Library. A Professor of English at Iowa State University, she lives in Ames and Kalona, Iowa, where she raises sheep and goats and tends a large organic vegetable garden.

NORTON
'98

PN
6071
.G27
B59
1997

Bloom & blossom

DATE DUE			

GARDEN LIBRARY
PLANTING FIELDS ARBORETUM